SAGE was founded in 1965 by Sara Miller McCune to support the dissemination of usable knowledge by publishing innovative and high-quality research and teaching content. Today, we publish over 900 journals, including those of more than 400 learned societies, more than 800 new books per year, and a growing range of library products including archives, data, case studies, reports, and video. SAGE remains majority-owned by our founder, and after Sara's lifetime will become owned by a charitable trust that secures our continued independence.

Los Angeles | London | New Delhi | Singapore | Washington DC | Melbourne

POST-MANDAL
POLITICS IN BIHAR

Thank you for choosing a SAGE product!
If you have any comment, observation or feedback,
I would like to personally hear from you.

Please write to me at **contactceo@sagepub.in**

Vivek Mehra, Managing Director and CEO, SAGE India.

Bulk Sales

SAGE India offers special discounts
for purchase of books in bulk.
We also make available special imprints
and excerpts from our books on demand.

For orders and enquiries, write to us at

Marketing Department
SAGE Publications India Pvt Ltd
B1/I-1, Mohan Cooperative Industrial Area
Mathura Road, Post Bag 7
New Delhi 110044, India

E-mail us at **marketing@sagepub.in**

Get to know more about SAGE

Be invited to SAGE events, get on our mailing list.
Write today to **marketing@sagepub.in**

This book is also available as an e-book.

POST-MANDAL

POLITICS IN BIHAR

CHANGING ELECTORAL PATTERNS

SANJAY KUMAR

SAGE SERIES ON POLITICS IN INDIAN STATES—I

SERIES EDITORS
SUHAS PALSHIKAR
RAJESHWARI DESHPANDE

Los Angeles | London | New Delhi
Singapore | Washington DC | Melbourne

First published in 2018 by

SAGE Publications India Pvt Ltd
B1/I-1 Mohan Cooperative Industrial Area
Mathura Road, New Delhi 110 044, India
www.sagepub.in

SAGE Publications Inc
2455 Teller Road
Thousand Oaks, California 91320, USA

SAGE Publications Ltd
1 Oliver's Yard, 55 City Road
London EC1Y 1SP, United Kingdom

SAGE Publications Asia-Pacific Pte Ltd
3 Church Street
#10-04 Samsung Hub
Singapore 049483

Published by Vivek Mehra for SAGE Publications India Pvt Ltd, typeset in 10/12 pts Times New Roman by Zaza Eunice, Hosur, Tamil Nadu, India and printed at Chaman Enterprises, New Delhi.

Library of Congress Cataloging-in-Publication Data

Name: Kumar, Sanjay, author.
Title: Post-Mandal politics in Bihar: changing electoral patterns/Sanjay
  Kumar.
Description: Thousand Oaks: SAGE Publications India Pvt Ltd, [2017] |
  Includes bibliographical references and index.
Identifiers: LCCN 2017051577| ISBN 9789352805853 (print (hb)) |
  ISBN 9789352805860 (e-pub) | ISBN 9789352805877 (web)
Subjects: LCSH: Elections—India—Bihar. | Politics, Practical—India—Bihar. |
  Bihar (India)—Politics and government. | Bihar (India)—Economic
  conditions. | Bihar (India)—Social conditions.
Classification: LCC JQ620.B5265 K86 2017 | DDC 324.954/123053—dc23 LC record available at
https://lccn.loc.gov/2017051577

ISBN: 978-93-528-0585-3 (HB)

SAGE Team: Abhijit Baroi, Alekha Chandra Jena, and Ritu Chopra

Contents

List of Tables

List of Figures

List of Abbreviations

AIAWU	All India Agricultural Workers Union
BJP	Bharatiya Janata Party
BLD	Bharatiya Lok Dal
BPP	Bihar People's Party
CPI	Communist Party of India
CPM	Communist Party of India (Marxist)
CPML	Communist Party of India (Marxist-Leninist)
CSDS	Centre for the Study of Developing Societies
CSO	Central Statistical Organisation
DISE	District Information System for Education
DMKP	Dalit Mazdoor Kisan Party
EBC	Extremely Backward Castes
ECI	Election Commission of India
GA	Grand Alliance
GSDP	Gross State Domestic Product
HAM	Hindustani Awam Morcha
INC	Indian National Congress
JD(U)	Janata Dal (United)
JMM	Jharkhand Mukti Morcha
LJNSP	Lok Jan Shakti Party
MCC	Marxist Coordination Committee
NDA	National Democratic Alliance
NES	National Election Study
OBC	Other Backward Class
PSP	Prajatantrik Socialist Party
RJD	Rashtriya Janata Dal
RLSP	Rashtriya Lok Samta Party
SBCs	Scheduled Commercial Banks
SSP	Samyukta Socialist Party

Series Note

The *SAGE Series on Politics in Indian States* aims at developing comprehensive, contemporary political histories of Indian states looking at the past two and a half decades. The series will consist of volumes covering important trends in the politics of the major states of India. Each volume, devoted to one particular state, would situate the politics of that state in the larger sociohistorical context and present a detailed analysis of the significant patterns of its competitive politics, with a focus on the framework of party competition, the rise of new social forces, the role of leadership, and the context of regional political economy. Going beyond state specificity, each volume would also attempt to situate the politics of the state in the larger all-India context.

Besides analyzing the state-specific trends in party politics that have led to the rise of many state parties, these volumes would also carefully look at the social bases of parties and their electoral fortunes in the backdrop of fluctuations in voter choices during the elections of the past quarter century, making use of the rich data archives of Lokniti.

The unfolding dynamics of politics at the regional level since the 1990s have forcefully brought back the states into the consciousness of the students of Indian politics. It has also led to a renewed interest among sociologists and economists about the political processes at the state level and their interconnections with socioeconomic developments in India. At the same time, there is a glaring absence of detailed documentation of the state-specific political processes of the past two decades. The series will address this gap in the literature on Indian politics. The series will also propel more informed cross-state comparisons as a starting point to truly grasp "all-India" politics.

Preface and Acknowledgments

It is not unusual to choose a field study of the place one belongs to. Being a native of Bihar, I always had a strong desire to write a book on the theme that is so dear to many *Biharis*: the politics of Bihar. Since the electoral politics in Bihar has witnessed a major churn after the 1990s with the advent of Mandal politics, I decided to focus on the state's post-Mandal electoral politics.

My journey of doing research on Bihar's electoral politics began during the 1995 assembly elections when, defying the predictions of many political analysts, Lalu Prasad Yadav became the chief minister of the state for the second time. During that election, I did my field study in Mokama assembly constituency, just 80 kilometers from Patna, the capital of Bihar.

Due to my deep interest in Bihar politics, I continued my engagement with research on this topic using surveys as my primary research tool. The Lokniti team of the Centre for the Study of Developing Societies (CSDS), of which I have been a core team member, conducted surveys for all the Lok Sabha and assembly elections held in the state since 1995, including the latest one held in 2015. This election halted the winning march of BJP, as the *Mahagathbandhan*—coalition of Janata Dal (United) (JD(U))–Rashtriya Janata Dal (RJD) and Congress—managed to defeat the Bharatiya Janata Party (BJP)-led alliance. The Lokniti team of CSDS and the state team in Bihar together conducted surveys during all these elections, which ultimately helped in the collection of a time series data on electoral choices of the people of Bihar over a period of time. This data is treasure trove for any researcher willing to trace the changing electoral politics in Bihar. I must thank the Lokniti teams, that at CSDS and that in Bihar, for working together on these surveys and collecting such valuable data.

Several researchers working at Lokniti helped me at various times and at different stages of writing this book. I express my gratitude to my colleagues Jyoti Mishra, Vibha Attri, and Shreyas Sardesai for helping me while writing this book. Other researchers, namely, Pranav

Gupta, Aaarushi Gupta, Sana Salim, and Asmita Aasawari, helped me with data and tables. Thanks are also due to the data unit team of CSDS that includes Himanshu Bhattacharya and Kanchan Malhotra. It will be unjust if I do not mention the name of Dhananjay Kumar Singh of Lokniti, who extended various kinds of administrative and logistic support to me whenever needed.

Surveys can never be possible without the active cooperation of the respondents. Over the last several years during various surveys, we interviewed large numbers of people living in different parts of Bihar. I must extend my thanks to all the respondents who agreed to spare their precious time for sharing their views on politics, elections, and related issues during the various rounds of surveys that we conducted during the elections. Thanks are also due to the team of investigators, who worked hard in the field for data collection. Without the hard work of these field investigators, collection of reliable data would not have been possible and I would have struggled hard to make sense of electoral politics during the post-Mandal period in Bihar. I would also like to extend my thanks to Rakesh Ranjan, the Lokniti coordinator of Bihar, who led the survey team in Bihar during most of these surveys.

With various surveys that I personally, and the Lokniti team collectively, embarked upon, I kept writing, both before and after elections, short pieces for newspapers, analytical articles for research journals, and at times forecasts, which got splashed in the national media. The media gave a lot of visibility to the studies and the data at times were also widely appreciated; however, what was missing was an output with a much longer shelf life, and in those terms, there is no substitute for a book.

The journey of my research on Bihar politics, which began about two decades ago, seems to be coming to a happy ending with SAGE, a publisher, with which I have most of my previous publications. My sincere thanks to the SAGE team for considering my manuscript worthy of publishing. I would also like to express my sincere thanks to Professor Suhas Palshikar and Professor Rajeshwari Deshpande, who have been instrumental in expediting the completion of the manuscript. I had begun to write this book leisurely, but their offer to consider publishing this book first in the *SAGE Series on Politics in Indian States*, which both of them are editing, encouraged me to complete the manuscript earlier than originally planned. Thanks are also due to valuable colleagues at CSDS, especially V.B. Singh, D.L. Sheth, Yogendra Yadav, and Ashis Nandy, who always encouraged me to write this book at different stages of my academic career. I would also like to acknowledge the encouragement and support that I received from all my other colleagues at CSDS while working on this book.

It is impossible to compensate for my frequent absences from my family for the various surveys that I conducted in Bihar. The least they deserve is a special mention here. My family has been very supportive to me, while I wrote this book. I would like to thank first my wife, Rashmi, who supported and encouraged me not only for writing this book but does so for all that gets published under my name. I am sure that without her moral support, it would not have been easy for me to complete this book. My daughters Vishakha Nandini and Manavi Nandini also deserve a special mention here; both of them have always been a source of inspiration for me. Their curious questions, especially from my younger daughter Manavi, about how one writes a book, have been very interesting. Appreciation from other family members has also been a source of inspiration, and I must acknowledge their invisible contributions to this book. There may be a few others who provided different kinds of support to me while writing this book; I may not have mentioned their names, but my sincere thanks to all of them as well.

Sanjay Kumar

Introduction

History testifies that Bihar has been at the center of politics in India since a very long time. Many significant political changes that have taken place in India during the last several decades have had their genesis in Bihar. Not only was Bihar the epicenter of pro- and anti-Mandal agitations in the 1990s, the state was also the epicenter of the anti-Emergency movement of 1975, popularly referred to as the "JP Movement" and led by the great socialist leader Jayaprakash Narayan when the then Prime Minister Indira Gandhi imposed a national emergency. It is important to mention that Bihar played an important role in bringing about political changes even during the British rule. Mahatma Gandhi began his famous Indigo movement—called the Champaran Movement in our history books—in 1817 against the Britishers from Champaran, a district in the northeastern region of the state. The nature of political contest and political representation in North Indian states during the post-Mandal period also had deep roots in Bihar.

In the past, Bihar's political landscape was largely dominated by the Congress party, like many other states of India. The Congress had an uninterrupted rule in the state for several decades until 1990, with only minor interruptions in 1967 and 1977 when the state had a non-Congress government. The nature of electoral politics and political representation in the state witnessed major changes during the post-Mandal period. This period witnessed the rise of regional political parties and regional leaders with a reasonable support base, especially amongst the voters belonging to the lower social strata—namely, the Other Backward Classes (OBCs), the Dalits, the Adivasis (in undivided Bihar), and the Muslims. The post-Mandal politics in the state marked the beginning of the decline of the Congress. Since the first post-Mandal assembly elections held in the state in 1995, the support base of the Congress has declined—election after election—ultimately reducing the age-old party to a very minor political player in the state.

The post-Mandal politics in Bihar that began with the national party—Congress—versus the regional party—the Janata Dal (JD)—in the 1990s has finally turned into an electoral battle between the two dominant regional political parties—the Rashtriya Janata Dal (RJD) and the Janata Dal (United) or JD(U), with the two national political parties—the Congress and the Bharatiya Janata Party (BJP)—playing secondary roles as alliance partners with the regional parties. While occasionally forming an alliance with the RJD, the Congress also went alone in a few elections. Moreover, the BJP and JD(U) led by Nitish Kumar managed to form a durable alliance since the 1996 Lok Sabha elections. Other regional parties such as the Ram Vilas Paswan-led Lok Jan Shakti Party (LJNSP), Left parties such as the Communist Party of India (Marxist) (CPM), the Communist Party of India (CPI), and the Communist Party of India (Marxist-Leninist) (CPML), and a few smaller regional parties contributed to electoral politics during the last three decades. These smaller regional parties normally played very minor roles but at times they have also played significant roles in the state's electoral politics. In the February 2005 assembly election, LJNSP's refusal to extend support—to any of the bigger parties with sizeable number of seats in the hung assembly—resulted in the state going to polls again in October 2005, which resulted in a change of guard. Nitish Kumar became the chief minister of Bihar for the first time, after forging an alliance with the BJP.

The nearly three-decade-long post-Mandal politics of Bihar has witnessed several twists and turns, the latest being the change of government in July 2017 when Nitish Kumar, after breaking alliance with the RJD, formed the government in alliance with BJP in less than 24 hours of his resignation. It is important to note that Nitish Kumar contested the 2015 assembly election in alliance with the RJD and Congress, a rather unusual alliance. The two archrivals in Bihar politics, Nitish Kumar and Lalu Prasad, came together and formed an electoral alliance, referred to as *Mahagathbandhan*, with the singular aim of preventing a BJP win in Bihar. The grand alliance (GA) managed to win the 2015 assembly elections by defeating the BJP and its allies LJNSP and Rashtriya Lok Samata Party (RLSP), and formed the government; however, this government was short lived. Nitish Kumar decided to break the alliance from the RJD due to the allegation of corruption charges and CBI raids on his deputy Tejashwi Yadav and other members of the ruling RJD. Nitish Kumar demonstrated his zero tolerance for corruption, but ended up forming the government with the party that he criticized as being communal during his campaign of the 2015 assembly election. If there was something unusual about Nitish Kumar forming a Mahagathbandhan with Lalu Prasad Yadav and the Congress before elections, it was no less strange than his forming the government with the BJP against whom he managed to win the mandate of the people of Bihar. The book analyzes in great detail these twists and turns in the electoral politics of Bihar during the post-Mandal period using empirical evidence from various surveys conducted by a team of research investigators in Bihar.

Politics of a state is the product of its society and economy. An understanding of the social and economic history of Bihar will help in understanding the changing nature of its electoral politics during the last several decades. Chapter 1 provides an introduction to the social and economic history of Bihar. At the time when Bihar was united, when Jharkhand was also part of the state, the state was divided into three broad regions: North Bihar, Central Bihar, and South Bihar. After the separation of Jharkhand from Bihar, a new geographical classification was worked out on the basis of social, cultural, and political differences. The chapter discusses in detail these differences in the five regions, namely, Tirhut, Mithila, Magadh, Bhojpur, and Seemanchal (East). Although these divisions are primarily cultural, they are also used for studying political orientations. Each of the regions exhibits its own unique blend of social and cultural values, with a language and tone different from the others. Caste plays an important role in the politics of the state, and the chapter rightfully pays attention to the various caste dynamics in the social and political spheres. From an upper caste dominated power structure, the politics in Bihar during the post-Mandal period, which this book is all about, has got transferred to the dominant middle castes, namely, the OBCs in general and the Yadavs in particular. The Yadavs and the Muslims constitute a sizeable portion of the voters in Bihar. The sizeable presence of Muslims in districts such as Katihar, Dharbhanga, Purnia, Siwan, and few others has resulted in political parties looking at the Muslims as their vote bank. The mobilization by some political parties centers around the Muslims. A section in this chapter gives a brief history of the important political parties in Bihar, its electoral history, and its leadership.

Even though the focus of the book is to analyze the electoral process and political changes in Bihar during the post-Mandal period, a political history is always important for an understanding of the present. Chapter 2 analyzes the political history of Bihar between 1967 and 1989. This period is also referred to as the Congress period in the Indian electoral history, though there were brief interruptions. For the first time, non-Congress governments were formed in many states including Bihar. A cursory review of the political history of Bihar in the post-Independence period unfolds three distinctive phases. The first phase (1947–1967) is marked by complete dominance of the Congress party with upper castes at the apex of the power structure. The second phase (1967–1990) could be designated as a transition period with the gradual decline in dominance of the Congress party as well as of the upper castes and the slowly but steadily emerging influence of the middle castes in the political arena. The third phase (1990 and after) is marked by complete reversal of the first phase, that is, marginalization of the Congress party and the upper castes in the politics of the state. The chapter analyzes in great detail the various phases of the electoral history of the state.

The 1990s marked the beginning of the political domination of regional parties in many states including Bihar. This in a way also hinted toward the beginning of OBC politics in Bihar after V.P. Singh became the prime minister of India following the 1989 Lok Sabha election. The state witnessed the first assembly election in 1990, after V.P. Singh becoming the prime minister. Chapter 3 discusses in detail the process of political mobilization and the political outcome of the 1990 and 1995 assembly elections. The 1990 assembly elections witnessed the formation of a non-Congress government after a very long time, with Lalu Prasad Yadav becoming the chief minister of the state for the first time. This victory of the JD ended the long rule of the Congress in Bihar. Not only did the Congress lose power in the state after being defeated in the 1990 assembly election, but this defeat also marked the beginning of a systematic decline of the Congress. The 1995 assembly election resulted in further domination of the JD under Lalu Prasad Yadav's leadership, winning a majority of its own, beyond the expectations of many. With the BJP's limited support base in the state, systematic decline in the electoral support of the Congress, and Nitish Kumar having left the JD to form Samata Party, the JD under the leadership of Lalu Prasad Yadav registered a massive victory in the 1995 assembly election. This was the first election in the post-Mandal period that witnessed the electoral contest centered around the OBC vs the OBC.

Chapter 4 traces a long period in Bihar's political history—beginning from the 1995 assembly election and going up to the 1999 general election. It examines various political upheavals that took place during that period. From Lalu Prasad Yadav's singular dominance during the 1990 and 1995 assembly elections to the swift rise in the BJP's electoral presence, the chapter analyzes significant events in the state's politics and posits them against the backdrop of the changing nature of political mandate at the Center. The rise of regional parties and the clout of backward castes are weighed against a declining Congress authority, and an in-depth analysis of both phenomena is done to understand its possible mechanics. Furthermore, the relation of caste and religious identities vis-à-vis political parties is analyzed with the help of rich evidence collected by the Lokniti–Centre for the Study of Developing Societies (CSDS) team through surveys to examine the dynamic nature of political alliances and the effects they have on political parties. Questions of voters' behavior and motivations take center stage as the chapter reflects on the nebulous nature of Bihar's politics, where change remains the only constant and the relationship between a voter, a party, and a leader is subject to a complex, multilayered society.

Chapter 5 primarily deals with the political scenario in Bihar post-1999 Lok Sabha elections. While the BJP–JD(U) combine won convincingly in these elections, by the time of the assembly elections in the state, there was damaging infighting that benefitted the RJD–Congress alliance, which registered a thumping victory. Thus, the chapter seeks to analyze this proverbial reversal of fortunes and tries to posit possible reasons for the same. In addition, it also delves into possible reasons for the surprising wins registered by the RJD in the 2004 Lok Sabha election. Given the substantial lack of developmental achievements under the Lalu–Rabri regime, the continued support of the poor backward classes to the RJD seems to be a paradox of sorts, but the chapter analyzes it through the lens of identity and social justice to argue that in spite of the poor developmental record of Lalu's government, his charismatic image as the "messiah of the poor" went a long way in ensuring his victory.

This chapter also deals with the bifurcation of the undivided state into Bihar and Jharkhand and examines its effects on the electoral politics of the state. Finally, the chapter ends with the 2005 victory of the BJP–JD(U) alliance in the assembly election and temporary halt of the Lalu juggernaut. In examining this victory, the chapter seeks to resist any oversimplifications on the nature of voter behavior to argue that it was a complex mixture of various caste, developmental, and economic factors that made both the rise of Nitish Kumar and the subsequent decline of Lalu Prasad Yadav possible.

Chapter 6 focuses on the 2005 assembly elections, and examines in minute detail the voting patterns and coalition politics that drove these momentous elections. For most observers of politics in the state, these elections marked the beginning of a new era for not just the politics in Bihar but also the social and economic life here. Nitish Kumar's rallying slogan, "*Nutan* Bihar," firmly established his name among stalwart leaders, not just of the state but also of the country. In the coming years, the story of an impoverished Bihar racked with inefficiency, corruption, and crime would undergo significant changes, which could be credited in large part to the rainbow coalition that Kumar sought to create.

The chapter offers evidence of the nuanced manner in which the dynamics of social justice were incorporated within state action, ranging from the creation of the Mahadalit Commission to the thrust on female empowerment and the resultant political gains. While examining caste-based mobilization in the state, the chapter consciously disparages any overarching macro theories about voter behavior of individual caste groups to make a case for the vitality and volatility that typifies voting patterns. For instance, while it is generally accepted that Muslims have remained staunch supporters of the RJD, Chapter 5, through careful analysis of the CSDS data generated from election studies in the state, argues that the relationship of the Muslim community with the RJD, too, has undergone significant changes between the 1995 and the 2005 elections. In doing so, the ostensible aim of the chapter is to constantly underline the importance of understanding the dynamism that characterizes the political life of the state. In addition, the chapter also focuses on landmark reforms introduced by the Election Commission of India (ECI) and interrogates possible repercussions that these reforms could have had on the level of voter turnout and the defeat of certain political parties (RJD) to the benefit of others (BJP–JD(U)). Both these aspects manage to give a cohesive picture of a period of visible reforms within the state and firmly establish Nitish Kumar as the face of changing politics of a new Bihar.

If the 2009 Lok Sabha elections were a powerful blow to the dominance of the RJD and its leader Lalu Prasad Yadav, then the 2010 assembly election was a cause of further embarrassment. Both the voter share and the number of seats declined steeply, causing many observers to believe that the people had finally and summarily rejected Lalu Prasad Yadav's politics of social justice and had put their faith into the model of development presented by Nitish Kumar. By making close observations of these claims in Chapter 7, an effort has been made to understand the efficacy of such an argument. Reflecting on the diverse social and political culture in the different regions of Bihar, the chapter argues for heterogeneity of reasons that exist for the popular verdict in favor of Nitish Kumar (and against Lalu Prasad Yadav). Analyzing the statistics and survey reports as well as the final voting figures, the chapter seeks to throw more light on what possible factors could have made the 2010 elections so resolutely one-sided. Debates around development, caste, and caste-based mobilization are each given relevant attention as the chapter examines the connection between caste identity, aspirational politics, and electoral politics.

The last chapter (Chapter 8) of the book analyzes the quick turnaround that Bihar politics had witnessed within a couple of years. It analyzes the political events from the BJP's alliance with the LJNSP and the RLSP registering a massive victory in 2014, the same alliance getting badly routed during the assembly election held the next year in 2015, and to the latest turnaround of Nitish Kumar switching alliance partners from the RJD back again to the BJP. The first section of the chapter analyzes the Lok Sabha election of 2014 that was unique in various respects. First, it marked the end of the decades-long alliance between the JD(U) and the BJP; second, the public mandate received by the BJP was the clearest mandate given to any political party at the national level during the past several decades; and finally, it brought unlikely alliance partners together to claim victory in Bihar. Breaking away from their successful partnership with Nitish, the BJP joined hands with Ram Vilas Paswan's LJNSP and Upendra Kushwaha's RLSP, which made the alliance the unchallenged victor from Bihar, winning 31 of the 40 Lok Sabha seats of the state. The results of the 2014 Lok Sabha election were popularly referred to as victory of politics of development over caste alliance. This chapter reopens the debate between caste and development, also mentioned in the previous chapter, but this time in favor of the BJP and against the success story of Nitish's transformative policies. Attributing the BJP's win to a number of factors such as anti-incumbency against the Congress and the promise of transformative, fast-paced development by the BJP, the chapter argues that while traditional caste loyalties changed, it is in no way a reflection of the absolute rejection of caste in favor of development.

The second section of the chapter deals with another landmark election—that of the Bihar Assembly in 2015—that managed to stall the BJP juggernaut for the first time and provided hope to a faltering opposition. The Mahagathbandhan or the GA, the chapter posits, was successful due to a multiplicity of factors, most of which managed to give the gathbandan a substantive edge over the BJP. Caste again played a crucial role, but the chapter also seeks to understand voter appraisal of the government's 10 years of positive reforms. In doing so, the chapter tries to challenge the false binary in development or caste identity, to reflect on ways in which they inform, affect, and reshape one another to make politics in the state very dynamic and versatile. It would be an injustice to the reader if the latest turnaround of politics is not mentioned in the book, so the last section of the last chapter analyzes in some detail the events that resulted in the breaking of the alliance between Nitish Kumar and Lalu Prasad Yadav over the issue of charges of corruption on Tejashwi Yadav, Nitish Kumar's deputy and leader of the RJD. The analysis ends with a hint at the future possibilities about electoral politics in Bihar in general and more so about the future of Nitish Kumar and his image, his popularity in particular. The questions remains: Will Nitish Kumar be able to gain electorally from his new political move in alliance with new alliance partners, or has he managed to burn his fingers while offering *Yagya* (*Havan*) to prove his zero tolerance for corruption?

1

Social and Economic History of Bihar

It is not just India—the whole world suffers from what may only be called "Bihar fatigue" (Das, 1992). All that seems to originate from this benighted state are stories of horror: economic backwardness, social inequity, electoral banditry, political cupidity, caste riots, and cultural degeneration. But much water has flowed down the Ganga in more than 20 years, as economic backwardness is gradually receding, violent electoral banditry in forms of booth capturing has become virtually nonexistent since 2014 and is being replaced by booth management, as it exists in rest of India, and the caste wars may have apparently institutionalized themselves in the state's political electoral battle in a more sublime way. Yes, the political cupidity or the urge to practice politics and the keenness to pursue it remains.

A Social and Economic History of Bihar

A voter's political preferences, attitudes, and political orientations toward sociopolitical issues have always been shaped by the kind of social environment in which he lives. Scholarly studies have also established the social context in which voters shape their electoral behavior and political preferences (Bartels, 2008). Such behavior is exhibited in the form of voting behavior during the elections. Political preferences are also impacted by the primary socialization that an individual experiences at his home and later among his peers.

Electoral behavior, which includes orientations and support for a political ideology, and voting behavior are impacted by a number of factors such as social class of the individual, gender, race, religious orientations, and social identities (Anderson & Heath, 2003; Butler & Stokes, 1974; Hout, Manza, & Brooks, 1999; Kelley & McAllister, 1985; Lipset & Rokkan, 1967). Social scientists have drawn a comprehensive relationship between electoral behavior of individuals and social positions and have come to the conclusion that differences in social positions of individuals, or a group of individuals, over various issues are associated with different concerns that transform into support for political parties that appear to champion their concerns (Kelley & Evans, 1995; Weakliem, 1993). Thus, electoral politics of a given political unit (nation or its parts) in a given point of time is assumed to reflect the prevailing social dynamics of that unit. India is a diverse nation with all its 28 provincial units called states no less diverse individually.

Bihar can be called one of the most politically dynamic states of India with one of the highest levels of politicization. When we say highest level of politicization, it means high levels of political awareness and a tendency to have strong political opinions. Seen in this context, it would be worthwhile to cast a glance at the political demography of Bihar.

Regions

Patna is the capital of Bihar, from where the state government functions. It is also a hub of political and cultural activities. Patna, situated on the banks of Ganga, lies in the Magadh region of the state. Besides being politically vibrant and socially conscious, Bihar is also very diverse geographically with various regions of the state representing a unique sociopolitical culture. The state is broadly divided into five main regions: Tirhut, Mithila, Magadh, Bhojpur, and Seemanchal (East). These divisions are primarily cultural but are also used for studying political orientations. Each of the regions exhibits its own unique social and cultural values with a language and tone different from the others (see Figure 1.1).

Maithili, an Indo-Aryan language, is the primary language spoken in the Mithila region of the state, while in the Bhojpur region, *Bhojpuri* is the main spoken language. In Patna and the adjoining region known as Magadh, *Magahi* language is spoken. Every region of the state has some sort of political and social domination of a particular caste group according to its numerical strength or political influence in the region. As caste groups have come to be associated with different political parties, the various regions have become strongholds of those political groups.

Figure 1.1

Major languages spoken in Bihar

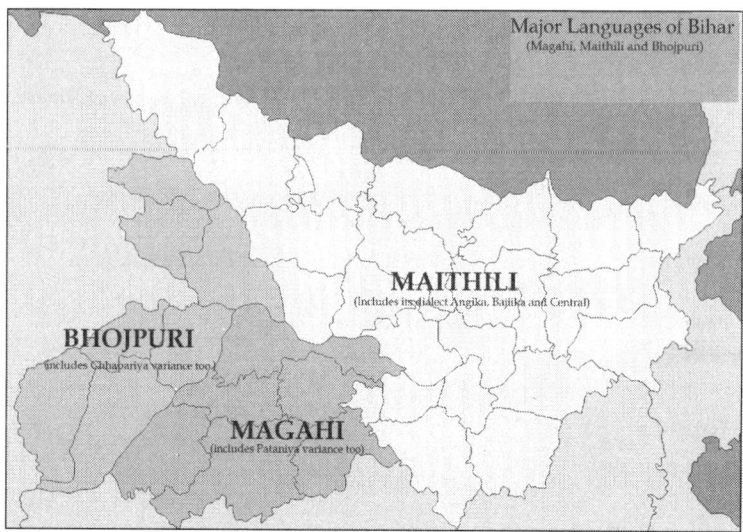

Source: http://en.wikipedia.org/wiki/Bihari_languages#/media/File:Languages_of_Bihar. gif (retrieved on May 13, 2015).

Note: Maithili includes its dialects Bajjika and Angika, Magahi includes Pataniya variance, Bhojpuri includes Chhapariya variance; image adapted from Google images. This map is not to scale and does not depict authentic boundaries.

For overlapping political and cultural reasons, Bihar has been divided into five zones—Tirhut, Mithila, Magadh, Seemanchal, and Bhojpur (see Table 1.1 and Figure 1.2).

Castes

Structurally, the population of Bihar comprises thousands of individual castes. Caste remains fundamental to the sociopolitical base of political parties, but it also decides how tickets will be distributed and how ministries will be allocated after elections among various caste groups who assert their political identities on the basis of caste.

The caste politics vis-à-vis electoral politics in Bihar may be looked at from two broad contexts: caste politics post-Independence and caste politics post-1990, after the Mandalization of the politics of the state.

Table 1.1

Regions of Bihar and districts within them

Regions	Districts
Tirhut	Bagha (SC), Bettiah, Motihari, Gopalganj, Siwan, Maharajganj, Chhapra, Hajipur (SC), Vaishali, Muzaffarpur, Sitamarhi, and Sheohar
Mithila	Madhubani, Jhanjharpur, Darbhanga, Rosera (SC), Samastipur, Saharsa, and Madhepura
Magadh	Barh, Balia, Munger, Begusarai, Nalanda, Patna, Aurangabad, Jehanabad, Nawada (SC), and Gaya (SC)
Seemanchal	Araria (SC), Kishanganj, Purnia, Katihar, Banka, Bhagalpur, and Khagaria
Bhojpur	Arrah, Buxar, Sasaram (SC), and Bikramganj

Source: Classified by the author.

Figure 1.2

Districts of Bihar

Source: http://gov.bih.nic.in/Profile/Districts.htm (retrieved on May 13, 2015).

Note: Adapted from Google images. This map is not to scale and does not depict authentic boundaries.

The pre-1990 social and political space in Bihar was dominated by upper castes such as Brahmins, Rajputs, Bhumihars, and Kayasthas among Hindus, and Syeds, Sheikhs, and Pathans among Muslims. The Bihar society was divided into three layers of social stratification among Hindus and two layers among Muslims.

Hindus are divided into upper castes, backward castes, and Scheduled Castes (SC), while Muslims are divided into upper castes and backward castes. The Brahmins, Rajputs, Bhumihars, and Kayasthas constitute the upper caste among the Hindus, while Yadavs, Kurmi–Koeris, and Banias constitute the backward castes. The Chamars, Dusadhs, and Musahars constitute the SC, also referred to as the untouchables. Untouchability continues to be practiced in some pockets of the state despite Jitan Ram Manjhi—belonging to the Musahar community—taking over as the chief minister of the state.

In pre-1990 Bihar, the upper castes (Brahmins, Bhumihars, Rajputs, and Kayasthas) dominated not only the social and political space but also the bureaucracy and the judiciary. It is alleged that the upper caste dominated the institutions of Bihar and subverted the land reforms in Bihar that would have been advantageous to the backward castes and the SC populations.

Thus, caste is the most durable mode of social identity and has become the basis of sociopolitical organizations. Based on the 1931 census, upper caste Hindus constituted about 13% of the total population of undivided Bihar. Although upper or forward-caste Hindus, estimated to be 21.5% of the population in 2001, are numerically small compared to OBCs, until recently, they are the ones who have dominated the social, economic, and political lives of the state. Traditionally, they constituted the most powerful section of society, for they possessed large chunks of arable lands and dominated bureaucracy, academia, big businesses, and until recently, political powers too (Blair, 1980; Robin, 2009).

It is important to note that neither the upper castes nor the OBCs constitute one monolithic group; rather, they are composed of various *jatis*. These groups (jatis) are politically divided and sometimes even vote for a party with whom they may not be known to be politically associated with. For example, upper caste voters may at times vote for an RJD candidate and ignore a BJP candidate if he does not belong to their caste. So, there may be variations in voting behavior, at times, which may be different from the set traditions.

While the Rajputs, Bhumihars, Brahmins, and Kayasthas constitute the upper castes, there are a larger number of jatis that are categorized as OBCs. The Yadavs, Kurmis, and Koeris constitute the upper OBC, while other jatis such as Kahar, Kumhar, Lohar, Tatwu, Teli, and Dhanuk constitute the lower OBC. Even within Muslims, there are upper and lower jatis. The question is: Is the voting pattern of various jatis within these three caste groups (the upper castes, the OBCs, and the Muslims) similar when there is immense social and economic disparity among them? Another question is: Do these caste groups show similar tendencies in voting behavior in face of deep class differentiation among them? There has been a tendency of the more affluent sections of society voting on different lines. Even backward caste people who are rich and affluent have at times preferred the BJP during the time of elections.

Backward castes or OBCs constitute the largest chunk of population. According to the 1931 population census, backward caste (Hindus) accounted for about 51% of the total population of Bihar. The backward castes—Yadavs, Kurmi–Koeris, and Banias—were in an advantageous position in the post-Mandal phase. During this phase, the upper castes were virtually replaced by backward castes as the political elite of Bihar. The Brahmins, Rajputs, Bhumihars, and Kayasthas were replaced by the Yadavs, Kurmi–Koeris, Banias, and Telis. Jagannath Mishra, a Brahmin, was replaced by Lalu Prasad, a Yadav, as the leader of Bihar in the post-1990 phase. The upper castes and the OBC community jostled with each other for political space in Bihar, and finally, the upper caste accepted the leadership of the OBCs after a long and protracted struggle.

Amongst the backward castes, Yadavs, Koeris, and Kurmis are quite important both numerically and in terms of socioeconomic mobility. Yadavs with 11% of total population were the single largest backward caste in Bihar and they continue to be so. The post-1990 phase made Yadavs the most socially and politically dominant caste in Bihar while also experiencing an upward social mobility that continues until date.

The Kurmis and Koeris, together called Luv Kush Samaj (group), constituted about 7.7% of total population in Bihar. Although the OBCs do not suffer social disabilities as the Dalits do, they seem to have been enjoying lower socioeconomic status compared to the upper castes. Both the Yadavs and Kurmi–Koeris were agrarian communities (pre-1990 phase) tilling the lands of the upper caste landlords, but after 1990, the situation gradually changed. With rise in their social mobility, their social and political positions drastically changed as they began to be the new political elites in the changing circumstances, even as they continue to lag in social, educational, and economic indicators in comparison with upper caste population. Traditionally, most of these OBC castes have been engaged in agriculture as either cultivators or laborers. In urban areas, most of them have been engaged in unorganized sectors.

Table 1.2

Landholding percentage of major social groups in Bihar (2011–2012)

Indicators	All	SC	OBC	Others
Size of Land Cultivated				
0	45.1	67.3	42.1	30.1
0.001–0.400 hectare	0.9	0.9	1.2	0.3
0.410–1.000 hectare	9.3	6.3	8.9	13.9
1.010–2.000 hectare	8.7	2.8	9.0	14.3
Above 2.000 hectare	3.8	5.0	3.6	7.3

Source: NSSO, Ministry of Statistics and Programme Implementation, Government of India (2015).

Educationally, they have been way behind the forward castes (NSSO 2011–2012; see Table 1.2).[1]

Although their access to socioeconomic resources has improved because of affirmative action in recent years, they still continue to lag behind the forward castes in many of the social and economic indicators. Until 1989, it was the upper castes who dominated Bihar politics with their virtual control over society and economy as well. But the OBCs rode on the Lok Dal party for their political emancipation. The upper backwards—Yadavs, Kurmis, and Koeris—virtually never formed a part of Congress electoral imagination as Congress party's power structure consisted of upper castes—Brahmins, Rajputs, and Bhumihars—in the leadership positions with Dalits, Muslims, and lower backwards as captive voters. But, when V.P. Singh's JD government announced the implementation of Mandal Commission recommendations[2] that reserved 27% seats for the OBCs, it led to a new kind of political and social empowerment in Bihar. Both Lalu Prasad Yadav and Nitish Kumar became ardent advocates of Mandal politics that handed out a huge blow to the

---

[1] According to NSSO (1999–2000) estimates, OBCs accounted for 54% of the total Hindu population in Bihar. It can be assumed that the proportion of individual castes such as Yadavs and Kurmis remains more or less the same as in 1931 census.

[2] Bindheshwari Prasad Mandal (1918–1982) was an Indian parliamentarian. He was Yadav by caste and had served as chairman of the Second Backward Classes Commission, which came to be known as the Mandal Commission. The commission's report triggered a mobilization in the "OBCs" segment of Indian population. The implementation of the report by the V.P. Singh government led to a fierce debate on the policy for underrepresented and underprivileged groups in the Indian polity and society.

mosque–temple politics perpetuated by the BJP in North India, primarily Bihar.

The SCs, the ex-untouchables, account for about 16% of the total population. About 93.3% of them reside in rural areas (Census 2001). They are unevenly distributed across the state, though their concentration is quite high in some districts such as Gaya, Nawada, Kaimur, Vaishali, Aurangabad, and Nalanda. Of the 23 SCs listed in the census, Chamars constitute about 31.3% of the total SC population in the state. Dusadhs, accounting for about 30%, are the second largest SC group. Other numerically significant SC groups are Mushar, Pashi, Dhobi, and Bhuia. Overall, the SCs or Dalits stand at the bottom of the socioeconomic hierarchy and thus form the most disadvantaged segment of society. The literacy rate among them is abysmally low. The vast majority of them are landless and poor (Table 1.2). Their living conditions are pathetic. However, in recent decades, there has been a growing consciousness among them about their rights and entitlements.

Religion

Religion is another important axis of social organization. Although Hindus constitute the dominant religious group, Muslims with 16.87% of the state's total population constitute a significant part. While they are not uniformly distributed, there are certain pockets where they are in majority or constitute a number that could be critically important for electoral outcomes. Table 1.3 shows the Muslim population in the districts of Bihar. In the recent decades, religion has re-awakened both as a political force and as a basis of collective action through the assertion of separate Hindu and Muslim identities. It is generally assumed that Muslims vote en bloc and thereby determine the electoral outcome in the state to a significant extent.

In brief, the society in Bihar reflects a great deal of diversity. The society is divided along several axes. Seen through the lens of social and economic development, Bihar depicts a dismal picture. There exist huge socioeconomic disparities among different segments of the population, especially among different social groups (see Tables 1.2 and 1.4). These differences and cleavages often form the basis of social and political mobilization and demobilization. The cleavages of economic disparity exist more between different caste groups than within the caste groups.

Table 1.3

Muslim population in the districts of Bihar

Districts	Muslim Population 2011 (%)
Pashchim Champaran	21.98
Purba Champaran	19.42
Sheohar	15.14
Sitamarhi	21.62
Madhubani	18.25
Supaul	18.36
Araria	42.95
Kishanganj	67.98
Purnia	38.46
Katihar	44.47
Madhepura	12.08
Saharsa	14.03
Darbhanga	22.39
Muzaffarpur	15.53
Gopalganj	17.02
Siwan	18.26
Saran	10.28
Vaishali	9.56
Samastipur	10.62
Begusarai	13.71
Khagaria	10.53
Bhagalpur	17.68
Banka	12.33
Munger	8.07
Lakhisarai	4.08
Sheikhpura	5.92
Nalanda	6.88
Patna	7.54
Bhojpur	7.25
Buxar	6.18
Kaimur (Bhabua)	9.55

(Continued)

Table 1.3

(Continued)

Districts	Muslim Population 2011 (%)
Rohtas	10.15
Aurangabad	9.34
Gaya	11.12
Nawada	11.01
Jamui	12.36
Jehanabad	6.73
Arwal	9.17

Source: Census report of 2011.

Table 1.4

Source of employment of major social groups in Bihar (2011–2012)

Indicators	All	SC	OBC	Others
Rural Occupation (% Households)				
Self-employed in agriculture	31.0	18.9	31.3	43.7
Self-employed in non-agriculture	18.4	14.0	20.4	16.9
Agricultural laborer	28.4	42.5	29.4	9.2
Non-agricultural laborer	9.8	15.5	8.9	7.0
Others	7.9	6.2	6.2	14.8
Urban				
Self-employed	43.8	28.6	49.8	34.9
Wage/salary earners	22.0	36.4	16.7	29.3
Casual laborer	13.2	25.4	12.3	8.3
Others	21.0	9.6	21.2	27.5

Source: NSSO, Ministry of Statistics and Programme Implementation, Government of India (2015).

The Brahmins, Rajputs, and Bhumihars were rich and held sway over large swathes of agricultural land, while the OBC communities such as the Yadavs and Kurmi–Koeris were tillers. This may be the unifying factor and paved the way for consolidation of caste as one homogenous group.

Land Use and the History of Zamindari Abolition

Bihar, as it stands today,[3] accounts for about 8.7% of total population of the country and ranks third among the states of India. The social life in Bihar heavily gravitates around the villages[4] where the vast majority of them are illiterate.[5] Over three-fourths of people secure their livelihood in agricultural and allied activities.[6] Even though the people of Bihar are excessively dependent on agriculture compared to other states, agriculture is not in good shape. Over the years, there has been stagnation in the agricultural sector (Sharma, 1995). While land still remains the measure of a family's prestige and social standing in rural areas, the distribution of operational landholdings is extremely skewed. In 2011–2012, about 45.1% of the rural households had less than 0.001 hectare to cultivate. Again, 10.2% of the rural households had cultivated land, which was more than 0.001 hectare but less than a hectare (marginal holdings), and rest 12.5% households cultivated land above 1.000 hectare each (Table 1.2).

The process of empowerment of the marginalized sections of society, however, is nothing new; it emerged suddenly in the 1970s and the 1990s, but was the culmination of long-drawn social and political movements that date back to the pre-Independence period. With nearly 80% of the population depending upon agriculture for their livelihood, it formed the mainstay of Bihar's economy. But agricultural land remained monopolized by the three upper castes—the Rajputs, the Bhumihars, and the Brahmins. The upper layer of the backward castes, namely, the Yadavs, Kurmis, and Koeris, were left with very little land. But for some exceptions, other lower castes were largely landless. Most of the zamindars

---

[3] Under the Bihar Reorganization Act 2000, Bihar was divided, and a new state of Jharkhand came into being on November 15, 2000, the birth anniversary of legendary Bhagwan Birsa Munda.

[4] Bihar is one of the least urbanized states of India. Only one-tenth of total population of the state resides in urban centers (Census of India, 2001).

[5] According to the Census 2001, only 48% of the population (7 years and above) returned as literate as against 65.3% for the country. Bihar is the least literate state in the country. There exists huge disparity in terms of gender, caste, religion, and residence. As against 60.3% male literacy rates, the female literacy rate was just 33.5%. Similarly, the rural literacy rate is much lower (44.4%) than that of urban (72.7%). The literacy rate of the SCs is much lower than that of the general population.

[6] About 80% of workers are engaged in agriculture and allied activities. About two-fifths of workers are cultivators and another two-fifths are agricultural laborers (Census 2001). About 90% of rural laborers are agricultural laborers.

were either from the Hindu upper castes or were *ashraf* (foreign) Muslims. The main caste groups were the Rajputs and the Bhumihars, besides the Brahmins in northern and western Bihar. The biggest landowner in the village wielded enormous authority on the everyday life of the villagers. Although it was an unwritten rule, villagers had to consult the biggest landowner on issues such as local agricultural wages, rights on land and other matters relating to the conduct of community's business (Sharma, 2005). The landowners had developed an exploitative agrarian system that placed vast majority of peasants in a debt trap. This led to a system of informal bondage that ensured the big landowning class' tremendous power to control the peasantry (Prasad, 1975). In brief, a large section of people belonging to the bottom strata of rural society in Bihar had to mortgage their freedom and dignity to the landlords because of indebtedness, poverty, and dependence for employment on landlords (Sinha, 1996).

During the pre-Independence period, the state witnessed strong movement for land reforms, which continued for a long time. The movement was led by Swami Vidyanand, Swami Sahajanand Saraswati, and Karyanand Sharma mainly in the north Bihar region, by leaders of the Kisan Sabha formed in the year 1920. They demanded abolition of the zamindari system, minimum wages for agricultural labor, licensing of the moneylenders' security to the tenant cultivator, and other reforms. Since it was mainly the upper castes that owned land and wielded social and political power, such movements inevitably got directed toward them. On the other hand, it was mainly the backward castes owning some land, which formed the backbone of the movement, as they perceived a direct benefit from such reforms. Though it could not be carried to its desired results, some redistribution of land as a result of the *Bhoodan* movement, led to the breaking of the upper castes' hold over land to a great extent.

The first 10 years of zamindari abolition did bring about some change in the social life in the countryside. The former zamindars were in the process of losing their extra economic feudal powers. This was a process complementary to the spread of democracy. On the other hand, abolition of zamindari coupled with vesting of ownership in tenants and land redistribution policies gave rise to a new class of peasant proprietors. The main beneficiaries were the middle peasantry and protected tenants. The landless laborers and the *bataidars* (sharecroppers) did not benefit much from the first two waves of land reforms in the Hindi heartland. In Bihar, it was the Yadavs, Kurmis, and Koeris (upper backward caste) who gained most from the reforms (Prasad, 1980).

In 1972–1973, the Ceiling on Landholding (Amendment) Act was enacted to prevent the transfer of surplus lands. Further, it included homestead, orchard, pastures etc. in the ceiling area prescribed in the Act. With these Acts in place, by 1970–1972, the state controlled about 22% of the land. The former zamindars, however, found a number of ways to retain large portions of their land, which were to be acquired as surplus land. The most popular way was that of holding *benami* land besides transforming land into ponds, gardens, and cold storages or by opening libraries and temples on their land (Nedumpara, 2004; Sinha, 1978).

The abolition of the zamindari system and vesting landownership in the hands of the tenants created a class of rural populace that would wish for better conditions for their enterprise through basic necessities such as roads, education, healthcare, farm extension, etc. But there was no plan for widespread provision of these in the rural areas. The central government's plan was mainly concerned with greater farm production and concentrated on the areas that had irrigation facilities for the purpose. Education was heavily concentrated on technical education at a higher level for the new industries under the plan. If this was the central government's plan, it was also the plan of the states, approved in detail by the Planning Commission. The central government's plan was also the plan of the central Congress authority. The provincial parties only followed the lead. To the forward caste leadership, this approach was also useful since their children could go into these new educational institutions to finally enter into the new jobs. This was where the failure of the state's party leadership originated from and remained unchanged, as we will see later in the following section, until the Congress was dislodged from power and even afterward.

In summary, during this phase, land reform was a major political initiative. Despite all their limitations, the land reform laws since 1948 have transferred ownership right in vast areas of land to the upper OBCs, mainly Yadavs and Koeri–Kurmis. This gave them the strength to ask for a larger share in political power, and by the late 1960s they seemed to have started asserting themselves politically, which is reflected in the slow but gradual rise of their representation in the *Vidhan Sabha* (Legislative Assembly). However, the lower OBCs and SCs were in a relatively weaker position since they remained largely landless and at most tenants-at-will, depending on the erstwhile zamindars as well as the new Yadav landowners. While the struggle for power was between the landowning forward castes and the new landowning class of Yadavs (they have their Thakur Sena, Bhumihar Sena, and Yadav Sena), these were united against the lower OBCs and the BCs.

The Process of Empowerment in Bihar

With a bit of land and with the diversification of their occupational patterns due to land reform, backward castes were able to improve their economic status and emerge as a newly rich rural agrarian class, popularly known as the *Kulaks* (high-income farmers/peasants), and they started to play an important role in the social and political spheres. On the other hand, such struggle also sowed the seeds of a sense of empowerment among the people.

This assertiveness kept growing with the various social and political movements, but took on a particularly intense form in the mid-1970s with the movement led by Jayaprakash Narayan in which, though it was an all-India movement, Bihar played a leading role and provided the backbone. This movement ultimately led to a change of guard at the Center. As a fallout, the newly emerging Kulaks, at least in Bihar, played an important role in the changed scenario.

Failure of Land Reforms in Bihar and Bloody Caste Wars

The enactment of the 1972–1973 Ceiling on Landholding (Amendment) Act to prevent transfer of surplus lands led to heightened tension between the landless class—mostly the SC population and the lower OBCs. The upper caste, allegedly with the active aid of bureaucracy, subverted the land reforms in Bihar leading to violent clashes between these two groups.

The ground realities in Bihar had the potential to enable mobilization of popular discontent over the years. However, resistance from the landed sections and from successive state governments, whether overt or covert, prevented the implementation of any substantial land reform measures. Organizations such as the All India Agricultural Workers Union (AIAWU) have raised the issue of plugging loopholes in the land ceiling legislation and the distribution of surplus land, including land caught in litigation, following the models of West Bengal and Kerala. The AIAWU had also been demanding the distribution of waste, Bhoodan, evacuee, and uncultivated lands to the landless, free of cost. In fact, the organized struggle for land rights goes back to 1929, when the Bihar Pradesh Kisan Sabha was founded under the leadership of the CPI leader Swami Sahajanand Saraswati. "Land to the tiller" was a popular slogan of the Kisan Sabha that forged strong ties with middle-level peasants and some upper caste groups as well. "Bihar was the first State in Independent India to legislate on land reforms, but it never proceeded to any meaningful implementation of the measures mainly because of the lack of political will and resistance from the landed sections" (Rajalakshmi, 2001).

The extent of resistance could be gauged from the fact that the Bihar Abolition of Zamindari Act, 1948, was challenged in court and later replaced by the Bihar Land Reforms Bill, 1949. The Bihar Land Reforms Act, 1950, faced legal obstacles because it challenged the interests of the zamindars who were mostly upper caste Hindus and Muslims. A study conducted by the Partnership Council of India, an organization supporting the Ekta Parishad, stated that "although it was implicit in the 1950 Act that the state was the ultimate landlord with exclusive proprietary interest, the issue of ultimate ownership of land remained controversial," the *Frontline* news report said. (Rajalakshmi, 2001)

The Bihar Land Ceiling Act, 1961, could not be implemented due to many loopholes in it that diluted its implementation.

The Council's study also quotes a Planning Commission report of 1964 which says that had the law been implemented properly, one or one and a half lakh acres of spare land could have been acquired. The ceiling process accumulated 3,85,013 acres of spare land, of which 2,77,491 acres was distributed among 3,52,703 families as of January 2001. In 2000–2001, 449.73 acres was distributed among 844 families. However, the extent of land distributed to each family works out to about 0.53 acres, which is too small an area for profitable cultivation. Besides, it was not specified what kind of land was distributed, giving rise to speculation that most of it was non-cultivable land. (Rajalakshmi, 2001)

The subversion of land reforms led to bloody caste wars in Bihar. The conflict that broke out in the late 1970s continued until the year 2000, in which over 700 people were killed. The dead belonged mostly to the SC section of Bihar's society.

To any old-timer, the earliest image of the Bihar caste wars is from 1977. Belchhi in Patna had seen 14 SC workers killed and the enduring image is of a visit by Indira Gandhi, who otherwise lay low since the post-Emergency defeat. She had to ride on an elephant to reach the smallest hamlet of Dalits, the monsoon having waterlogged the approach road (Singh, 2012).

Belchhi triggered caste wars that continued to rage in the hinterlands of Bihar until 2000. At least 700 people were killed in 91 attacks carried by various caste groups. Majority of the people were killed during 1994–2000 when the army of upper caste landlords, *Ranbir Sena*, was at the peak of its power.

The now defunct Ranbir Sena, CPML, and Maoist Communist Centre (MCC) were at the forefront of the caste and class wars in Bihar. While the Ranbir Sena represented the interest of the upper caste, the CPML and the MCC vouched support for lower caste and lower class people.

Upper caste members of Ranbir Sena—an organization founded by Brahmeshwar Mukhia, who was murdered in 2012—sparked violent protests in Patna, and were charged in 22 massacres.

"It was the media and the police who called it Ranbir Sena. The organization I formed was Rashtrawadi Kisan Sangharsh Samiti," Mukhiya, acquitted in 16 of the 22 cases before getting bail, was quoted as saying in a media report in Patna in 2012. His claims notwithstanding, an organization that called itself the Ranbir Sena left its signature on the killings. Its letter-pad carried an image showing "blood-about-to-drop" besides a logo that said "virodh, adlav aur balidaan." Ranbir Sena diaries seized by police revealed code words such as "'A++' for group killings, 'A+' for a family killed and 'A' for individuals murdered," the media report said (Singh, 2012).

Private Armies

The Ranbir Sena was formed in August 1994 after land disputes between the upper caste landlords, the SC and OBC working class reached its zenith. The SCs and OBCs were actually encouraged by the formation of JD government led by Lalu Prasad Yadav, and the upper caste feared that now the working class may strike back and usurp their lands. The later part of 1994 was a period when the CPML Liberation was pitching for class justice and another extreme-left group MCC (now CPI-Maoist) was gearing to take on the upper class with threats of violent movement if they did not give up their land to the tillers and the poor. Certainly, the rise of the extreme-left movement was a result of the state's failure to implement land reforms in letter and spirit, which was obviously under the influence of the upper caste lobby. Over a dozen private armies surfaced and disappeared between the late 1970s and the mid-1990s. In 1978, OBC Kurmis formed the Bhumi Sena whose areas of influence were Patna, Gaya, Jehanabad, and Nalanda. The Kuwar Sena of upper caste Rajputs came up in 1979, with its strongholds in Bhojpur (Arrah) and Buxar. In 1980 came the Brahmarsi Sena of Bhumihars, allegedly responsible for the massacres in Paras Bigha (Jehanabad) of 11 OBC members and Pipra (Patna) of 14 SC members. OBC Yadavs formed the Laurik Sena in 1985. There also were the Brahman Sena, the Satyendra Sena, the Srikrishna Sena, the Samajwadi Krantikari Sena, and the Azad Sena of various caste groups; the Savarna Liberation Front and Searchlight did not last long. In 1986, the then Chief Minister Chandra Shekhar Singh banned all such private armies (Singh, 2012).

In 1987, the MCC killed 52 people belonging to the upper caste in an Aurangabad village dominated by Rajput caste men. Vinay Singh, an upper caste villager, lost 20 members of his family in this violent attack.

Ranbir Sena was formed in Belaur village—the scene of many land disputes—in Bhojpur district, after a clash between a CPML Liberation leader and a fellow villager.

On July 11, 1996, alleged Ranbir Sena men killed 21 Dalits including women, children, and infants in Bathanitola village in Bhojpur district. Close to 60 Ranbir Sena men armed with swords, lathis, and firearms descended on the village and carried out the killings. This was apparently a revenge attack for the killing of at least nine Bhumihar upper caste people in Nadhi village in Bhojpur district.

The authorities and the government were not able to stop this kind of massacres in the killing fields of Bihar. Next year, on December 1, 1997, at least 58 SC members were killed in Lakshmanpur Bathe village in Jehanabad district by upper caste militiamen.

"The RJD government was selective about the victims it reached out to. Lalu Prasad Yadav and Rabri Devi would visit mostly where Dalits were killed," said an old-timer. In 1999 came the killing of 23 Dalits at Shankarbigha village of Jehanabad. MCC cadres, gaining in power by now, hit back by killing 35 landlords at Senari, Jehanabad. The last major strike by the Ranbir Sena came in 2000, when it killed 35 OBC and SC members in Mianpur (Aurangabad). "The Senari massacre marked the growth of the MCC and the diminishing influence of the Ranbir Sena, whose activities started to ebb after Mianpur," says a police officer who has long worked in Naxal areas (Singh, 2012).

These gruesome caste terror activities in Bihar have affected all the people in the state. The caste violence was highest against the SCs with 201 deceased, lowest against OBC with 35 deceased, and moderate against upper caste with 129 deaths (Table 1.5).

Impact of Industrialization in Bihar

After the bifurcation of the state, the process of industrialization in Bihar has gone down, since industrialization was more concentrated in the Chota Nagpur belt which is currently part of Jharkhand. Moreover, the net domestic product in Bihar is ₹32,004 crore, of which the share of the industrial sector is a mere ₹1,020 crore. Industry thus accounts for

Table 1.5

Some prominent incidents of caste violence in Bihar

1977	Becchi (Patna): 14 killed, upper backward landlords attack SC laborers
1980	Pipra (Patna): 14 killed, upper backward landlords attack SC laborers
1984	Danwar–Bihta: 22 killed, upper castes attack SCs
1987	Dalelchak– Baghaura: 52 killed, MCC attacks upper caste villagers
1992	Bar (Gaya): 34 killed, upper backward class attacks upper castes
1996	Nadhi (Bhojpur) 8 killed, CPI(ML) attacks upper castes/landlords
	Nadhi (Bhojpur): 9 killed, attack this time by upper castes on SCs
	Bathanitola (Bhojpur): 22 Dalits killed by landlords, the worst of that year's many attacks
1997	Haibaspur (Patna): 10 killed in attack by landlords on SCs
	Ekwari (Bhojpur): 10 killed in attack by upper castes on SCs
	Khadasin (Jehanabad): 8 SCs killed in attack by landlords
	Lakshmanpur Bathe (Jehanabad): 61 killed in attack by upper castes on SCs
1999	Senari (Jehanabad): 35 killed, MCC attacks landlords, first strong sign of MCC gaining strength
	Sendani (Gaya): 12 killed in attack by landlords on OBCs/SCs
	Shankarbigha (Jehanabad): 23 killed in attack by upper castes on SCs
2000	Mianpur (Aurangabad): 35 OBCs killed in attack by Ranbir Sena
2014	Bhojpur: Rape of 6 Dalit women and minors by Ranbir Sena and all members of all three upper castes

Source: CSDS Data Unit.

only 3.2% of the state domestic product in contrast to the national average of 20.1%, making Bihar one of the least industrialized states in the country (Das Gupta, 2007). Due to bifurcation, regional representation of several industries has also been altered; currently, food, tobacco, leather, and non-metallic mineral products form the industrial base of Bihar. It lost coal, refined petroleum products, basic metals, motor vehicles, and trailers, which earlier formed the base of Bihar's industry.

Further, of a total of 1,528 industrial units in the state, only 236 are medium or large units. The geographical spread of these units is also skewed. Out of the 38 districts in Bihar, as many as 10 districts have no medium- or large-scale industrial units and another 11 districts have less than five units each. Most of the medium- and large-scale units are concentrated in Patna, Magadh, and Tirhut divisions. The situation regarding small-scale industry is no different, though the tiny sector and artisan units are more evenly spread throughout the state.

The lack of industrialization has often been explained by factors such as natural endowment, infrastructure support, local availability of skilled manpower, size of local and export markets, and industrial policies of both the central and state governments. Each of these factors opens up a plethora of questions as to the role of "policy" failure to overcome these limits to industrialization in the state, crucial in a scenario where agriculture is overcrowded due to the dearth of employment opportunities in the rural non-agrarian sector.

In many ways, Bihar is a classic case of an enclave economy, illustrative of the contradictions between investments—public and private—and the prevalence of non-capitalist predatory accumulation. Thus, while there were centers of heavy industry—steel in Jamshedpur, iron and coal in Dhanbad, cement in Dalmianagar and Dehri on Sone, and oil in Barauni, to name a few—these were either under the control of a few families or, worse, the mafia, as in Dhanbad. Most of the big industry was not just regionally concentrated; it also developed few linkages—upstream and downstream—with the local market. The only exception, if at all, was sugar, with nearly 40% of sugar capacity falling in the cooperative sector. In most other cases, from heavy industry to leather and paper, both the ownership and the spillover effects remained narrow. Overall, thus, the industrialization process failed to have an impact on the agrarian misery and exploitation; and post-bifurcation, most industries went to Jharkhand.

Similarly, a steady supply of Bihari migrant labor was vital to the needs of the Indian industry that developed around textiles in Bombay and Ahmedabad in the first three decades of the twentieth century. Simultaneously, the warped nature of absorption of the agrarian surplus meant that there was no incentive for landlords to diversify into trade or industry. Thus, the lack of industrialization in Bihar, except for the efforts of the Tata group in Jamshedpur, was a product of the explicit colonial policy toward maintaining the hinterland as a feeder economy for the main centers of colonial capital.

There were other ways in which the post-Independence policy regime worked against both a broadening and deepening of the industrial base. Central to it was the Freight Equalization Policy of 1948 for coal and iron. Essentially the policy denied the eastern zone of the country any advantage of proximity to these mineral resources, indirectly facilitating further industrial development in the already advanced western regions of the country. To make matters worse, similar policies were not introduced for other intermediary products produced in the western regions, thereby increasing cost for industries elsewhere using these resources. This double bias crippled industrialization in Bihar, with available capital shifting to the western regions of India.

Overall, thus, Bihar's lack of industry is a direct product of apathetic national policies that created structural and institutional constraints for industrialization in the state.

The Bihar economic survey argues that the high level of industrial sickness in Bihar is due to inadequate infrastructure facilities: the lack of working capital, non-availability of raw material, inadequacy of road network and communication services, poor and uncertain power position, and weak research support. Besides, unsatisfactory credit availability, abnormally high interest rates, delay in granting term loans, and rigid attitude of banks and other financial institutions in the state are also some other inhibiting factors.

While all these policy announcements have generated substantial enthusiasm, there is some skepticism about how well they will work as also about the commitment of the state government to vigorous industrialization. It bears repetition that the ruling National Democratic Alliance (NDA) is a coalition of the BJP and the Janata Dal (Secular)— JD(S). The former draws heavily on the upper caste/class elite, unwilling and unable to challenge the power of the landed elite, who have historically neither invested in agricultural modernization nor diversified into non-farm activities. The JD(S), in turn, draws on socially backward and marginal groups who not only have little investible surplus but for the moment seem more interested in pursuing a politics of "social justice." The only agenda that the two can agree on is *sushasan*, good governance.

On the whole, the Industrial Incentive Policy is a product of this sushasan initiative. It is a standard package of concessions with substantial incentives to encourage new investments in line with the policies pursued by more developed states. Such policies have become necessary under the current neoliberal economic order in which the states are competing for investments. However, given the historical causes of non-industrialization in Bihar, the likelihood of this policy to significantly change the industrial landscape is marginal. The reasons for non-industrialization in Bihar are complex and have more to do with national policy for the last 60 years or more. These have to do with institutional structures of landholding patterns, the undermining of competitiveness through policies like freight equalization and an abysmal infrastructure scenario.

Thus, the problem of industrialization cannot be solved by a one-time incentive policy at the level of the state. When more developed states offer similar concessions and are also in a position to provide better infrastructure, why would new investments come to Bihar? Moreover, policies of land acquisition for mega industrial parks seem to be totally misplaced when such efforts have met with little success in Bihar in the past. In the current conjuncture, when the basis of such industrial agglomerations is being questioned with respect to the effects on agriculture, acquisition of such large amounts of land appears even more suspect.

For states like Bihar, industrialization will remain a distant dream unless we can visualize an alternative industrial structure. Not only does the state have to set right historical wrongs, but national policies also have to be revised to specifically encourage investment in backward states and regions. How far this will happen in a situation in which the state seems keen to recede from its developmental role remains an open question.

Educational Developments Since Independence

In comparison to other states, education has improved in Bihar. One thing that development economists agree on is the importance of education. Put simply, if development is to be sustainable, people need to be well educated. Just looking at economic output, education contributes to growth by increasing the level of human capital of the workforce—as India has discovered in the IT sector. Looking beyond the statistics, education can equip people with the tools for a more fulfilling and enjoyable life (Table 1.6).

The Government of Bihar has lately undertaken numerous policy initiatives to make education more reasonable and reachable to children. These enterprises have focused on reducing the "opportunity cost" of schooling and providing incentives for enrolment and performance (Ranjan & Prakash, 2012).

According to the District Information System for Education (DISE) data for 2006–2007, the enrolment rate at the primary level in Bihar has been increasing and is now higher than the median of the 20 major states in India. However, in terms of the enrolment rate at the upper primary level, Bihar is right at the bottom of the list of these 20 states, with less than half of the eligible children attending school. However, the DISE enrolment data for primary grades are not available for Bihar after 2007. In the case of dropouts, Bihar has a higher out-of-school rate than the median state in India, though the percentage has been declining over time. In line with the enrolment numbers, the out-of-school rate is higher among older children.

In addition to the infrastructural challenges, Bihar needs to consider other important determinants of a good education. Previous studies highlight the problem of teacher-absenteeism in several developing countries, including India. This body of research highlights a strong

Table 1.6

Educational levels of major social groups in Bihar (2011–2012)

Indicators	All	SC	OBC	Others
Educational Levels (% Persons)				
Not literate	41.9	58.9	43.9	20.5
Literate and up to primary	20.5	21.3	21.5	17.6
Middle	13.1	7.6	14.0	14.8
Secondary	12.7	5.9	12.3	20.2
Higher secondary	7.1	3.4	5.5	15.6
Diploma/certificate	0.3	0.4	0.1	0.9
Graduate and above	4.3	2.1	2.8	10.5

Source: NSSO, Ministry of Statistics and Programme Implementation, Government of India (2015).

connection between poor school infrastructure, such as lack of drinking water and teacher-absenteeism, but also suggests that improved monitoring by authorities can improve teacher attendance. Indeed, data from a field experiment in Kenya suggests that scholarship incentives, where good grades were rewarded with grants and payment of school fees, helped to motivate both students and parents as well as reduce teacher-absenteeism.

Focusing on the teachers themselves, most studies on the link between performance-related pay and educational outcomes find the effects to be positive. An essential prerequisite to the implementation of any kind of incentive pay scheme, however, is to set up a data system for monitoring the performance of schools and teachers. Such a data system is essential in linking student performance to teacher effectiveness. Developing such a data system will have the additional benefit of allowing the administrators to monitor the performance of schools and take remedial action in poorly performing schools. Put simply, if Bihar is to implement a policy to incentivize teachers and measure school performance, it needs to have a data system in place first.

The problem, though, is not just with the teachers. There is also a problem with parents and children demanding enough education. Our survey of existing research suggests that many parents and children perceive the returns on schooling to be much less than the returns from starting work earlier in life. The result is people choosing to "undereducate" themselves in many developing countries (otherwise known as "underinvestment" in education). Experimental studies suggest that public campaigns aimed at informing parents and children of the benefits of education are extremely cost-effective at increasing school enrolment. Given the current lack of public information in Bihar, it is strongly recommended that the government launch such a campaign. In Bihar in particular, it would be a good idea to emphasize on the development of English language skills, given their high returns in the job market.

Recent policy initiatives and improvements in primary school enrolment show that Bihar is making progress in improving its education levels. These policies have focused on lowering the cost of schooling through subsidizing or providing textbooks, uniforms, bicycles, and cash transfers for attendance. While these have reduced the costs of schooling in Bihar, much remains to be done to boost schooling infrastructure and improve conditions for both students and teachers.[7]

---

[7] See http://www.livemint.com/Home-Page/vkRlJ8u3T6OzWccTpJslrI/Education-in-Bihar-Still-a-long-road-ahead.html (retrieved on November 10, 2017).

Profile of Major Political Parties

The major political parties in Bihar are being distributed on national and regional basis. There are two national political parties in Bihar, the Indian National Congress (INC) and the BJP, and two regional parties, the RJD and the JD(U).

Congress (INC)

The Congress party had been the foremost political force in Bihar before the rise of the JD. The party had held power in the state for numerous years and 16 chief ministers of the state have been Congressmen. Numerous leaders from the state have served in the Union Council of Ministers in the Congress governments since Independence. This list includes one of the most popular Congress leaders outside the Nehru–Gandhi family— former Defense Minister Late Babu Jagjivan Ram (who left the party in 1977 to form Congress for Democracy, which later merged with the Janata Party) who hailed from Arrah in Bihar. Jagjivan Ram had been instrumental in helping the party consolidate support among Dalit voters and countering the rise of socialist parties in the state.

Since 1990, the party has faced a massive decline in the state and has been reduced to a minor player. It has hardly managed to win seats when it has contested alone in the state elections. Hence, it has contested numerous Lok Sabha and assembly elections in recent years in alliance with the RJD.

In the 2015 Vidhan Sabha election, the Congress leadership was instrumental in bringing the RJD and JD(U) together. The party itself contested for merely 41 seats, but managed to win in 27 constituencies— its best performance in the state since 1995.

Bharatiya Janata Party

The BJP is currently one of the prime players in Bihar's politics. The party has never led a government in the state and has only been a "junior partner" in ruling coalition with the JD(U) on multiple occasions. Before the formation of Jharkhand, the BJP was one of the foremost political forces in state politics due to a concentration of support in Jharkhand. Post-bifurcation, the BJP ceased to be a dominant force in the state. The BJP and Samata Party (later renamed as the JD(U)) formed an alliance in 1996. This alliance stood for close to 17 years and even managed to form the government between 2005 and 2013 (in 2013 the JD(U) had unilaterally ended the alliance). Senior party leader Sushil Modi had then served as the deputy chief minister under Nitish Kumar.

In the 2014 Lok Sabha election, the BJP won a plurality of seats, 22 seats, in the state and had re-emerged as a dominant force in state politics. Even in 2014, the BJP had contested in alliance with the RLSP, the Hindustani Awam Morcha (HAM), and the LJNSP. At present, the BJP remains an important independent political player in state politics. This was indicated by the party's vote share in the 2015 assembly election. The NDA may have lost terribly, but the BJP still managed to win over 50 seats with a vote share of 24.4% (Table 1.7).

Rashtriya Janata Dal

The RJD was formed on July 5, 1997, after a formal vertical split in the JD. Senior leaders such as incumbent Chief Minister Lalu Prasad Yadav,

Table 1.7

Vote share of the BJP in alliance

	BJP	*Overall Vote Share of Alliance*
1996 Lok Sabha election	20.5	35
1998 Lok Sabha election	24	39.7
1999 Lok Sabha election	23	43.8
2000 assembly election	14.6	39.9
2004 Lok Sabha election	14.6	37
Feb. 2005 assembly election	11	25.6
Oct. 2005 assembly election	15.7	36.2
2009 Lok Sabha election	13.9	37.9
2010 assembly election	16.5	39.1

Source: CSDS Data Unit.

Note: All figures are in percent.

Raghuvansh Prasad Singh, and Kanti Singh left the party to form the RJD. Lalu Prasad Yadav retained support of MLAs in the Bihar assembly and managed to continue as the chief minister. Numerous Lok Sabha and Rajya Sabha MPs of the JD from Bihar also left the party with him, which made the RJD an important constituent of the ruling United Front government. Later that year, Lalu Prasad Yadav had to resign as the chief minister of Bihar due to ongoing CBI investigations against him. He was replaced by his wife Rabri Devi who served as the chief minister of Bihar until February 2005.

The party has contested all national elections in the state, except 2009, in alliance with the Congress party. Its best performance came in the 2004 Lok Sabha election when it had won 24 seats and Lalu Prasad Yadav became the country's railway minister. The party was granted the status of a national party by the ECI in 2008, as it had the required level of support in Bihar, Jharkhand, Manipur, and Nagaland. After consecutive electoral debacles in the 2009 Lok Sabha election and the 2010 Bihar assembly election, this status was eventually withdrawn by the ECI.

The party contested the 2015 assembly election as part of the Mahagathbandhan (GA) with the JD(U) and the Congress party. Contesting 101 seats, the RJD won in 80 and emerged as the single largest party in the state. The election brought back Lalu Prasad Yadav and the RJD to the center stage of Bihar politics. While Nitish Kumar again became chief minister, Lalu Prasad Yadav's younger son Tejashwi Yadav became the deputy chief minister of state. Lalu Prasad Yadav's elder son Tej Pratap Yadav also holds important portfolios in the state. In early 2015, senior leader Pappu Yadav left the party to form a new party—the Jan Adhikar Party.

Janata Dal (United)

The JD(U) was officially formed in 1999 after a split in the erstwhile JD. The faction led by Sharad Yadav, J.H. Patel, and Ram Vilas Paswan formed the JD(U), while H.D. Deve Gowda formed the JD(S). In 2003, there was a merger between the JD(U) and the Samata Party. The latter was a splinter group of the JD and was formed in 1994 by George Fernandes and Nitish Kumar after differences with Chief Minister Lalu Prasad Yadav became irreconcilable.

The JD(U) was an important partner of the NDA government between 1999 and 2004 and senior leaders such as Sharad Yadav and Ram Vilas Paswan had held important portfolios in the government. The party has contested numerous Lok Sabha and state assembly elections in alliance with the BJP. In October 2005, the two parties had managed to form the government in alliance under the leadership of Nitish Kumar. The JD(U) unilaterally snapped ties with the BJP in 2013, in opposition to Narendra Modi's elevation in the BJP.

Over the years, three major splinter groups have left the JD(U) and formed separate political parties in Bihar. The first split in the JD(U) took place in 2000 when Ram Vilas Paswan left the JD(U) to form the LJNSP. In 2013, due to growing differences with Chief Minister Nitish Kumar, senior Koeri leader Upendra Kushwaha left the JD(U) and formed the RLSP. In 2015, after Jitan Ram Manjhi was ousted from the chief minister's position, he left the JD(U) and formed the HAM. All three splinter groups are currently members of the NDA.

Lok Jan Shakti Party

The LJNSP was formed in October 2000 by senior JD(U) leader Ram Vilas Paswan. Its president Ram Vilas Paswan belongs to Pasi caste, a sub-caste within the Dalits, and is currently one of the senior most leaders in Bihar politics. Being a minor player in the state with a solid support base among a section of Dalits and Muslims, the LJNSP is known for shifting allegiance between alliances.

At the time of its formation, the party was a member of the NDA at the Center. After the 2002 Gujarat riots, Ram Vilas Paswan resigned from the Union Cabinet and his party left the NDA. Later his party joined the United Progressive Alliance (UPA) and Ram Vilas Paswan again became a central minister. The party's best performance in a state assembly election was in February 2005. It received 12.6% votes and had won 29 seats. As both the RJD and the JD(U)–BJP alliance fell short of the majority, the LJNSP found itself as the kingmaker in that election. Ram Vilas Paswan made his support conditional on the appointment of a Muslim chief minister in the state. This was rejected by both sides and re-election took place in the state. The decision backfired as the LJNSP won only 10 seats in the subsequent October election.

Currently, the LJNSP is a member of the NDA and had won six out of the seven seats that it had contested in the 2014 Lok Sabha election. Ram Vilas Paswan is a member of the Union Cabinet.

References

Anderson, R., & Heath, A. (2003). Social identities and political cleavages: The role of political context. *Journal of the Royal Statistical Society, 166*(3), 301–327.

Bartels, L.M. (2008). The study of electoral behavior. In Jan E. Leighley (Ed.), *The Oxford Handbook of American Elections and Political Behavior* (pp. 239–261). New York, NY: Oxford University Press.

Blair, H.W. (1980). Rising Kulaks and backward classes in Bihar. *Economic & Political Weekly, 15*(2), 64–74.

Butler, D., & Stokes, D.E. (1974). *Political Change in Britain: The Evolution of Electoral Choice*. London: Macmillan Press.

Das, A. (1992). *The Republic of Bihar*. Delhi: Penguin Books.

Das Gupta (2007). Industrial structure. In *Road Map for Rural Industrialization in Bihar: A Report of the Special Task Force in Bihar*, 14. New Delhi: Government of India.

Hout, M., Manza, J., & Brooks, C. (1999). Classes, unions, and the realignment of US Presidential voting 1952–1992. In G. Evans (Ed.), *The End of Class Politics: Class Voting in Comparative Context* (pp. 83–96). Oxford: Oxford University Press.

Jafferlot, C. (2003). *India's Silent Revolution: The Rise of the Lower Castes in North India*. London: C. Hurst & Co.

Kelley, J., & Evans, M.D.R. (1995). Class and class conflict in six western democracies. *American Journal of Sociology, 83*, 386–402.

Kelley, J., & McAllister, I. (1985). Social context and electoral behavior in Britain. *American Journal of Political Science, 29*(3), 564–586.

Lipset, S.M., & Rokkan, S. (1967). Cleavage structures, party systems and voter alignments: An introduction. In S.M. Lipset & S. Rokkan (Eds.), *Party Systems and Voter Alignments: Cross-national Perspectives* (pp. 1–64). New York, NY: Free Press.

Nedumpara, J.J. (2004). *Political Economy and Class Contradiction*. New Delhi: Anmol Publications.

NSSO, Ministry of Statistics and Programme Implementation, Government of India. (2015). *Employment and Unemployment Situation among Major Social Groups in India, July 2011–June 2012* (Report No. 563). Retrieved December 4, 2017, from http://mospi.gov.in/national_data_bank/pdf/NSS_68Round-563.pdf

Prasad, P.H. (1975). Agrarian unrest and economic change in rural Bihar: The three case studies. *Economic & Political Weekly, 10*(24), 931–937.

———. (1980). Rising middle peasantry in North India. *Economic & Political Weekly, 15*(5/7), 215–219.

Rajalakshmi, T.K. (2001). Land rights and wrongs in Bihar. *Frontline, 18*(22). Retrieved November 16, 2017, from http://www.frontline.in/static/html/fl1822/18220460.htm

Ranjan, Priya & Prakash, Nishith (2012). Education policies and practices. Discussion Paper No. 6614 June 2012.

Robin, C. (2009). Bihar: The new stronghold of OBC politics. In C. Jaffrelot & S. Kumar (Eds.), *Rise of the Plebeians? The Changing Face of Indian Legislative Assemblies* (pp. 65–102). New Delhi: Routledge.

Sharma, A.N. (1995). Political economy of poverty in Bihar. *Economic & Political Weekly*, *30*(41/42), 2587–2602.

———. (2005). Agrarian relations and socio-economic change in Bihar. *Economic & Political Weekly*, *40*(10), 960–972.

Singh, S. (2012). A lasting signature on Bihar's most violent years. *The Indian Express*. Retrieved November 16, 2017, from http://archive.indianexpress.com/news/a-lasting-signature-on-bihar-s-most-violent-years/957421/

Sinha, A. (1996). Social mobilisation in Bihar: Bureaucratic feudalism and distributive justice. *Economic & Political Weekly*, *31*(51), 3287–3289.

———. (1978). Legal Loopholes: To landlord's rescue. *Economic & Political Weekly*, *13*(42), 1758–1750.

Weakliem, D.L. (1993). Class consciousness and political change: Voting and political attitudes in the British working class 1964 to 1970. *American Sociological Review*, *58*(3), 382–397.

2

Electoral History of Bihar

Political Processes in Bihar: Of Caste, Party, and Political Power

> Our tall claims about social transcendence apart, the results of this election were influenced heavily by caste. I don't say people have not voted above caste. But casteism has played a very important role.... Casteism worked as much against us as it did in our favour because some castes voted as much in solidarity for us as the Yadavs did for RJD. (Sinha, 2011, p. 9)

The then Bihar Chief Minister Nitish Kumar was quoted as saying by noted journalist Arun Kumar. Surprisingly, the Kurmi strongman was commenting after the landslide win he got in the 2010 assembly elections in which the NDA (of which the JD(U) was a part) got over 200 seats.

"We will have to fight one more battle against casteist forces—casteist forces in all castes" (Sinha, 2011, p. 11). Nitish said little realizing that after four years, realpolitik would force him to join hands again with his friend-turned-foe-turned-friend Lalu Prasad Yadav and redraw the caste algebra in the state to check the surging BJP under the leadership of OBC leader and now Prime Minister Narendra Modi.

This election had virtually knocked out caste arithmetic of Lalu Prasad Yadav to tatters, with Nitish Kumar replacing it with his own caste algebra. What we still see is that 60 years since Indian independence and more than 20 years of economic liberalization, the centrality of caste in the social and political choice of electorate remains unchallenged. Although Nitish Kumar got votes from across the caste and communities who did not form part of his arithmetic, for a large chunk of voters caste was the primary factor in making an electoral choice. After Mandalization post-1990 phase, power shifted from upper castes to OBCs in Bihar, who are now at the center of the political structure. A cursory review of political history of Bihar in the post-Independence period unfolds three distinctive phases. The first phase (1947–1967) is marked by complete dominance of the Congress party with upper castes at the apex of the power structure. The second phase (1967–1990) could be designated as a transition period with gradual decline in dominance of the Congress party as well as the upper castes and slowly but steadily emerging influence of the middle castes in the political arena. The third phase (1990 and after) is marked by complete reversal of the first phase, that is, marginalization of the Congress party and upper castes in the politics of state. Let us glance through each phase to understand the political transformation in Bihar which was impacted by social churnings taking place at its grassroots.

We treat it as a separate section as it denotes a paradigm shift in political equations in Bihar.

The Dominance of Congress (1947–1967)

As the INC was the dominant player in the freedom struggle, eventually liberating the country from the colonial power, the party became the natural political heir of the British in the state, as elsewhere in India. Other parties, namely the Left parties, which had some pockets of support in districts such as Begusarai, Muzaffarpur, Madhubani, Gaya, and Sitamarhi, could not consolidate their mass base. Thus, the Congress party was, in effect, without political rivals. It occupied almost the entire political space of the state. Until 1962, the party, in the absence of organized opposition groups, combined with the towering leadership of Srikrishna Sinha, the first chief minister of Bihar, and a low voter turnout, enjoyed monopoly of political space.

While the Congress was dominated by the upper castes—Brahmins, Rajputs, Bhumihars, and Kayasthas—and drew support from them, other castes/communities also supported the party. The SCs (ex-untouchables) were loyal to the Congress, because for them it was the Congress under the leadership of Mahatma Gandhi that had fought for their dignity and incorporated many provisions in the Constitution to liberate them from atrocities. The practice of untouchability was made a punishable offence.

In order to ensure their fair representation in the central and state legislatures, reservation was granted to them; provisions of reservation in other public spheres such as educational institutions and public employment were also embodied in the Constitution and various laws relating to discrimination against them also followed. All these measures were seen and propagated as a gift of the Congress to the Dalits, who rallied behind the Congress (Frankel & Rao, 1989).

A large chunk of Muslims also supported the Congress, though their representation in the party organization as well as in the ministry was not adequate. After the partition of India, Muslims carried the burden of being disloyal to the country. Their loyalty was suspected by many Hindus. Further, there were no major and viable political formations that could have been an alternative to the Congress. In brief, they had no option but to go with the Congress and vote for it.

Despite the fact that the Congress was a party dominated by the forward castes and landed aristocrats, it took a reformist path despite the fact that some of its policies would go against the interests of the upper castes. The abolition of zamindari system and passing of the Land Reforms Act could be cited as an example in this regard.[1] According to NSS 1953–1954, the top 10% of rural households owned 52.36% of the land, while the bottom 40% households owned mere 1.25% of land. And most of the 10% households that owned about half the land in the state belonged to the upper castes (Prasad, 1987), except for some Muslims. During this period, the forward castes held most of the lands and there was a patron-client voting system in which tenants and agricultural laborers voted at the behest of their landlords. Hence, any legislation on

---

[1] Bihar became the first state to bring out a law against Zamindari immediately after Independence. The state government was quick at enacting the Zamindari Abolition Act in 1948. The government issued notices to zamindars asking them to surrender the documents of their estates. However, most zamindars did not respond to the government's demand and no major change took place. One of the reasons for this was that many politicians and bureaucrats came from affluent zamindar families. In 1950, the Bihar Land Reforms Act was passed and was upheld by the Supreme Court after being challenged by the Bihar Landlords Association under the leadership of the Maharaja of Darbhanga. The refusal by the zamindars to surrender the land records of their erstwhile zamindaris was challenged in the courts. But the Supreme Court of India, in a brief judgment, upheld the zamindars' stand. The result was that the state was without any records of landholding in the zamindari areas. Whatever the landowners could produce became the documents accepted by the courts. The pace of Survey Settlement operations was so slow that they virtually were nonexistent. By 1983, only 6 out of Bihar's 50 districts had been surveyed and settled with new land records.

land reforms was, therefore, bound to hurt the interests of the forward castes and jeopardize the prospects of the Congress.

Bihar is economically, educationally, and socially one of the most backward states but is also politically one of the most important states. This is not simply because this state once accounted for 54 Lok Sabha seats (now 40 after formation of Jharkhand) but also because the long process of democratization has inculcated a sense of empowerment among the people. The backward castes started sensing this empowerment as early as the mid-1970s, a feeling which, in a way, bloomed fully in the early 1990s with the advent of Lalu Prasad Yadav as the chief minister. When Lalu Prasad Yadav, during his tenure as the chief minister, implemented welfare programs for lower sections of the society, especially the Dalits, even they began sensing the change.

The defeat of the Congress in 1990 marked the end of an era in Bihar's politics which can be best described as "feudal democracy" (Witsoe, 2011). Congress failed to deliver the promises of land reforms, independence, poverty alleviation, removing humiliation, discrimination, and indignity of the OBCs and Dalits, while the Bhagalpur riots virtually knocked the Congress party out of Muslim electoral imagination.

In a state where traditionally, political power had remained monopolized by the upper castes for a long time, this desire to share power among the middle caste groups was bound to bring forth a process of social and political change leading to the realignment of newly emerging social forces. This process started in Bihar in the mid-1970s, initially a bit falteringly, but came into its full form in the first half of the 1990s. But very soon, during the mid-1990s the process of "de-alignment" of these social and political forces begun and the middle caste no more remained as one political group.

The social struggle in the mid-1980s and 1990s, particularly in central Bihar, certainly inculcated a sense of empowerment among the deprived people actively associated with it, though it could not bring about major changes in the social, political, and economic spheres.

In other words, the politics that followed since 1990 is largely the politics of reassertion and reaffirmation of old caste cleavages, deepened further to capture political power. People now tended to vote more for identity (of caste) than for non-parochial issues such as good governance, improvement in the material conditions of people, betterment of and universal access to health and educational facilities and universal provisions of basic amenities. (Kumar, Alam, & Joshi, 2008)

At the best, the sense of empowerment led to more number of contestants in various elections vying for political power. But it certainly led to an urge for participation in the electoral process with voter turnout in various elections also rising phenomenally. In the pre-1990 phase during the upper castes' domination of Bihar's polity, to come out and vote was a big challenge.

This has been reflected in the various elections held during the 1990–2010 period. The increasing number of contestants in the successive assembly and Lok Sabha elections, and the increasing turnout over the years, bears testimony to it. From 1,594 contestants in the 1952 assembly election, the number went up to 8,410 in 1995. However, there was a sharp decline in the number of contestants in the 2000 assembly elections with only 3,941 contestants (see Table 2.1). It remained virtually steady in the three assembly elections that followed. In 2005 February

Table 2.1

Candidates' performance: Assembly elections, 1952–2015

Year	Total No. of Candidates	Average No. of Candidates per Constituency	Candidates' Forfeited Deposit (%)
1952	1,594	4.8	61.6
1957	1,393	4.4	51.5
1962	1,529	4.8	53.0
1967	2,025	6.4	64.1
1969	2,154	6.8	63.4
1972	1,983	6.2	63.0
1977	2,994	9.2	76.8
1980	3,002	9.3	74.7
1985	4,237	13.1	83.3
1990	6,629	20.5	88.9
1995	8,410	26.0	91.6
2000	3,941	12.2	80.7
2005 February	3,193	13.1	82.6
2005 October	2,135	8.8	73.3
2010	3,523	14.5	85.7
2015	3,411	14.0	85.11

Sources: Up to 1985, Singh and Bose (1988); 1990, Election Commission of India (1990); 1995, Shah (2004); 2000, Election Commission of India website.

elections, the number of contestants were 3,193, while in the October elections it declined to 2,135, apparently due to two elections in a year. In the 2010 assembly elections, it increased to 3,523, an indication that electoral participation and enthusiasm to take part in the political process continues in Bihar.

Similarly, from 189 contestants in the 1952 Lok Sabha election, the number went up to 1,448 in 1996. However, their numbers declined to 469 in 1998 due to several restrictions imposed for contesting the election. Since 1998, the number of contestants in Bihar Lok Sabha elections remained stable with 497 contestants in 1999, 462 candidates in 2004, 672 in 2009, and 647 in 2014 (see Table 2.2).

The turnout of voters also increased phenomenally during this period. From 39.7% during the 1952 assembly election, the turnout went up to 61.8% in 1995. The 1998 Lok Sabha election witnessed a 64.6% turnout as compared to 59.5% in the 1996 Lok Sabha election. The state which

Table 2.2

Candidates' increasing number and performance: Lok Sabha elections, 1952–2014

Year	Total No. of Candidates	Average No. of Candidates per Constituency	Candidates' Forfeited Deposits (%)
1952	189	3.6	43.9
1957	189	3.6	47.1
1962	233	4.4	46.3
1967	315	5.9	61.3
1971	421	7.9	71.0
1977	340	6.3	70.3
1980	594	11.0	76.9
1984	676	12.5	83.0
1989	711	13.2	81.0
1991	1,216	22.5	90.1
1996	1,448	26.8	91.5
1998	469	8.7	72.9
1999	497	9.2	76.7
2004	462	11.6	81.2
2009	672	16.8	86.8
2014	647	16.2	85.5

Sources: Up to 1984, Singh and Bose (1986); 1989–1991, Shah (2004).

had witnessed only a 39.7% turnout in the 1952 Lok Sabha election had certainly moved ahead in the process of democratization. Hence, this struggle by different sections of society led to the alignment, realignment and further de-alignment of various castes in the state.

Although the country started witnessing political change in the mid-1960s in the form of various non-Congress governments coming to power in different states in 1967 (Bihar being one of them), it was in 1977 that it witnessed a major political change for the first time. Not only was the monopoly of the Congress party broken at the center and the Janata Party came to power, in a large number of states, non-Congress governments were installed with thumping majorities. This central government did not last long and the Congress returned to power in 1980. It was only nine years later that once again a new formation in the shape of the JD came to power at the center. Bihar played a major role in the formation of both these non-Congress governments, returning a large number of non-Congress representatives to Parliament in 1977 and 1989 Lok Sabha elections. The Congress drew a blank and its votes went down to 22.9% in the 1977 Lok Sabha elections as compared to 39 seats won and 40.1% votes polled in the 1971 election. In the assembly elections of 1977, the seats for the Congress were reduced to only 57 as compared to 168 seats won in the 1972 assembly elections. The Congress lost nearly 10% votes in these two elections as its votes went down to 23.6% in 1977 as compared to 33.1% in the 1972 assembly elections. The Congress regained much of the lost ground in the 1980s but again suffered a major setback in the 1989 Lok Sabha elections. As compared to 48 seats and 51.8% votes in 1984, the party managed to win only 4 Lok Sabha seats and its votes went down to 28.1% in the 1989 election, while the JD won 31 seats with 36.4% votes and the CPI and CPM won 4 seats and 1 seat respectively with 7.9% and 1.4% votes (see Table 2.3).

Traditionally a Congress stronghold, the success of a large number of non-Congress representatives in the state was primarily on account of the realignment of the backward castes who had generally voted against the Congress in both the 1977 and 1989 Lok Sabha elections.

A new consciousness in the peasantry grew alongside the political mobili-zation of the OBC in Bihar by the socialists in the 1930s and 1940s. Bihar became the first state to abolish the zamindari system in 1950 and the ben-efits of the limited redistribution were reaped by those who owned some land, mainly the upper OBCs. An early challenge to Congress domination in Bihar sprang up in the mid-60s in the form of the Triveni Sangh—an

Table 2.3

Performance of parties: Assembly elections, 1967–1977

Year/Party	INC	BJS	CPI/CPM	PSP	SSP	JNP	JKD	IND
1967	128	26	24+4=28	18	68	—	13	33
1969	118	34	25+3=28	18	52	14	—	24
1972	167	25	35+0=35	—	—	—	—	17
1977	57	—	21+4=25	—	—	214	—	24

Source: Election Commission of India.

Note: PSP: Praja Socialist Party, SSP: Samyukta Socialist Party, JNP: Janata Party, BJS: Bharatiya Jana Sangh, JKD: Jan Kranti Dal, CPI/CPM: Communist Party of India/Marxist, IND: Independent.

alliance of Yadavs, Kurmis and Koeris. The ferment created fertile ground for backward caste mobilizations by Lohiaites in the 1960s and for the JP-led anti-Congress movement that acquired the character of a backward caste consolidation against the upper caste-dominated Congress in the 1970s. (Mishra, 2011)

There are three important reasons why Congress party could never build a social coalition in Bihar that included backward castes in its fold. First, until 1990 their social coalition which included the landed gentry cutting across castes, the upper castes, the SCs and the Muslims hardly faced any formidable challenge. The social coalition was enough to ensure electoral victories. Second, in the first three general elections it had virtually no opposition.... Its dislike for the upper backward castes was no secret. These upper backward castes were their tenants and stood to be the main beneficiary of the zamindari abolition because of their status as superior tenants. The antagonism zamindari abolition created between the upper caste landed gentry and the OBCs, particularly Kurmis and Koeris, could never be overcome.... It is no exaggeration that Yadavs have suffered maximum humiliation among the three upper OBCs. (Jha & Pushpendra, 2012)

Control over Congress: Upper Castes vs Upper OBCs

The upper castes exercised dominant control over the organization and structure of the Congress party since its inception, and rebuffed any attempt by the upper OBCs to gain any share of power within the organization or through it.

> The upper backward castes (Yadavs, Kurmis and Koeris) had tried to gain
> a share of state power through the Congress for over four decades but had
> been terrible disappointed.... The party had failed to feel the pulse of the
> backward castes who wanted nothing short of a share in state power. The
> neglect hurt them. (Sinha, 2011, p. 95)

The upper caste leaders of the Congress knew that their political rivals
are not the Muslims, Dalits and lower OBCs as they are not in a position to throw challenge to their political, social, and economic power but
upper OBCs—Yadavs, Kurmis, and Koeris, who were next to them on
political, social, and economic indicators.

In 1970, Daroga Prasad Rai, a Yadav, became the first backward caste
Congress chief minister of Bihar sending feelers to the OBCs that the
party is willing to share power with them and give importance to them
in institutions of politics and governance.[2] Rai, in his bid to empower the
OBCs, had set up the State Backward Classes Commission in 1971 to
identify the economically and socially deprived sections of the society
and give suggestions in the form of reservations in educational institutions and government jobs. But the hopes of OBCs, particularly the
Yadavs (numerically the strongest caste in Bihar), were dashed, as Rai
was removed after upper caste leaders plotted against him. This episode
made the OBCs push the Congress out of their political imagination
permanently.

In the early 1970s, the OBCs were neither politically organized nor
they had any political institution which could spearhead their social and
political ambitions. Politically, they were dispersed and fragmented and
their political choice hinged on individual candidates according to the
situation in the various Lok Sabha and assembly segments. Some sections of the OBCs also supported the SSP (United Socialist Party).

> In a bid to improve the lot of more deprived section among BCs the then
> Bihar Chief Minister Karpoori Thakur in 1978 implemented the Mungeri
> Lal Commission report. The Commission divided the BCs into two cate-
> gories so far job in the state government is concerned. The first category is
> as usual called the Other Backward Castes (OBCs) and the second one the
> Extreme or Most Backward Castes (EBCs or MBCs). Karpoori himself

---

[2] Satish Prasad Singh was the first backward caste Congress chief minister but was in chair
for only five days. So we consider Daroga Prasad Rai as the first backward caste chief
minister retained in office.

came from Nai (Barber), an Extremely Backward Caste of Samastipur district of north Bihar. (Ahmed, 2010)

The early 1970s also saw the rise of the prominent, charismatic Koeri leader Jagdeo Prasad, who commanded impressive following among the upper OBCs, the lower OBCs, and the Dalits. He was popular as "Lenin of Bihar." The movement that he led in central Bihar had drawn the ire of upper caste landlords in that region. At that time, central Bihar had become a flashpoint between the upper caste and upper OBCs for exercising social and political control. Jagdeo Prasad was brutally killed by police on September 5, 1974 while he was leading a peaceful protest with about 20,000 people during the peak of the Bihar Movement (a 1974 student movement in Bihar led by the veteran Gandhian socialist Jayaprakash Narayan—known as JP, against the misrule and corruption in the Congress government of Bihar).

> There was widespread suspicion among the backward castes that Jagdeo Prasad had been killed at the instance of a Bhumihar minister in the Congress government. His martyrdom was to sharpen the sense of alienation of the backward castes from the Congress and give a huge impetus to their crusade against upper caste hegemony in the state. (Sinha, 2011, pp. 95–96)

Bihar Movement and Emergency

Bihar Movement was an agitation launched by the students of Bihar in 1974, against the alleged misrule and graft of the Congress-led state government. The protests were led by the veteran socialist Jayaprakash Narayan. This later took the shape of a protest movement against Congress-led central government of then Prime Minister Indira Gandhi. The backward castes supported the movement for two broad reasons: first, they wanted to dislodge the upper caste-dominated Congress from power in the state and second, the ideology of Jayaprakash Narayan of empowering the backward castes was similar to their political goals and interests. In the middle of the Bihar Movement, alignment of political forces took place in Bihar with Karpoori Thakur merging his SSP with Bharatiya Kranti Dal of Charan Singh. The prominent Jat leader was twice the chief minister of Uttar Pradesh and champion of the cause of farmers.

Rise in Anti-Congress Sentiments Among the Upper Backwards

Following Loknayak's call for "total revolution," Indira Gandhi imposed emergency.[3] Narayan was popular as Loknayak among his supporters and admirers, and his launching the movement was one of the factors that prompted Gandhi to impose draconian provisions that suspended civil liberties and curbed political freedom.

The imposition of emergency led to further strain in ties between the upper backwards and the Congress party in Bihar. Indira Gandhi's "authoritarian" government started patronizing the Dalits and lower backwards during the emergency. The minimum wages of farm laborers were raised, debt-bonded laborers were freed, and land grants were given to the Dalits. These steps of the government, though positive, further alienated the upper backwards and even the forward castes—Brahmins, Rajputs, Bhumihars, and Kayasthas who formed the core of the Congress leadership in the state—because it impacted them economically and socially. So, when the general elections took place in March 1977, these two rival caste combinations—the upper castes and upper backwards—joined hands to defeat the Congress. The anti-Congress vote during the emergency in case of Bihar could be attributed to two factors—muzzling of civil and democratic rights, as well as the perception among the upper caste and upper backwards that the Congress government is showing "undue favor" to lower backwards and Dalits.

The establishment of Janata Party government in Delhi after the virtual electoral demise of the Congress in the 1977 polls (see Figure 2.1)

---

[3] The emergency was imposed on June 25, 1975 when the president passed an ordinance about how the state was in danger. All the fundamental rights were suspended, politicians were arrested and a heavy censorship was imposed on the media. It began with the case against Indira Gandhi for election malpractices in Allahabad High Court. The verdict of the same was later challenged in Supreme Court which granted Gandhi a conditional stay. It allowed her to be an MP but not preside over parliamentary proceedings. This was viewed as the first step to emergency. The second step was the 'Total Revolution' initiated by Jayaprakash Narayan who demanded the resignation of Indira after the Allahabad High Court gave its verdict. It was on the same day, June 25 that JP declared the nationwide plan of daily demonstrations in every state capital. The police, army and the people were asked to follow the Constitution than Indira Gandhi. The emergency is regarded as the outcome of a systematic failure as India was facing social, economic and political crisis. (Daily News & Analysis, June 25, 2014)

Figure 2.1

JNP overpowered Congress after Emergency

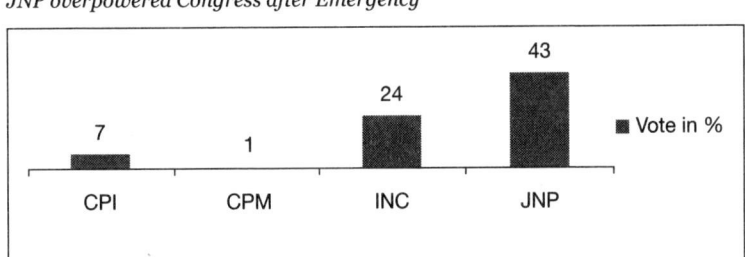

Source: Election Commission of India.

emboldened the upper backwards and upper castes so much that they started hitting hard at the lower backward castes and the Dalits. Most of these massacres were agrarian in nature and were a result of conflict between the landowners and the peasants, primarily in the central districts of Bihar. The upper backwards' killing of 14 SC people in Belchhi in Patna district started a trail of violence that continued for many years. The Dalits were facing onslaughts from two powerful cast combinations, the upper castes and the upper backwards. Yadavs, Kurmis, and Koeris were the rising class of peasants who faced hostilities from both the lower castes and the upper castes, who wanted to marginalize them.

The abolition of zamindari had helped these three jatis to attain upward social and economic mobility as they now had lands at their disposal. Pushed by laborers from one end for higher wages and marginalized by the upper castes on the other, the upper backwards had become a militant community by now. Most of the massacres that followed in the coming years (1977–2001) were orchestrated by upper backwards and upper castes and the victims were Dalits and sharecroppers, who mostly came from lower backward communities.

Following the national and state assembly elections, Janata Party came to power in both New Delhi and Patna. Janata Party was a conglomerate of many conflicting and complex political groups who shared only one aspect of ideology—an urge to remove the Indira Gandhi–led Congress government from power. Once that mission was accomplished, internal differences started resurfacing. During the 1977 elections, even the upper castes had supported and voted the Janata Party along with the upper backwards; this organization became a flashpoint of social and political conflicts between the ambitions and aspirations of these two classes and caste groups. The upper backwards did not like the presence of upper castes in the Janata Party conglomerate as, despite their best attempts, the Brahmins, Rajputs, Bhumihars, and Kayasthas did not allow them influence in the Congress party.

The upper backwards were led by Bharatiya Lok Dal (BLD) and socialists in the Janata Party, while the upper castes interests were taken care by BJS and the Congress (O). The clash between these two classes, upper castes and upper backwards, was primarily for the ownership of the Janata Party. The upper castes, realizing the numerical strength and the newly gained clout of upper backwards, had by now become conciliatory toward them as they felt that if the Congress came back to power, it will again start pampering the Dalits and lower backwards at their interest and cost. Meanwhile in Delhi, the then Prime Minister Morarji Desai had faced hostilities from the upper OBC Jat leader Charan Singh and Lohiaite leader Raj Narayan, who were hell-bent to assert themselves in the government. Charan Singh, who commanded immense support base among the peasants in the northern India, particularly Uttar Pradesh, had openly declared his ambitions to become the prime minister of the country. To apply pressure on the then Prime Minister Morarji Desai and other leaders, Charan Singh used to organize huge caste rallies in Delhi to flaunt his support base and popularity. Socialists' leaders and Charan Singh had by now started pitching for reservation for OBCs on the line extended to SCs and Scheduled Tribes (STs).

At the same time, the upper castes of the Janata Party allowed Bihar's Chief Minister Karpoori Thakur to give maximum representation to the backward castes in the Bihar ministry. At least 42% representations were given to backward castes in ministerial berths, while 29% were given to upper castes. It was the largest share ever given to the lower caste groups.

Under tremendous pressure from the backward groups, both the central government in New Delhi and state government in Patna stepped up efforts in the direction of providing quota to the OBCs. The Janata Party-led central government of Prime Minister Morarji Desai constituted the second Backward Commission under the chairmanship of B.P. Mandal, the first OBC chief minister of Bihar. The commission was given a mandate to identify the OBC communities and suggest measures for reservation in central government services and educational institutions.

In Bihar, the OBC Chief Minister Karpoori Thakur—who belonged to the lower backward Nai caste—announced acceptance of the Mungeri Lal Commission report submitted to the Congress government in 1976. The report was gathering dust since its submission, as Congress, apparently under pressure from the dominant upper caste groups, did not dare to implement it. The Karpoori Thakur government accepted the recommendation of providing 26% reservation in government jobs for OBCs in early 1978, opening the split wide open between the upper caste and lower caste lawmakers and leaders. The split in Bihar was all-pervasive as it vertically divided the discourse in educational institutions, government offices and public transport among others, taking the class- and caste-conflict to the urban space. It was a different kind of polarization that Bihar was experiencing in its society, with the political parties and cultural institutions vertically divided on the lines of "forward" and "backward." The move—of the Janata government—led to conflicting social mobilizations in Bihar that would shape the politics of the state on caste-based assertions in the coming decades, and would see the emergence of Lalu Prasad Yadav, Nitish Kumar, Sushil Modi, and Ram Vilas Paswan in the political map of Bihar.

Cutting across party lines, the upper caste and lower caste MLAs had extended support to the youth of their castes to spearhead agitation on the streets, leading to rallies and counter-rallies. Patna was the epicenter of such protests. The city witnessed many violent clashes among youth belonging to both segments of the society. Anarchy had prevailed in the streets of Patna, as mob violence and clashes had become the order of the day for at least two months. An organization called "Forward League" was formed to agitate and protest against the reservation policy while the backwards came under the banner of All India Backward Classes Federation. Both these organizations were at the forefront of agitation for their respective stands. Anti-quota protesters took to streets, destroyed public property, burnt buses, and even derailed train while pro-quota protesters even hurled abuses at Jayaprakash Narayan for his statement that only economically weaker sections of the OBCs should be extended the benefit of the reservation.

Amid this socioeconomic and political turmoil in Bihar, the upper caste MLAs and ministers stepped up campaign for the ouster of Karpoori Thakur from the position of the chief minister of Bihar, and demanded that his quota policy be indefinitely rolled back. This led to a political deadlock and saw youth leader Nitish Kumar (who later became the chief minister of Bihar) coming up and presenting a compromise reservation formula which was accepted. Nitish Kumar was noticed and appreciated for this move to end the deadlock, though he was too young to make an impact. His reservation formula had suggested four amendments to Karpoori Thakur's reservation policy, which included that the economically affluent sections of the OBCs should be kept aside from reservation benefits in jobs and educational institutions. To break the impasse, Nitish Kumar, who was then the national executive member of Yuva Janata, convened a meeting of different groups in Patna and came out with a compromise formula which was accepted by all. His other suggestions included quota benefits for the economically weaker sections of the upper castes, the enshrinement of right to employment in the Constitution, and efforts from the state institutions to improve educational standards of the backward castes so that they were eligible enough to avail the advantages of the reservation.

> Nitish's suggestions were aimed at bridging the forward–backward chasm created by quota announcements. His formula took care of the three major concerns of the upper caste youth; one that there were economically backward people among the upper castes: two that with very high unemployment, the Karpoori quota would further reduce job opportunities for them; and three the quota would benefit only elite section of the backward castes. (Sinha, 2011, p. 99)

Nitish Kumar was noticed by Chief Minister Karpoori Thakur after the compromise formula was published in "Samayik Varta," though he was never called by the leader or the senior members of the Janata Party for further discussions or deliberations on the vexed policy issue.

Nitish Kumar's deliberations and ideas were amply enriched by the social and economic philosophy of Ram Manohar Lohia and Jayaprakash Narayan. The "Loknayak," as Jayaprakash was known, agreed with the youth leader, as he wanted the reservation to benefit the needy among the backward castes besides being an ardent votary of constitutional guarantee for education and employment.

In its bid to end the deadlock, Bihar government announced a revised formula in November 1978 that imposed an income ceiling for OBC beneficiaries, while it also accommodated the concerns of the poor among upper castes and women by extending 3% reservation to each of these two groups. This was done by curtailing the OBC quota from 26% to 20%.

The debates and deliberations on reservation policy by the Janata Party government, led by Karpoori Thakur in Bihar, impacted its polity at two broad levels—it led to the backward castes rallying under the leadership of upper backwards which did not go down well with the upper castes, and it paved way for a negative perception among the electorates at large that this government is using the bogey of quota as a diversionary tactic to hide its failures on the issue of non-performance, price rise, rising unemployment, and poor law and order situation.

Impact of Caste Issues on Bihar Movement

The biggest casualty of the reservation fiasco was the Bihar Movement, whose main aim was to fight corruption in the central government. The movement, after 1977, vertically split into "forward" and "backward" politics amid a strong realization among the latter group that they too deserve a share in the social, economic, and political space of Bihar which was historically dominated by the former. This fissure, in coming decades, would shape the politics of Bihar.

Youth leaders like Nitish Kumar, who believed in casteless polity and was keen on the extension of reservation benefits on economic terms, attempted in vain to bridge this divide in the Bihar polity. He organized a rally under the banner of Yuva Janata on March 18, 1978, which was attended by youth across the caste and community spectrum. The rally ended up as a "symbolic affair," just an attempt by an idealistic leader who dreamt of a "casteless approach to social revolution" because the wounds were historically too deep.

We could now divide Bihar society into five broad political spectrums—upper castes, upper backwards, lower backwards, Dalits, and Muslims. The Congress had been running the show in Bihar since 1947 with upper castes as leaders and Dalit, Muslim, and lower backwards as voters. The upper backwards had been attempting to upset this applecart by weaning away substantial chunk of the lower backwards, Dalits, and Muslim support base.

Amid this milieu in Bihar's social and political spectrum, the upper caste Janata Party MLAs kept up with their effort to dislodge Karpoori Thakur as Bihar's chief minister. Karpoori Thakur drew his political strength from OBC Jat-peasant leader and Home Minister Charan Singh was by now losing to Brahmin Prime Minister Morarji Desai in the game of political one-upmanship. Caste fissures had been making the central government look very weak and fragile by the time it completed two years in March 1979, prompting the upper caste Janata Party MLAs to wean away Dalits and SC legislatures by propping up Ram Sunder Das, a Dalit, as Bihar's chief minister in April 1979. Karpoori Thakur was forced to resign as his support base had shrunk in the Janata Party legislature group.

Ram Sunder Das obliged the upper caste support by announcing an amendment to Karpoori Thakur's reservation formula, though he did not completely dump it. In a bid to restrict the OBC share in government jobs and educational institutions, Ram Sunder Das government's reservation quota for OBCs now included the candidates who were selected even from the general seats. For example, if there are 100 seats, 20 will be reserved for OBC candidates and if 5 candidates from that group are selected in the general category, the quota would become 15. Under any circumstance, the OBC reservation would not exceed 20%. The upper caste would still corner 53% of government jobs, which included 3% from the economically weaker sections among them, along with an additional 3% women quota. Majority of the women preparing for civil services belonged to the upper caste and upper class strata of the society, so it would have resulted in upper caste's share in the cream jobs to 55%.

This move checked the influx of OBCs in the bureaucracy, key to controlling government policy and its implementation, and allowed the perpetuation of upper caste domination on that institution. But soon Ram Sunder Das' government plunged into a political crisis, as Charan Singh and Raj Narayan brought down the Morarji Desai government in New Delhi. The Janata legislature party split as Charan Singh's BLD and Raj Narayan's Socialist Party walked out of the Janata Party. The developments in New Delhi had a direct impact on the political situation in Patna, with Janata Party splitting into two groups, one lead by Charan Singh and other by Raj Narayan. The Janata Party youth wing also saw a division with youth leaders Lalu Prasad Yadav and Nitish Kumar joining the Charan–Raj Narayan formation. The other wing of the Janata Party was headed by Chandra Shekhar and comprised of the supporters of BJS, some former Congressmen and members of Prajatantrik Socialist Party (PSP). Charan Singh had taken oath as prime minister with the support of Congress, led by "sworn enemy" Indira Gandhi, which discredited the government in the eyes of the public, leading to the grand old party coming back to power in 1980. In Bihar, the Congress was backed by strong support from the upper caste groups—Brahmins, Rajputs, Bhumiars, and Kayasthas. Muslims and division of backward votes handed out a crushing defeat to the Janata Party formations and walked away with 30 seats out of 54 from the state, 3 years after the Indira Gandhi-led dispensation was wiped out from the political map of Bihar. The student hero of 1977, Lalu Prasad Yadav, was also defeated from Chhapra parliamentary constituency in 1980 parliamentary polls.

Later, Raj Narayan and Charan Singh also split, with two youth leaders Lalu Prasad Yadav and Nitish Kumar—who would be making imprint on Bihar politics in coming decades—joining Lok Dal led by the veteran Jat leader. The repeated splits of the Janata Party led to scarcity of candidates in the Lok Dal which was a blessing in disguise for both the youth leaders, who got tickets from Sonepur and Harnaut, a Kurmi-dominated constituency. The irony for Nitish Kumar was that he being known as a close associate of Karpoori Thakur alienated the upper castes from him, while he became a despised figure among Kurmis for his earlier stance that economically affluent among OBCs should be kept out of purview of the reservation. His caste men from Harnaut were at the forefront of the statewide pro-reservation movement for OBCs which was opposed to Nitish Kumar's formula of economic-based reservation. Nitish ultimately ended on wrong side of both Kurmis and upper castes, losing the Harnaut assembly election in 1980 by 5,000 votes to Arun Kumar Singh, an accused in the infamous Belcchi massacre (Mishra, 2013).

The sorry part of the saga was that Nitish was a Kurmi for upper caste, and seen with contempt by his own caste for his ideal stand of reservation on economic criteria. On the other side, Lalu Prasad Yadav romped home from Sonepur in a triangular contest.

The Belcchi massacre, in which at least 14 SC people were killed, was the first among the series of violent assaults in Bihar. The gory incident was apparently perpetuated by Kurmi landlords and it led to the caste men being dubbed as "scoundrels." The Congress used this opportunity to reconsolidate the Dalits in its favor.

The Yadav–Kurmi rivalry which split the JD in Bihar in the mid-1990s, leading to the formation of the RJD under Lalu Prasad Yadav and Samata Party under Nitish Kumar, had its seeds in old rivalry among the two upper backward caste groups that allied with each other and split many times to fight the upper caste's hegemony both socially and politically. What apparently kept them politically united was the upper caste's domination over the social, economic, and political system of Bihar.

Commenting on the traditional rivalry between the three upper backward caste groups—Yadavs, Kurmis, and Koeris post 1977—Arun Kumar Sinha says: "The pro-reservation campaign brought about solidarity of backward castes under the leadership of upper backwards. With that happening, the upper backwards—the Kurmis, Yadavs and Koeris—began to fight over the mantle of leadership. Old social rivalries between them were accentuated" (Sinha, 2011, p. 103).

Bihar Politics 1980: Congress Returns to Power

The repeated fragmentation and splits of Janata Party into many political constituents, and the withdrawal of BJS from the conglomeration had considerably weakened the Janata Party leading to the revival of the Congress party. When the elections took place in 1980, the upper castes had by that time returned to the Congress fold as they realized that their interests were best served within the Congress fold, and the upper OBCs who had played a pivotal role in the Janata Party movement would resist their attempts within the Janata organizations. Simultaneously, the 1977 Belcchi bloodbath allegedly perpetuated by upper OBC caste group of Kurmis and Mrs Indira Gandhi visiting the Dalit village on an elephant had made headlines consolidating her Dalit vote base.

When the assembly elections were held in mid-1980, the Congress romped home crushing the fragmented Janata Party groups in Bihar. The once Jayaprakash Narayan-led dispensation had fragmented into three parts—Lok Dal, Janata Party, and the BJP. The Congress victory was not impressive as it was aided by a fragmented opposition. The party, for the second time, gave the mantle of chief ministership to Jagannath Mishra, a Brahmin by caste, giving a message to its upper caste core constituency that it values them. Jagannath Mishra was the chief minister of the state from April 1975 to April 1977.

In the June 1977 assembly polls post-emergency, the Congress had faced a massive erosion of vote base and could only win 57 seats. The division of anti-Congress votes in 1980 assembly polls led to the victory of the grand old party. In a house of 324, the Congress returned with figures of 169. There were many reasons for the victory of the Congress. It benefitted due to fragmented opposition, there was disappointment with the Janata government, and Karpoori Thakur's idea of OBC reservation had antagonized the upper caste from the Janata Party. Karpoori Thakur was one the most hated figures in the eyes of the upper castes. The most surprising element of the 1980 assembly poll was that the Lok Dal could not come back to power despite playing the OBC quota politics. The polls were a virtual referendum on Karpoori Thakur's quota politics. Despite the OBC population exceeding 50%, the demographic majority could not be transformed into an electoral majority. It could be gauged from the fact that from out of the 254 candidates that were fielded by the Lok Dal, 132 forfeited their security deposits. Only 42 candidates were victorious. The strike rate of the Lok Dal was under 17% while it garnered 15.63% of the total votes. So, the OBCs could not consolidate in favor of Lok Dal, despite their best of efforts. The underlining message of the 1980 assembly polls was also that only a united opposition could stand before the might of the Congress party. A successful anti-Congress coalition should be prompted by a conglomeration of left-right-centrist parties and not a single party identifying itself with one caste or class segment. The Janata Party had defeated Indira Gandhi's Congress in 1977 assembly elections due to it being a united front of opposition parties wherein it had received 42.68% of the total votes, while in the 1980 elections the combined vote share of the Janata splinter groups were 32.92%. Lok Dal got 15.63%, Janata Party got 7.21% of votes, while the BJP received 8.41% of votes. This opposition disunity was further aided by negative swing due to the "non-performance" of the state government.

From Table 2.4, it is amply clear that Congress returned back to power only due to a fragmented opposition. There were numerous contenders for the OBC votes, even if the segment was the largest political group. The Congress was able to revive its old alliance among the upper caste, Dalits, Muslims, and some share from the OBCs. If the Janata Party groups would have fought together, they would have won many seats and it would have even denied the Congress party a majority of its own.

Table 2.4

Seat share of parties: Assembly elections, 1980 and 1985

Name of the Party	1980 Assembly Elections	1985 Assembly Elections
BJP	21	16
CPI	23	12
CPM	6	1
INC	169	196
INC (U)	14	—
Janata Party (JNP)	13	—
Janata Party (Secular) Chaudhary Charan Singh	42	—
Janata Party (Secular) Raj Narayan	1	—
Jharkhand Mukti Morcha (JMM)	11	9
Independent	23	29
Lok Dal	—	46

Source: Election Commission of India.

The Congress got just 169 seats which were only 6 seats more than a simple majority. This and many more elections repeatedly proved one thing that there is a huge electoral base for a non-Congress politics and it was the fragmentation of that voter base that was time and again sending the grand old party to power.

> The Lok Dal leaders—Charan Singh at the National level, Karpoori at the State level and emerging ones as Lalu (Prasad Yadav) and Nitish (Kumar)—understood this very well but they had their own difficulty: in a conglomerate they were dwarfed and repressed by upper caste leaders. They were not averse to working with upper castes but they had to come before them. (Sinha, 2011, p. 107)

Quota politics was more a psychological tool for upward social mobility. Despite being in a minority, the upper caste groups wielded enormous strength in the society and institutions of the state. They virtually controlled the bureaucracy and the judiciary. The largest number of lawyers belonged to the Kayastha caste because traditionally and historically, they had taken up education for the service and judicial sector.

The reason why the Socialist Party and BLD leaders continued on the quota politics is because it gave them a sense of empowerment, and the whole community or class within a social set-up felt pride if anyone from their community was able to find a place in the elite civil services or, for that matter, qualify in the government jobs. If a Yadav or Kurmi got selected in the services, it was a matter of achievement for the entire community. The government jobs, even those of a primary teacher or a clerk, had always been something that brought social prestige in Bihar's society. Whenever the results of medical, engineering, or civil services were announced, the community people would start looking for candidates selected among them.

The politics in Bihar, since time immemorial, have been shaped by this kind of social response toward the share in social, educational, and economic resources. Although the leaders of the Lok Dal were disappointed with the results of the assembly polls, their strategy was ready for the future. They had firm conviction that with this kind of quota politics, they would gradually be able to carve a constituency for the party and themselves in the coming years. As such, despite the setback they received in the 1980 assembly polls, they persisted with reservation as central to their political program. This was the best way to build a political constituency that would be mobilized during elections and other political exercises.

The kind of politics that the Lok Dal wanted to pursue got a shot in the arm in late 1980, when the Second Backward Commission headed by B.P. Mandal submitted its report to Prime Minister Indira Gandhi's government, recommending 27% job reservation to OBC categories and segment. Indira Gandhi kept delaying the recommendation of the commission, while the Lok Dal stepped up pressure on the government for implementation of the report. In the backdrop of demand for implementation of the recommendation of the Mandal Commission, former Prime Minister Charan Singh organized a huge backward caste rally in New Delhi on February 18, 1982. Indira Gandhi understood the political challenge thrown by her rivals and political adversaries, but she could not afford to antagonize the upper castes. She had to choose between the upper castes and the upper OBC, so she thought that it was politically expedient to remain with the upper caste constituency who have traditionally been supporting the Congress. She had realized that the upper castes had returned back to the Congress after 1977 elections, in which they had deserted the Congress party, and now she and her government were not in a position to take such a political risk. Her pro-Dalit instances during the emergency had made the upper caste vary of her, but they had again come back to support her as they had also realized that upper backwards will not share power with them in the Janata Party conglomerates. Also, with the Lok Dal persisting with its demand for implementation of the Mandal Commission, they had no option but to seek the social, economic, and political security within the Congress party and organization. "Indira knew that the upper castes, comprising most of the rural gentry and urban intelligentsia, formed the head of the Congress voter base, and the Dalits and the Muslims its voter base" (Sinha, 2011, p. 108). According to eminent political scientist Paul Brass, the coalition of extremes—upper castes, Muslims, and Dalits—was not invented by Indira Gandhi but by Mahatma Gandhi as a strategy to counter the British moves to divide the society and weaken the freedom movement.

Thus, in a bid to please and appease the upper caste, Indira Gandhi made Jagannath Mishra the chief minister of Bihar. Not stopping with that, the upper caste MLAs were also given a lion's share of cabinet postings and positions. When after three years Jagannath Mishra had to bow out as a result of factionalism, he was replaced by Indira Gandhi with Chandra Shekhar Singh, a Rajput by caste.

By the beginning of early 1980, politics in Bihar was in a state of flux. The upper castes were back in the center stage and with the revival of the Congress and its coalition extremes, the upper backwards were pushed to the fringe of the electoral and political battle. On their part, Indira Gandhi and Congress took efforts not to push with her extreme Dalit agenda that had alienated the upper castes. The Dalits and Muslims had no option other than to vote for the Congress. The Belchhi massacre had given a message that the upper backwards or Lok Dal party would not treat them differently, so a Dalit–upper backward alliance was not a pragmatic phenomenon. But the Congress' appeasing the upper caste again after 1980 elections, combined with the rise in Dalit consciousness as a result of reservation in bureaucracy and legislature, were prompting them to break out of this unnatural coalition. The upper caste–Dalit–Muslim alliance was based on the concept of vote for security. The Dalits were a socially very weak community to pose any kind of opposition to the upper caste. The state institutions which were controlled by the upper caste did not allow empowerment of Dalits. The upper caste used these institutions to maintain the hegemony over the social, economic, and political life of the Dalits. The Dalits' need for social responsibilities like marriage or any other economic need were taken care by the upper caste, and in return they were supposed to stamp the ballots on the symbol of the Congress party. They controlled the economic life of the Dalits, thus commanding their political submission. This is the reason that despite scores of massacres perpetuated on the Dalits by the upper castes between 1977 and 2001, the conviction rate by the judiciary was extremely low. The reason for this was that the upper caste dominated the institution. With the aid from police and administration, Dalit booths were also stationed in the upper caste-dominated areas, while most of the times they were not even allowed to exercise their franchise. The upper caste, in collusion with booth officials and administration, rigged those booths.

Much of the caste wars that bloodied the rural hinterland of Bihar since 1977 was a result of Dalit assertion of their rights, rise in consciousness due to their representation in bureaucracy and legislature due to the quota extended to them, the rise of radical left ideology, and awareness about land and voting rights among other things. The rise of radical and intellectual left ideology among the Dalits gave them momentum to fight the tyranny of the landlords.

Just like tribal, the Dalit in certain states are greatly influenced by LWE (left wing extremism) due to plethora of socio-economic and political factors, especially their naked exploitation by the rich landlords and other influential sections. The SCs/Dalit constitute 17.5 per cent of total population of the country and is concentrated in 17 states. Except Bihar and Jharkhand the left wing extremists could not make any decisive influence among Dalits in other states. (Thomas, 2014, pp. 103–104)

Thus, the Dalits' disenchantment with the Congress also started in the beginning of the 1980s as Indira Gandhi, after coming back to power, went soft on her "hyper" Dalit welfare agenda. This move had a disjunctive impact on the Dalits. Thus, a gradual process of Dalit alienation from the Congress had already begun, which in the coming years witnessed the dumping of the grand old party by the Muslims, virtually marginalized the party in the political process of Bihar.

Split in Lok Dal 1982

By the beginning of the early 1980s, the Bihar Movement which had galvanized people against corruption had virtually faded, Jayaprakash Narayan, the architect of the movement against Indira Gandhi during emergency, had passed away, and Kishan Patnayak had also moved out of Patna. Idealism gave way to pragmatism. Lalu Prasad Yadav and Nitish Kumar had stepped up their political activities, and they were organizing rallies to demand the implementation of the Mandal Commission recommendation. During this period, Lok Dal had organized a big rally in Delhi in which both Lalu Prasad Yadav and Nitish Kumar participated. This was a period when both the young leaders cooperated with each other. In 1982, the Lok Dal experienced a vertical split leading to instability in the opposition camp. Now, it was the turn of Bihar leader Karpoori Thakur and Jat leader Charan Singh to part ways. The Jat leader had expelled Thakur, Devi Lal, H.N. Bahuguna, and Biju Patnaik among others, for conspiring against him. The two groups Lok Dal (Karpoori) and Lok Dal (Charan) later merged as Dalit Mazdoor Kisan Party (DMKP). It was again known as Lok Dal. Both the youth leaders—Nitish Kumar and Lalu Prasad Yadav—also joined one or the other socialist group. Lalu Prasad Yadav joined Lok Dal (Charan), while Nitish hopped from one party to another. He first joined Janata Party of Satendra Narayan Sinha. Nitish also went to Lok Dal (Karpoori), SSP, BLD, DMKP, and then back to Lok Dal.

Bihar Politics: The Era of Rajiv Gandhi (1985–1990)

Rajiv Gandhi took over the premiership of the country after his mother Indira Gandhi was assassinated on October 31, 1984. The subsequent Lok Sabha elections saw a Congress wave in which it clinched 50 out of the 54 parliamentary seats from the state. The Congress (Jagjivan), Lok Dal, Janata Party, and CPI bagged one seat each. As far as both the rising Janata youth leaders were concerned, Lalu Prasad Yadav fighting on Lok Dal ticket was roundly defeated from Chhapra and came third. Nitish could sense the Rajiv wave post-Indira Gandhi assassination and chose not to test himself in the electoral battle.

Bihar Assembly Elections, June 1985

A similar story was repeated in Bihar assembly elections too, which were held nearly a year later, in June 1985. The Congress party's honeymoon with the voters continued and the party won 196 seats in the assembly elections. It was an increase of 27 seats compared with assembly polls of 1980. The brunt of the Congress wave was borne by the Left and the Right, with the BJP shrinking to 16 seats from 21; the CPIM from 6 to 1, and CPI from 23 to 12, but the Lok Dal was able to not only hold its fort but even increased its tally from 42 to 46.

Yadav Consolidation Within Lok Dal in 1985

The striking part of the Lok Dal victory in the 1985 was the consolidation of Yadavs in the party. About half of the 46 MLAs who were elected on the Lok Dal ticket were Yadavs, who were hell-bent on undermining the position of the other caste groups in the party including its leader Karpoori Thakur. But the results of the 1985 assembly polls indicated that the quota politics pursued by the Lok Dal and Karpoori Thakur had failed to cut much ice with the electorates. The reason for the failure was attributed to less ground work done by the Lok Dal for mobilization of various OBC caste groups. It is not easy to turn a social caste into a political caste, and it requires a lot of efforts right from a neatly run campaign combined with sound mobilization strategy. Thus, though Karpoori Thakur had announced 26% reservation for OBCs, he had no mobilization strategy on how to unite "sainkre saath" or the 60% of the state's population which was backward castes—upper and lower, Muslims, Dalits, and tribals.

It was a dream of the great socialist Ram Manohar Lohia to weave these five segments into one thread and create a social coalition that would challenge the upper caste hegemony over the social, economic, and political system of the country. The social and political relation-ships between these five segments were not only complex but some or the other way they were rivals for shrinking of social, economic, and political space of Bihar. Everyone in the segment had problems with the upper castes: the upper backwards and the lower backwards did not see eye to eye; the upper backwards and Dalits had their own set of problems; and the Muslims—as a community—had their own set of problems. During the communal riots, backward castes, Dalits, and even tribals formed mobs that looted and murdered Muslims. So, the kind of social coalition that Ram Manohar Lohia had envisaged, its time had not come yet. Women, then, did not exhibit the political or social behavior rising above caste or community due to the patriarchal set-up of the society.

Thus, the socialist movement that was envisaged by Ram Manohar Lohia, Jayaprakash Narayan, and Karpoori Thakur ended up empower-ing mostly the upper backwards because they were economically sound, politically aware, were capable of taking on the muscle power of upper castes, and socially more conscious. If any (class/caste) could compete with the upper castes in terms of the social, economic, and political muscle, it was these three upper backward castes—Yadavs, Kurmis, and Koeris. The social coalition of the 1980s was much more politically oiled than the coalition of the 1930s during the days of "Triveni Sangh." The reason was that these three castes had improved their economic status during the last four decades and the resultant social upsurge impacted their political ambitions in the politics of Bihar in the 1980s.

Lok Dal, the Party of Upper Backwards

The Lok Dal virtually represented the political ambitions of the Yadavs, Kurmis, and Koeris besides that of the lower backwards. Karpoori Thakur, a lower backward leader belonging to the Nai (barber) caste, through his quota politics nurtured the socialist movement through its thick and thin. Even the upper caste leaders of the Lok Dal, who were Lohiaite in their ideology and believed in reverse discrimination in the form of reservation, had to play second fiddle to the backward castes in the political structure of the Lok Dal. The backwards were so vary of the upper caste leaders that they were unwilling to share power with even such leaders who supported their ideology of social emancipation. If the political atmosphere of Bihar in the early 1980s represented infancy of

the ambitions of the upper backwards through their political vehicle—
the Lok Dal—the situation in the mid-1980s represented its adolescence.
Through the years under auspicious leadership of Karpoori Thakur, the
party was traversing the dichotomies of even the upper caste leaders of
the Lok Dal.

In terms of population, the Yadavs were the largest Hindu caste group
in Bihar with their population being pegged at about 13%. But after Lalu
Prasad Yadav became the chief minister in 1990, he virtually started
what could be called "Yadavization" of Bihar politics and in the process
he antagonized the Kurmis and Koeris forcing his friend and associate
Nitish Kumar to part ways and ally with upper caste-dominated BJP. At
present, the Yadavs are the most politically empowered caste group in
Bihar with the caste men enjoying key positions in all the three powerful
political institutions, the BJP, RJD, and JD(U).

Thus, the process of realignment, which started in the mid-1970s and
took full shape in the early 1990s, is now giving way to a process of de-
alignment among the forces of backward castes. This is reflected in the
form of the consolidated backward castes' further breaking apart, and
a section of them aligning with the upper castes to put up a challenge
to the dominance of one section of backward castes represented by the
Yadavs.

Bihar has a history of playing an important role in most of the alternative political transformations that have taken place at the national level.
Going back to the formation of the Janata government in 1977, Bihar
played an important role, when the Janata party won all the 54 Lok Sabha
seats. Again, during the 1989 Lok Sabha elections which witnessed the
formation of another non-Congress government under the prime ministership of V.P. Singh, large numbers of non-Congress MPs got elected
from Bihar, while the Congress managed to win only four Lok Sabha
seats. Few years later, during the 1996 Lok Sabha elections which witnessed the formation of another non-Congress government led by H.D.
Deve Gowda, Bihar played an important role in electing many non-BJP
MPs. Similar drama had been enacted during the 2004 Lok Sabha elections, but with minor differences. On previous occasions, it had been the
Congress party which had been opposed by the voters of Bihar, but both
during the 1996 and 2004 Lok Sabha elections, it is the NDA–JD(U)
which had been seen as the main opposition parties, the enemy, by the
voters of Bihar. That is to say that the actors have changed, from the
Congress in earlier days to the NDA in recent years.

References

Ahmed, S. (2010). Nitish victory cast(e) in a different mould. *TwoCircles.net.* Retrieved December 5, 2017 from http://twocircles.net/2010nov27/nitish%E2%80%99s_victory_caste_different_mould.html#.VWgG5NKqqko

Election Commission of India. (1990). *Statistical Report on the General Elections to the Legislative Assemblies, 1989–90*, vol. I. New Delhi: Author.

Frankel, Francine, & Rao, M.S.A. (ed). (1989). *Dominance and State Power in Modern India: Decline of a Social Order.* New Delhi: Oxford University Press.

Jha, M., & Pushpendra. (2012). Governing caste and managing conflict—Bihar, 1990–2011. *Policies and Practices*, (48), 6–7. Retrieved from: http://www.mcrg.ac.in/PP48.pdf

Kumar, S., Alam, S., & Joshi, D. (2008, January–June). Caste dynamics and political process in Bihar. *Journal of Indian School of Political Economy*, *20*(1&2), 1. Retrieved November 16, 2017, from http://www.ispepune.org.in/jis108pdf/Bihar.pdf

Mishra, L.K. (2013). After initial failure, Nitish is now setting India's political agenda. *Times of India.* Retrieved November 16, 2017, from http://timesofindia.indiatimes.com/city/patna/After-initial-failure-Nitish-is-now-setting-Indias-political-agenda/articleshow/19608081.cms

Mishra, V. (2011). The long road to nootan Bihar. *Seminar Magazine*, (620). Retrieved November 16, 2017, from http://www.india-seminar.com/2011/620/620_vandita_mishra.htm

Prasad, P.H. (1987). Agrarian violence in Bihar. *Economic & Political Weekly*, *22*(22), 847–852.

Shah, Ghanshyam (ed). (2004). *Caste and Democratic Politics in India.* London: Anthem Press.

Singh, V.B., & Bose, S. (1986). *Elections in India.* New Delhi: SAGE Publications.

———. (1988). *Elections in India.* New Delhi: SAGE Publications.

Sinha, A. (2011). *Nitish Kumar and the Rise of Bihar.* Delhi: Penguin India.

Thomas, K.V. (2014). *Left Wing Extremism and Human Rights.* New Delhi: SAGE Publications.

Witsoe, J. (2011). Corruption as power: Caste and the political imagination of the postcolonial state. *American Ethnologist*, *38*(1), 73–85.

3

Emergence of OBC Politics: Elections During 1990–1995

Prime Minister V.P. Singh's government in New Delhi had run on the support of the BJP and the Left, and these parties had problems with the JD-led United Front government. Despite all these, the JD followed the model of unofficial alliance with the Left and the Right during the 1990 assembly elections in eight states, including Bihar. It did not put up candidates in 11 seats where the chances of the BJP's victory were high, while at the same time it left 25 seats for the CPI and 8 seats for CPM in Bihar in the 1990 assembly elections.

Lalu Prasad Yadav and Nitish Kumar played a defining role in the 1990 assembly election's campaign. The scenario was very confusing with JD teaming up with the BJP which had put the Ram Mandir campaign at the center stage, with the JD, at times, maintaining silence on the issue. The main target that drove this unnatural coalition was the fear of Congress and how to put the Congress on the dock, thus was formed this opportunistic alliance of Left, Right, and Center-Left. Both Nitish and Lalu attacked the Congress party at its upper caste leadership for graft, law and order, backwardness of Bihar, and perpetuation of upper caste hegemony. The Congress was the main rival for this unnatural alliance. The V.P. Singh government, at the center, was planning to implement the Mandal Commission report that would have given reservations to the OBC communities. This issue was also mentioned in the JD parliamentary elections' manifesto. Thus, a protest started all over India, including in Patna, by upper caste students against the implementation of the report. The anti-quota protesters, on December 15, 1989, blocked the roads in Patna and boycotted classes, attacked government offices and properties, and set them on fire.

The Mandal Commission in its 1982 report submitted to Indira Gandhi had recommended 27% job reservation for OBC categories in the central government services, even as 22.5% jobs were already reserved for SCs and STs. The former Prime Ministers Indira Gandhi and Rajiv Gandhi never tried to implement the recommendation fearing an upper caste backlash, and for the reason that the core of the Congress party's leadership consisted of upper castes. V.P. Singh, while campaigning for the Lok Sabha elections, had promised the electorates of Bihar, particularly the OBCs, that he would implement the recommendations of Mandal Commission if voted to power.

Campaigning and Strategy for 1990 Assembly Polls

The JD aimed at garnering the support of the backward castes, Muslims, and a section of upper castes. The major difference between the approach of the two leaders, Lalu Prasad Yadav and Nitish Kumar, was that the Yadav strongman was very open about perpetuating Yadavization, while Nitish Kumar was very reluctant to identify himself with the Kurmi caste. Lalu Prasad Yadav, in his bid to consolidate his position in the state unit of JD, nominated at least 100 Yadavs as candidates in the 1990 assembly elections out of the 270 seats on which the party fought the elections.

> This was highly disproportionate allocation (37 per cent) to a caste that had a total share of 11 per cent in the state population. It exposed the duplicity of the party in attacking the upper castes for enjoying 40 per cent or more share in the Congress with a population of less than 15 per cent. (Sinha, 2011, p. 139)

There was an internecine clash and scramble between the upper castes, Yadavs, and Kurmi–Koeris for tickets for the assembly elections. The upper castes, especially the Rajputs, considered the JD as their party as it was nationally led by Prime Minister V.P. Singh.

During his election campaign, Lalu Prasad Yadav had mobilized the masses on the promise of implementation of the recommendations of Mandal Commission and had attacked the upper caste leadership of the Congress party for the chronic backwardness of the OBCs and Dalits.

There was virtually no attack on the BJP during the campaigning for the 1990 assembly elections as the saffron party was an ally at the center and had some seat-sharing adjustments with the JD in Bihar.

The opposition parties continued with their winning spree during the assembly elections and rode on the anti-Congress wave. As a result, the reunited JD, which in 1985 poll comprised Janata Party and Lok Dal (B), won 122 seats. Both the Janata splinters in 1985 polls had together won 59 seats in the earlier assembly polls. The Congress was reduced to 71 from 196 seats. The BJP increased its tally from 16 to 39, the CPI from 12 to 23, and the CPM from 1 to 6 seats. Even the radical left Indian People's Front won 7 seats, mostly in central Bihar. The JD was short of majority in Bihar by 41 seats; thus, it depended upon the right (BJP) and the left (CPI/CPM) for survival of its government in Patna. In Bihar, the Mandal affair strengthened the emergence of a secular alternative to the Congress party in the form of JD, as the former was not able to build an OBC leadership (see Table 3.1).

Scramble for Chief Minister's Post, 1990 Assembly Polls

There were three candidates for the post of the chief minister of the state, each of them enjoying support from a particular faction of the central leadership. Lalu Prasad Yadav was backed by Devi Lal, Raghunath Jha

Table 3.1

Election results: Assembly elections, 1990 and 1995

Party/Year	1990	1995
INC	71	29
BJP	39	41
JD	122	167
CPI/CPM	23+6=29	26+6=32
Samata Party	—	7
JMM/JMM-S/JMM-M	19	19
CPML	7	6

Source: CSDS Data Unit.

Note: Seat share of parties in assembly elections of 1990 and 1995.

was backed by Chandra Shekhar, former Bihar chief minister (April 1979–February 1980), and Dalit leader Ram Sunder Das was backed by V.P. Singh, who, like the Congress' mindset, was unwilling to share power with upper backward castes. He appeared to model the JD on the pattern of the Congress with upper castes, Dalits, and the Muslims, where backwards could only be leaders but could not lead from the front.

> VP Singh's preference for Ram Sunder Das suggested that he had no immediate plan of engineering the social revolution of Lohia's dream and his ex-socialist colleague's obsession yet. His plans seem to be Janata replica of the Congress coalition model with upper castes, Dalits and Muslims. In this model the backward castes would have to play subordinate roles, but be projected as leaders. (Sinha, 2011, p. 141)

For about a week, the central JD members could not come to a decision even after hectic parleys with JD MLAs on the issue of chief ministership. Nitish Kumar was very instrumental in enlisting support for Lalu Prasad Yadav at this juncture, and he mobilized the backward MLAs of the party in favor of the Yadav strongman. V.P. Singh's emissaries wanted a consensus and no election, but Lalu Prasad Yadav forced an election. In a triangular contest, Lalu Prasad Yadav won the chief minister's position as Raghunath Jha was able to cut the upper caste, primarily Rajput MLAs, in his favor, thus handing out victory to the Yadav strongman. Lalu Prasad Yadav got 59 votes, Ram Sunder Das 56 votes, while Raghunath Jha polled 12 votes. During the candidate's selection, Lalu Prasad Yadav had given maximum tickets to the backwards, primarily the Yadavs, and this helped him in enlisting their support during the battle of Bihar's chief ministership.

Lalu's Years as the Chief Minister

Lalu Prasad Yadav who took over as the chief minister of Bihar on March 10, 1990, was a person who disliked elitism as he considered it politically incorrect. He wanted common people to identify him as a person from among them. That was the reason he took oath in the historic Gandhi Maidan—in the heart of Patna, in the middle of the common people and JD supporters—and not at the traditional Raj Bhavan in the presence of selected guests and dignitaries.

Lalu struck at the psyche of the backward and upper caste voters by slogans like "Vote hamara, Raj Tumhara, Nahi chalega, Nahi chalega" (Sinha, 2011, p. 145). Traditionally, the lower castes and backwards had been subjected to sneering remarks and double-meaning epithets by the upper castes for many centuries, and after 1990 the backward castes asserted themselves not only politically but also socially. They conveyed to the upper castes that "step aside, we have the land, we have the numbers, stop ill-treating us and now we are going to rule" (Sinha, 2011, p. 145).

Consolidation of Lalu Prasad Yadav's Rule in Bihar

There were two main factors that led to the consolidation of JD under Lalu Prasad Yadav. First, Yadav virtually walked away with all the electoral credit and advantages that emanated with the implementation of Mandal Commission report. Second, with his rhetorical speeches, he was able to convince the electorates of Bihar, primarily the Dalits, OBCs, and the Muslims that it was he who was the guarantor of their security from the upper castes and the rioters.

On August 7, 1990, the then Prime Minister V.P. Singh announced the acceptance of the recommendation of Mandal Commission report which gave the OBCs 27% reservation in central government jobs. The move came as a boon to Lalu Prasad Yadav. The BJP and the left wanted the United Front government to incorporate economic criteria into the reservations. Their idea was to frame on the basis of Karpoori Thakur's Bihar formula which instead of providing full quota to the OBCs broke it into two—extremely backward castes (EBCs) and backward castes. The upper backwards were placed in the backward castes category and the lower backwards in the EBC category, so that the educationally ahead upper backwards do not appropriate the entire quota. Second, it excluded the wards of income-tax paying citizens and provided for 3% reservation for economically poor among the upper castes.

But Lalu Prasad Yadav was against the formula to be implemented with a subcategory, on the grounds that it will fragment the backward caste movement against the social and political hegemony of the upper castes. There were violent clashes in the streets of Patna and other cities, and the unrest had even spread to rural areas of Bihar.

Instead of mediating and making peace between the forwards and the backwards, Lalu gave speeches that widened the chasm. Political profit could be maximized only in conflagration. This was the time when Lalu ranted most vituperatively against the upper castes and turned a Pied Piper for the backward castes. (Sinha, 2011, p. 146)

Mandal and Mandir virtually attempted to dominate the political landscape of India and tried to outdo each other. The Mandal debate had led to serious social tensions in mohallas and villages of Bihar, with clear polarization between the backwards and the forwards. Amid these social tensions, BJP leader L.K. Advani announced his controversial Rath Yatra for building the Ram Temple at Ayodhya on the disputed site of Babri Masjid.

The upper caste leadership of the BJP was somehow not comfortable with the Mandal report, even as the saffron party was aware of the political cost of going against the OBCs, who saw the reservation as an opportunity for their social and economic emancipation.

Thus, Lalu Prasad Yadav and Nitish Kumar were able to swing the mood of the OBCs in favor of JD and charging the BJP of sabotaging the Mandal project by propagating the Ram Mandir–Babri Masjid issue. Lalu's anti-BJP rhetoric was no less than music to the ears of the Muslims. This helped Lalu Prasad Yadav in consolidating the backward castes as well as the Muslims in his favor. Lalu Prasad Yadav was successful in demonizing the BJP for its alleged anti-Mandal stand.

Advani's rath yatra is nothing but a conspiracy to stonewall Mandal. The BJP represents the social diehards who attack Mandal because they want the old social system based on injustice to continue. Mandal has fulfilled the aspirations of the oppressed classes and given them social esteem. There is no way anyone can turn back the clock of social justice, Nitish Kumar told a pro-reservation rally in Gandhi Maidan in Patna. (Sinha, 2011, p. 148)

In Bihar, the Mandal affair strengthened the emergence of a secular alternative to the Congress party in the form of Janata Dal as the former was not able to build an OBC leadership. Besides, due to the Bhagalpur riots of October–November 1989, Muslims felt that Congress had acted decisively against them by permitting Ramshila processions pass through sensitive areas. These two events accelerated the decline in the popular vote of the Congress party in the eve of the 1990 Bihar legislative assembly elections. (Robin, 2009, pp. 85–86)

Arrest of Lal Krishna Advani in Bihar's Samastipur

Lal Krishna Advani's Somonath (Gujarat) to Ayodhya (Uttar Pradesh) Rath Yatra led to a surge in communal tensions leading to communal riots across the country, particularly in Uttar Pradesh, Karnataka, Gujarat, and Andhra Pradesh. Prime Minister V.P. Singh directed Bihar's Chief Minister Lalu Prasad Yadav to stop the yatra, and thus the BJP patriarch was arrested in Bihar's Samastipur district on October 23, 1990 by the JD-led state government. Lalu Prasad Yadav walked away with all the political accolades in terms of vote bank politics and projected the arrest of the Hindutva leader as his personal feat. This single incident made him the darling of the Muslims. No other leader in the history of Bihar was so outspoken in his support for the Muslims. Lal Krishna Advani's arrest led to the withdrawal of BJP support to the V.P. Singh government in New Delhi as well as Lalu Prasad Yadav-led government in Patna. The BJP withdrew the support of its 39 MLAs reducing the Lalu Prasad Yadav government to minority but it was rescued with the support of Left parties CPI—23, CPM)—6, Marxist Coordination Committee (MCC)—2, Indian People's Front (IPF)—7, besides JMM—19 and independents—30.

After winning the trust vote in Bihar assembly, post withdrawal of support of the BJP, Lalu Prasad Yadav emerged as the champion of not only social justice but also secularism. The Left support, whose voters were primarily Dalits and the lower backward castes, also strengthened the facade of social justice of Lalu Prasad Yadav. The Yadav leader did not allow the political tempo over upper caste hegemony subside down even after the Supreme Court putting a stay on the recommendations. He attacked the upper castes over their hegemonic control over Bihar state bureaucracy, as eight out of top 10 IAS officers were from the upper castes. His government issued an ordinance which entailed even imprisonment of officers ignoring the reservation provisions during recruitment of services in the state government.

Lalu Prasad Yadav Revises Karpoori Thakur's Quota Formula

The Karpoori Thakur's quota formula which was practiced in Bihar for the last 13 years was redone by Lalu Prasad Yadav. The Extremely

Backward Castes (EBC) leader's formula had provided 3% reservation for the economically weaker among the upper castes while 3% reservation was provided to women, which most of the times also went to the upper castes. Lalu Prasad Yadav annulled the 3% upper caste reservation provided under Karpoori formula and also reduced the women quota to 2% from 3%. The JD government under him equally distributed 4% between the backward classes and the extremely backward classes. The revision led to the increase in backward classes quota from 8% to 10% and EBC quota from 12% to 14%. The JD government, under Lalu Prasad Yadav in 1993, also passed the Bihar Panchayati Raj Act which reflected this new formula in the grass-roots-level institutions in similar proportion. For the backward classes, 10% seats were reserved; for the EBCs, 14%, and 2% for women.

> He (Lalu Prasad) was quite aware that Mandal and the revised Karpoori formula combined could at best bring few thousand jobs to the state's OBCs in a year, which could only create a very tiny oasis in the desert of OBC disability…. The novelty and uniqueness of Lalu was that he took Mandal beyond quota jobs; he converted it into psychological machine. Through his decisions, speeches, appearance, and public behaviour he was able to portray himself as *apna admi*, "one of our own" to the masses. The only other politician of Bihar before him who had been identified by the poor as "apna admi" was Karpoori Thakur. Lalu went beyond Karpoori…. He depicted his election and tenure as Chief Minister as a triumph of the downtrodden, making them feel it was actually gharib raj, rule of the poor. (Sinha, 2011, pp. 150–151)

Mandal Was Empowerment Scheme and Not Employment Scheme

The politics that surrounded the implementation of the Mandal Commission was not merely an employment scheme, as it only provided few thousand jobs, but a psychological game of social superiority. The backwards and Dalits under the leadership of upper backwards, primarily the Yadavs, led this social churning which marked this great shift in the society of Bihar. Lalu demonized the upper castes and built his sociopolitical structure on it. Karpoori Thakur had sought equality with the forwards but Lalu Prasad Yadav wanted complete social and political dominance over them. The gradual impact of Lalu Prasad Yadav's sloganeering backed by electoral strength was that the upper castes real-ized that their days were over and they became unadventurous/disadvan-taged in not only urban centers but also small towns and villages where the poor and backward caste people started asserting themselves more in government offices and police stations. Virtually, the entire backward caste upsurge during the phase was led by Yadavs, but the Kurmis felt left out. What made Lalu Prasad Yadav different from other OBC politi-cal leaders of his generation was his combative mode of dealing with upper castes. He did not believe in reconciliation with the upper castes but wanted to dominate over them.

Lalu Prasad Yadav Behind the Social Transformation in Bihar Since Independence

Under the banner of the communist parties CPI and CPML, the Dalits and the lower backwards had fought a decisive battle for their rights from the upper caste-dominated Congress party governments in Bihar. In the Mithilanchal region and the central Bihar belts of Gaya, rural Patna, and Jahanabad areas, the CPML had successfully won electoral battles against the feudal forces represented by the Congress party gov-ernments. Lalu Prasad Yadav, after his ascent as Bihar's chief minister, through his communication not only marginalized his contemporaries but also the communist parties. He started speaking in the language of the radical left even though/as worst violence was perpetuated against the Dalits and lower backwards by the upper caste and upper backward militias such as Ranveer Sena and Sunlight Sena. During the first five years of Lalu Prasad Yadav's rule, at least 17 massacres of Dalits and backwards took place in which nearly 150 rural poor were killed. But it was also the first time that the rural poor were getting a feeling of fresh political and social air in Bihar.

> Moreover, for the first time, the rural poor who were victims of a semi-feudal order cast their votes in very large numbers, resisting intimida-tions. They were obviously galvanized by the speeches Lalu Prasad Yadav against the upper caste landlords, giving the Dalits a new sense of izzat (dignity). (Robin, 2009, p. 87)

Lalu Prasad Yadav Overshadowed the JD

After becoming the chief minister, Lalu Prasad Yadav started showing instincts of a feudal lord. The maverick politician, the top youth leader of the anti-emergency movement in 1977, did not make any serious attempt to check corruption, institutionalize governance, or revamp the education system. The education system, particularly the higher education system, saw serious decline with semesters getting extended due to teachers' strike and other issues. Lalu Prasad Yadav started believing that the JD existed due to his personality and charisma among the masses. He started openly snubbing and sidelining serious leaders and advisers. These were the issues that forced Nitish Kumar to part ways in April 1994 which resulted in the formation of Samata Party. This was also the period which saw the emergence of Lalu Prasad Yadav's two brothers-in-law—Subhash Yadav and Sadhu Yadav (brothers of Rabri Devi, who became Bihar's chief minister after Lalu resigned over the fodder scam in 1997)—as power centers. The duo had developed a chain of syndicate across the districts of the state for distributing contracts and government tenders. This was combined by open Yadavization that was perpetuated in the Lalu Prasad Yadav regime in each and every space of political, social, and economic sphere. Nitish Kumar and his Kurmi caste men, along with Koeris, were feeling sidelined as the entire leadership was overwhelmed by the Yadavs under Lalu Prasad Yadav. The chief minister, in his bid to sideline Nitish Kumar among the Kurmis, during 1993 used his insistence on Karpoori formula (entailing separate quota for EBCs within OBC) instead of the Mandal Commission which resulted in gains for the lower backwards at the cost of upper backwards.

Later, when Nitish Kumar became the chief minister of Bihar in 2005, he implemented the Karpoori formula during his tenure and even demanded that the formula be implemented at the national level. The formula reserved separate seats for EBCs within the OBC category.

"Even my castemen (Kurmi, an OBC) were provoked against me for seeking quota for EBC within OBC. But, without bothering for the consequence I stood my ground," Nitish Kumar was quoted as saying (*The Economic Times*, 2014).

1995 Bihar Assembly Elections

The 1995 assembly elections of Bihar were a watershed as it followed the GA of the upper backwards' disintegration. The vision of Karpoori Thakur, Ram Manohar Lohia, and Jayaprakash Narayan which had already traversed through different paths, was to witness a new twist. The political ambitions of two of their iconic disciples—Lalu Prasad Yadav and Nitish Kumar—saw the upper backward movement splitting into two rival camps. By 1995, Lalu Prasad Yadav was the undisputed leader of the powerful Yadav caste and Nitish Kumar that of Kurmi–Koeri combine. The rivalries between these upwardly mobile upper backward groups were decades-old, but only the fear of upper castes had kept them united all these years. The 1990 Bihar assembly elections saw the consolidation of three upper backward castes: Muslims, some upper castes, and a segment of Dalits. This resulted in the victory of JD in Bihar.

CPML Response to Lalu Prasad Yadav's 1995 Victory

The CPML which had spearheaded the cause of the Dalits and the lower backward farmers against the upper caste landlords looked at the JD victory under Lalu Prasad Yadav with contempt.

It should not be forgotten that a large number of JD MLAs are renowned criminals and several of them come from upper castes, particularly Rajputs, with notoriously feudal backgrounds. The other face of Lalu was revealed in garnering the support of upper caste gentry with the plea that only he can save them from Naxalite violence. During his five-year rule, by distributing privileges and favors with impunity he won over several powerful feudal elements to his fold who originally belonged to the Congress(I) and BJP. To win Muslim support religious fundamentalism was invoked to the extreme, and barring a few exceptions, the Muslim gentry too solidly backed Lalu Yadav. In short, beneath Lalu's individual charisma is hidden a social coalition of various power groups and landed interests of several dominant castes including a significant section of upper castes. If these social dynamics are not understood one is liable to be trapped in a one-sided, liberal and social-democratic interpretation of Lalu's victory. Lalu Yadav is nothing but the ruling class response to the growing revolutionary struggle in Bihar. This is the secret behind the support given to him by the administration as well as by the majority of dominant power groups: Lalu Yadav is quite conscious of his mission and one can find him simultaneously projecting himself before the upper-caste landed gentry as the alternative to the violent Naxalites. When he claims that Naxalites handed over guns to the poor and he has handed them books he exposes his mission of disarming the people mentally and physically in the otherwise highly violent and armed society of Bihar. (Mishra, 1995)

In his book *Community Warriors: State, Peasants and Caste Armies in Bihar*, Ashwani Kumar says that the unity between the Samata Party and the BJP, who forged a powerful coalition of the Kurmis and the Koeris against the Yadav-dominated coalition, proved disastrous for the Lalu-led JD in the long run. A year later, Mr Prasad quit the JD and floated the RJD.

Split in JD: Birth of Samata Party

Since taking over as the chief minister of Bihar in 1990, Lalu Prasad Yadav backed by strong support from men of his caste and Muslims started the Yadavization of the party and the government, so much so that his close associate Nitish Kumar was forced to part ways with him. Lalu not only encouraged Yadavization but was also dictatorial in his outlook. The problems in Bihar led to a split in JD in July 1994. "It is a revolt against overlordship of Lalu," Nitish Kumar said after splitting the party (Ansari, Farz, & Ahmed, 1994). At least 14 MPs, including three prominent Muslim parliamentarians—Syed Shahabuddin, Mohammad Yunus Saleem, and Mohammad Taslimuddin—formed a separate group in parliament under the banner of Samata Party. At least 10 out of 14 MPs were from Bihar.

After taking over the reign as Bihar's chief minister, it saw Yadav's assertion under the leadership of Lalu Prasad Yadav in JD and in 1994 saw the breaking away of Kurmi–Koeri combine from the upper back-ward leadership of the party. After Nitish Kumar formed the Samata Party, the battle lines between these two camps were drawn, Yadavs on the one hand and Kurmi–Koeris on the other. The Samata Party forged an alliance with the BJP for the 1996 general elections.

For the first time in the political history of Bihar, two rival politi-cal camps were led by upper backward leaders. Since independence, the ruling and the opposition camps were mostly led by the upper caste groups. Then gradually, the opposition camp was led by a backward leader, and the treasury benches by the upper castes, but now both the poles of the state politics were virtually at the hands of the backward caste leaders, primarily upper backward leaders and the upper castes were reduced to the political margins who were forced to ally with one or the other camps as per their individual preferences and conveniences. In the 1995 elections, Samata Party led by Nitish Kumar won only seven seats and the BJP emerged as the principal opposition party replacing the Congress. The BJP won 41 seats and the Congress was reduced to 29 from 71. The BJP saw only marginal improvement from its 1990 tally with a rise of only 2 seats from 39 in the 1990 assembly elections.

The JD got 167 seats in the 1995 assembly elections, a decent jump from 122 in the last elections. There was a consolidation of Muslim, lower backwards, Dalit, and Yadav votes in favor of JD in 1995, though it lost some percentage of the Kurmi–Koeri votes due to Nitish Kumar factor. By this time, the upper castes had realized that their days of political dominance in the politics of Bihar were over. A lot of upper caste strongmen were elected as JD MLAs. The one thing that needs to be understood is that the upper caste were only losing to the upper backward castes in the political space, but their control over the education system, judiciary, and bureaucracy was undisputed. The upper backward leaders such as Lalu Prasad Yadav and Nitish Kumar knew that the upper castes were not only economically more affluent, but their control at the social and grass-roots levels was also still strong. At the social and rural levels, the Yadavs were still mere milkmen and the Kurmi–Koeris were farmers of the tilled lands.

In the 1995 assembly elections, the upper caste voters virtually had no place to go. They had supported the JD and the Congress in the 1990 assembly elections, but when Lalu Prasad Yadav took over as the chief minister, he left no stone unturned to heap insults on the upper castes. He allegedly said in 1992, "Bhura Baal Saaf Karo," meaning "Remove Bhumihar, Rajput, Brahman, Lala (Kasyahthas)" and in 1996 he allegedly referred the Kurmi–Koeri community as *Kukur* (dog) (*The Times of India*, 2008).

The upper caste Kurmi–Koeri alliance that culminated in later years was the result of such attitude of the Bihar strongman (Gaikwad, 2013). On February 12, 1994, a huge Kurmi Chetna Maha Rally was organized, supported by the Kurmi leaders from across the political spectrum from Right to Left. Patna's Gandhi Maidan is not only the symbol of political protest but also a place to show political might and strength. Lalu Prasad Yadav had organized huge protests and rallies at the ground to show off his political might for nearly two decades beginning in the 1990s. Before the Kurmi Chetna Maha Rally in 1994 in Gandhi Maidan, many other caste groups—mostly backwards—had organized rallies to flaunt their might. Many of these rallied were addressed by Nitish Kumar and Lalu Prasad Yadav. Backward caste groups such as Lohars, Kumhars, Nishads, Koeris, and Dhanuks had also organized rallies at the historic Gandhi Maidan in the heart of Patna, and now it was the turn of Kurmis— the second most powerful backward caste group after Yadavs—to do so.

> The idea (Mahachetna) was supported from leaders belonging from all political parties—Janata Dal, Congress, BJP, and CPI—who had not failed to note the growing sense of betrayal in the Kurmi community against Lalu. We fought shoulder to shoulder in the battle for Mandal. We were cheated was the common Kurmi refrain. (Sinha, 2011, p. 164)

The name of Kurmi caste was also found absent from the list of central services for Mandal reservations and also from the list of reservation for Bihar's Panchayat elections. Even as these "errors" were corrected later, it led to huge Kurmi unease and unrest. Thousands of Kurmis protested at the JP Circle in Patna.

Nitish was reluctant to go to the Mahachetna rally due to his aversion to caste politics, but he feared that Kurmis will declare him as an outcaste if he does not stand with them at this juncture, especially as Lalu Prasad Yadav was hell-bent on promoting the Yadavs. This was also the time when Nitish Kumar virtually declared himself as the leaders of the Kurmis in Bihar. Addressing the mammoth rally attended mostly by people from his own caste, Nitish Kumar told the crowd: "The Kurmis must step forward to take the leadership of the social justice movement. No power on earth can deny job reservations to Kurmis.... They (Kurmis) need to form a broader coalition with the OBCs and EBCs for their own political survival" (Sinha, 2011, p. 165).

The chasm between Nitish Kumar and Lalu Prasad Yadav grew to such an extent that it became difficult for the Kurmi leader to stay in JD. In the JD parliamentary party meeting in Delhi, Nitish Kumar had revolted against Lalu Prasad Yadav. On April 21, 1994, Nitish formed a new party namely Janata Dal (George)—JD(G)—splitting the JD. He walked away with 13 MPs including veteran socialist leader George

Fernandes. The JD(G) was dissolved in October 1994, and it paved the way for creation of the Samata Party.

JD Under Lalu Prasad Yadav Crushes Opposition: Congress, BJP, and Samata Party in Bihar 1995 Assembly Polls

Lalu Prasad Yadav was at the peak of his charisma during the 1995 assembly elections. He single-handedly led the JD to a majority of its own, winning 167 assembly seats out of 324. Nitish Kumar miserably failed to dent the vote share of Lalu Prasad Yadav, despite his best efforts. It was simple arithmetic that led to the victory of the JD. The opposition parties were fragmented which led to the JD winning a simple majority of its own, despite garnering only 28% of the votes. But the victory of the JD was overwhelming in the sense that despite poor parameters of performance on development and law and order, Lalu Prasad Yadav had notched a victory which the JD could not even achieve during V.P. Singh's wave of 1990, when virtually the entire media was supportive of it and forces right from Right to Left were in its favor. It was Lalu Prasad Yadav's personal victory, as he had achieved this feat even with heavy weights like Nitish Kumar being in the opposition. The Samata Party under Nitish Kumar was decimated with 303 candidates losing their seats out of the 310 they fought. At least 270 Samata candidates lost their security deposits, and only 21 of them were runner-ups in their constituencies. The Samata report card of the 1995 assembly elections read 7 seats and 7% vote share. The Samata in 1995 proved to be a sub-regional force, only having stronghold in Kurmi-dominated Nalanda district where it won three seats. Nitish Kumar won the election from Harnaut with a margin of just 13,000 votes against his JD rival.

In the 1985 Bihar assembly, the upper castes constituted 38.5% of total MLAs in the state, but in the Congress party their share was 41.8%. The three castes—Rajputs, Bhumihars, and Brahmins—constituted the bulk of the upper caste legislators. The backward castes comprising Yadavs, Kurmis, Koeris, and Baniyas formed 25.2% of total strength of the assemblies, but were only 17.4% in the Congress party MLAs. Meanwhile, the Muslims constituted 14.3% of the total Congress MLAs, but were only 10.8% of the total assembly's strength.

In the 1990 Bihar assembly elections, JD emerged as the dominant party replacing the Congress; simultaneously, the OBCs replaced the upper castes as the dominant caste in Bihar politics with the backward caste representation increasing to 34.3% in the assembly and 43.9% in the JD. While the share of upper caste in the assembly came down to 34.6% from 38.5%, in the JD they constituted 25.6% of total party MLAs. The Muslim representation saw a dip with only 6.2% of them getting elected, while they were 9.1% strong in the JD. The 1995 Bihar assembly elections were landmark moments for the OBC politics as 43.7% backwards constituted the Bihar legislative assembly. The share of forwards were at an all-time low with only 21.8% getting elected as MLAs, while their share in the JD legislators dipped to 16.1% from 25.6% in 1990 (see Table 3.2). The Muslim representation virtually remained stagnant with 7.1% getting elected as MLAs, though in the JD they were 9.2% strong. "The 1995 elections marked an acceleration of change in the social composition of the political class of Bihar with upper caste MLAs representing less than half of the OBC MLAs in the Vidhan Sabha" (Robin, 2009, p. 87).

Development and Izzat Under Lalu

While various combinations and recombination of castes and communities kept the JD as well as Lalu Prasad Yadav in power during the period 1990–2000, the political changes ushered in 1990 were not bereft of tangible issues. Although social justice, however vaguely understood, and self-respect of hitherto politically and socially marginalized sections had

Table 3.2

Changing pattern of assembly from 1985 to 1995: From upper caste domination to OBC emancipation

	Congress (1985)	Total % in Bihar Assembly	JD (1990)	Total % in State Assembly	JD (1995)	Total % in State Assembly
Upper castes	41.8	38.5	25.6	34.6	16.1	21.8
OBCs	17.4	25.2	43.9	34.3	52.6	43.7
Muslims	14.3	10.2	9.1	6.2	9.2	7.1

Source: Survey by Robin (2009).

formed the populist electoral slogans, rural development and law and order too figured prominently in the campaign of these two assembly elections. After winning the 1995 assembly elections, Lalu Prasad Yadav declared that his second term would focus not only on social justice for the poor, stability, and communal harmony but also on economic development (Hauser, 1997). His trips to many Southeast Asian nations, to the United States, and a conference of NRIs in Patna were seen as serious moves toward economic development in the state. Let us briefly discuss what changed for the better or worse in Bihar during a decade-long regime of Lalu Prasad Yadav.

In his first stint, Lalu Prasad Yadav not only provided political stability but also kept the state away from communal riots which occurred during the Congress regime at almost regular intervals. Undisputedly, security of life and property happen to be major concerns for minorities and marginalized section. Other priorities such as bijli, sadak, pani (electricity, road, drinking water) come up only after this. Lalu Prasad Yadav was able to ensure that there would be no communal riots; the houses of the backward castes and the Dalits would not be burnt, and there would be no violence against the underprivileged. This instilled confidence among the minorities and marginalized communities, and they hoped that a new Bihar of prosperity and social harmony was in the offing. With security to them and their life and property, economic prosperity would always follow.

If a comparative study is done on the composition of ministries in Bihar between the Congress government led by Chandra Shekhar Singh in 1983 and Lalu Prasad Yadav in 1994 (see Table 3.3), it could be observed that upper castes were replaced by the OBCs as the dominant group in the ministries, for the simple reason that their representation

Table 3.3

Caste composition of ministries in Bihar (in percent)

Caste/Community	Chandra Shekhar Singh (1983)[a]	Lalu Prasad Yadav (1994)[b]
Upper castes	44	27.0
OBCs	24	46.5
Dalits and Adivasis	13	15.5
Muslims	19	11.3
Number of ministers	—	71

Sources: [a]Frankel (1989) and [b]Choudhary (1999).

also jumped after the 1990 assembly elections. At least 44% of ministers belonged to the upper caste in 1983, but 46.5% of OBCs donned the ministries in Lalu Prasad Yadav's cabinet. Only 24% OBCs were part of the state cabinet in 1983, whereas only 27% upper caste became ministers during Lalu's regime.

While structural changes in political representation, providing stable government, ensuring communal harmony, and bringing the hitherto marginalized groups into political mainstream were major achievements of Lalu Prasad Yadav, he failed to keep other promises such as better roads, electricity, pensions, brick houses, and the subsidized saris and dhotis for those below the poverty line. Toward the end of his second term, there were growing number of incidences of kidnapping and extortion. Besides, there was also the rise of what Hauser calls "phenomenon of Yadavization" (Hauser, 1997, p. 2602), whereby Lalu himself was involved in widespread transfers and postings to the narrow interests of his caste fellows and party supporters.[1]

Even a casual look at the policies/programs meant for the poor and their implementation suggests that nothing substantial had happened during 1990–2000 that would have ensured a measure of economic betterment of the toiling masses, leave alone overall socioeconomic development of the state. For example, acquisition of surplus land and its redistribution would certainly have given a measure of empowerment to those having no land at all. Although data pertaining to how much surplus land was acquired and redistributed in the 1990s are not easily available, one can make an assessment of the situation indirectly with the help of other data sources. In 1991–1992, about 14.19% of the rural household had no operational holdings (NSSO 1991–1992), but this proportion increased to about 30% in 2002–2003 (NSSO 2002–2003). It can thus be assumed that land reform, and a major political agenda in the state in the pre-1960s and 1980s and what still could be a pro-poor policy, had taken a back seat.

On the economic front too, Bihar appeared to paint a dismal picture during the 1990s. For example, the annual growth rate of Gross State Domestic Product (GSDP) was 4.66 per cent during the period between 1980–81

---

[1] Some observers, having their eyes set on Bihar politics, commented that it was the Yadavization phenomenon that angered the upward mobile Koeris and Kurmis among whom there were more professionals and bureaucrats than among the Yadavs. And finally it caused the split between Lalu Prasad and Nitish Kumar (who formed Samata Party in 1994).

and 1990–91. It fell to 2.69 per cent during the period between 1990–91 and 1999–2000. Similarly, annual growth rate of per capita GSDP fell from 2.45 per cent to 1.12 per cent during the same periods. (Ahluwalia, 2000)

During the 1990s, the law and order situation had worsened and as a result crime rates increased considerably. In 1990, about 4,166 cases of murder, 2,138 cases of kidnapping and abductions, and 3,164 cases of dacoity were reported in the state. With this, the percentage share of Bihar in total cases of murder, kidnappings, and dacoity reported for India as a whole was 11.9%, 11.6%, and 28.5%, respectively. In 1999, Bihar had accounted for 14.0% of murders, 11.2% of kidnappings, and 30.9% of dacoity of total cases of murder, kidnapping, and dacoity reported for India as a whole (Crime in India, 1990, 1999). In short, macro-level statistics suggest that things rather worsened in the 1990s in Bihar.

The declining popularity of Lalu Prasad Yadav's regime and loss of many seats in the election could, in part, be attributed to the declining socioeconomic conditions of people in the state. However, by and large, the supporters of Lalu Prasad Yadav still had confidence in him and voted for him. It can be argued that development means differently to different people and the common people may not see development the way development economists do. It is more likely to be the case, where social structure restricts socioeconomic mobility of those at lower rungs or those that constitute the bulk of social "others." For them, the issues of being "social/political equals" may be more important than being "economic equals" until sociopolitical processes aimed at offering social justice/self-dignity get saturated. If this was the case, it could be argued that the rhetoric of social justice/self-dignity had not reached its saturation point until now.

The Politics of Bihar in the 1990s: Political Ascendancy of Backward Castes and Rout of the Congress

The 1990s era could also be seen as a new beginning in the politics of Bihar, which was marked by several features. First, the absolute decline of the Congress; second, the emergence of the JD/RJD; and finally the people having the experience of various forms of government: minority government, single-party majority rule, and also coalition governments. During the last two decades, though, there had been various forms of government, but coalition government had been the dominant form of government in Bihar. This second phase of coalition era may be seen as a new beginning in the politics of the state, which had remained sharply polarized in the form of pro- and anti-Lalu forces in Bihar.

The politics in Bihar until the 1980s was virtually dominated by one party, the Congress, except for brief interludes on two occasions during 1967–1971 and 1977–1979. Before the 1980s, there was hardly any meaningful role for the opposition parties or forces to play in the politics of the state. The Congress party was dominated by upper castes in both the party's organization and elected members to legislature (Jaffrelot, 2003). Thus, the power sharing among different social groups was disproportionately in favor of the upper castes. But, the end of the 1980s had ushered in a new era in the politics of Bihar with the doors shut for the Congress, a party that was so far the darling of the people. Yet another important thing that took place was the mobilization of marginalized sections of the society (Yadav, 1999).

The Lok Sabha elections held in 1989, in fact, signaled who would not rule the state in future. The Congress had suffered a major setback and not only had the Congress lost most of the parliamentary seats, but it also lost its traditional support base—the upper castes, the Dalits, and the Muslims. The Muslims in Bihar had started drifting away from the Congress following the Bhagalpur communal riots. The demolition of Babri Masjid in 1992 under the Congress regime at the center made the drift and alienation complete.

On the other hand, the "Mandal Wave" in the late 1980s had been sweeping over the country. The "Mandal Tangle" took a serious political turn in Bihar and also in most parts of North India. It had led to the polarization of masses along the forward–backward lines. The Congress was not ready to give in to the demand of implementation of Mandal Commission report, which had recommended reservation for OBCs in public employment and educational institutions. The handling of Shahbano Case in the late 1980s was seen as Congress' attempt to appease Muslims. This gave the Ram Mandir movement fresh impetus and momentum. The BJP's aggressive campaign was getting into the psyche of certain section of masses, namely the upper castes, who grew disenchanted with the Congress and had started tilting toward the BJP. Thus, while "Mandalization" of politics offered the backward castes a rare opportunity to get united and capture power, the Ram Mandir movement broke the upper castes away from the Congress to fall into the lap of the BJP. Added to Mandal–Mandir–Masjid factors that had contributed to the fast-losing popularity of the Congress was the charge of corruption against the then Prime Minister Rajiv Gandhi, which had boiled into the infamous "Bofors Scandal." V.P. Singh, who had recently drifted away from the Congress, had made it an election issue. Although there is no standard literature explaining how far and whether the Bofors deal played any part in the defeat of the Congress, it can be reasonably assumed, particularly in the context of Bihar, that it was one of the contributory factors.

Apart from these macro factors, the Congress had by now become a divided house, internal factionalism had reached its nadir, and the party was in shambles. The Muslims had deserted Congress following the Bhagalpur riots. Dalits and OBCs were getting mobilized under the umbrella of the JD with leaders such as Ram Sunder Das, Lalu Prasad Yadav, Nitish Kumar, and Ram Vilas Paswan, to name a few, at the helm of party affairs. In South Bihar, the movement for a separate state for tribals had grown too intense. The JMM that had been spearheading the movement of a separate state, by 1990, was a force to reckon with its own pocket of influences in the Jharkhand region of Bihar. In short, given these series of political, social, and economic developments that had already taken place, the only need of the hour was exchange of political elites and when the 1989 general elections took place, the formality of the role-reversal was complete. Another major factor for the loss of the 1989 general elections in Bihar and 1990 State assembly elections was that the united might of opposition from Right to Left had ganged up against the Congress party to dislodge it.

The Congress had lagged much behind the Janata and Left parties in terms of both vote and seat shares in Bihar. The Congress had secured 28% of valid votes and won merely 4 Lok Sabha seats out of 54. As against this, the JD got 37.6% of valid votes and 32 seats. The rest of seats were shared by the BJP, JMM, and a few independents.

The Mandal (Commission report) was the biggest game changer for the regime of Lalu Prasad Yadav and as he had successfully appropriated all credits for the empowerment of the backwards and the Dalits, the 1995 assembly polls saw the JD getting a majority of its own under his leadership. In a pre-election study done by the Lokniti-CSDS in 1995, a clear polarization was visible between backwards and forwards over the issue of Mandal which gave 27% reservation to OBCs. About 68.5% of the upper caste respondents had opposed Mandal tooth and nail (see

Table 3.4

Caste voting pattern in 1995 election

Caste and Voting Patterns in Bihar—Rise of OBCs	OBC	Upper Caste
Disapprove	13.4	68.5
Approve	75.5	27

Source: CSDS Data Unit.

Note: All figures are in percent.

Table 3.4), while 13.4% of the OBCs were opposed to it. Among the OBCs, at least 75.5% of voters supported implementation of the Mandal Commission report entailing reservation for the backward classes in educational institutions and government jobs in the state and central government agencies. Only 27% of the upper caste respondents had favorable opinion for the Mandal Commission report.

Thus, the 1995 assembly election in Bihar during the post-Mandal period had witnessed the electoral contest on forward–backward axis, which had also resulted in consolidation of the backward castes in favor of the JD led by Lalu Prasad Yadav. In this, the backward caste consolidation of the three dominant OBC castes—Yadav, Kurmi, and Koeri—took the lead, while large numbers of OBCs were left out of the process of social, political, and electoral mobilization. But the phase of the OBC consolidation was short-lived, and cracks had appeared among the OBC castes just before the 1995 assembly elections, with the formation of Samata Party and Nitish Kumar as its leader, and thus his party failed to make a mark in the state assembly elections.

Realizing the limitation of electoral success based only on support of their own caste, both the RJD led by Lalu Prasad Yadav and Samata Party (now JD(U)) led by Nitish Kumar had tried to make alliance with other political parties, with an eye on electoral support of other caste groups. While the Nitish Kumar-led Samata Party in Bihar formed an alliance with the BJP, the Lalu Prasad Yadav-led RJD formed alliance with different parties in different elections. The 1990s also marked a complete breakdown of the Congress in the state, resulting in forming alliance with Lalu Prasad Yadav-led RJD at times, and at times contesting elections alone. The Congress, from the position of Bihar's ruling party in 1990, was struggling for opposition space by 1995 as its seat share drastically fell to an all-time low of 29 seats—much below the BJP's 41 seats. The saffron party replaced the Congress as the principal opposition party in the state assembly. This period also witnessed major transformation in the social basis of political power in Bihar and in some other states of North India[2] (Jaffrelot, 2003; Yadav, 1999). Consequent to the decline of the Congress party, there emerged different political formations. However, the JD not only emerged as a party of prominence but also had managed to snatch power from Congress in the assembly elections held in 1990. The support base of the JD constituted an overwhelming proportion of backward castes, the Muslims, and the Dalits. The BJP had also made inroads into the electoral scene in Bihar, and it drew major support from the upper castes. However, it was not able to bring the entire upper caste bloc into its fold; a significant part of the upper caste was still with the Congress in the 1995 assembly polls.

The JD under the leadership of Lalu Prasad Yadav in Bihar continued its impressive performance in the Lok Sabha Elections of May–June 1991. The JD alone won 32 out of 54 Lok Sabha seats in the state. Surprisingly, the Left Front managed to win nine seats. The BJP could win only five seats in that election. However, soon after the regime change in Bihar, it appeared that the consolidation of the backward castes was neither so compact nor was the upper–lower castes divide a durable feature of politics in the state. The internal squabbles among the ambitious champions of backward castes finally led to the division of JD. The backward castes got divided into two blocs, one represented by Lalu Prasad Yadav under the JD and other by Nitish Kumar under the Samata Party. Both the leaders, in fact, represented two dominant backward castes, namely the Yadavs and the Koeri–Kurmi. The rift between Lalu Prasad Yadav and Nitish Kumar largely on the issue of selective favoritism practiced by Lalu Prasad Yadav finally led to the splitting of the grand coalition of backward castes. This led to a decline in the vote share of the JD in subsequent parliamentary elections.

The victory of the JD in Bihar in 1995 assembly elections (167 seats) under the leadership of Lalu Prasad Yadav made him one of the tallest leaders within the party. In January 1996, he became the national president of JD. But as Lalu was enjoying the peak of his political power with a robust win in assembly elections and was making an impact on national politics as the JD president, the fodder scam was detected in which his name also cropped up. In the first report on fodder scam, Lalu Prasad

---

[2] Around this time, in fact, entire North India underwent a major political transformation with declining political influence of upper castes and rising political prominence of the backward castes and Dalits. This resulted in the shrinking of political space for national parties still dominated by upper castes and gaining salience among regional parties, often dominated by one caste or the other.

Yadav was also figured in the list of those involved in the scam. This unexpected development brought him under intense political pressure. His name-cropping handed out a big political blow not only to his public image but also to his prime ministerial ambitions.

Fodder Scam and Its Impact on Bihar's Political History

Fodder scam or Chara Ghotala amounted to fictitious purchase of cattle, cattle feed, and vehicles for cattle transportation by the officials of the state's animal husbandry department, with active connivance of its politicians. The scam had started in the 1980s during the Congress rule. According to rough estimates, between 1993–1994 and 1995–1996, the Bihar government paid ₹253 crore for the purchase of cattle feed in Jamshedpur, Gumla, Patna, Ranchi, Chaibasa, and Dumka whose real value was just ₹10 crore.

> Whenever history discusses Bihar's former chief minister Lalu Prasad, the fodder scam, or Chara Ghotala, as it is popularly known in Bihar, is bound to come up. The scam not only changed the political future of Prasad, but also changed Bihar's politics. It is the scam which ended Lalu's prime ministerial ambition, and dethroned him as the Chief Minister of Bihar, observed a report in Sify Finance. (Mishra, 1995)

There were demands for his resignation both from within his party and outside, including the Left Front, one of the credible electoral allies of the JD in Bihar. Eventually, he resigned from the post of national president of the JD and formed his own party called "RJD."

Formation of the RJD

By 1997, despite his name cropping up in the fodder scam and denting his public image, Lalu Prasad Yadav had emerged as the undisputed leader of not only the Yadavs and Muslims but also a section of the lower backwards. As pressure mounted on him to quit as the chief minister, he split the JD—its parliamentary party as well as Bihar state legislature party—leading to the creation of the RJD in a convention held in Delhi on July 5, 1997. He walked away with 18 MPs out of 45 and 137 Bihar JD MLAs out of 167. He struck a deal with Congress and gave ministerial births to most of its 30 MLAs. The CPI (26) and CPM (6) also extended support to him to keep the communal forces at bay, while the JMM's 19 MLAs also favored him with the promise of a separate state. Most of the 26 independents were also drawn to his camp. Thus, Lalu Prasad Yadav saved his political legacy in Bihar. He resigned as the chief minister on July 25, 1997, and his wife Rabri Devi replaced him on the same day.

Era of Coalitions

The 1990 Bihar government under Lalu Prasad Yadav was also a coalition government which was run on the support of the BJP, CPI, CPM, and JMM besides the independents. Bihar had already entered into a phase of coalition after the defeat of Congress in the 1990 assembly polls, but it appeared in 1995 after the JD getting majority that one party would be able to provide stability. The 1995 JD victory appeared to be short-lived as the party was split by Lalu Prasad Yadav for perpetuating his rule. With his 1997 resignation and elevation of Rabri Devi, the state again witnessed a coalition government.

The second phase of coalition era in Bihar (after 1990) was somewhat different from the first phase in the mid-1960s. Although during both these periods the coalition governments were more or less the result of the decline of the Congress, the difference lay in the fact that while in the first phase of coalition era the Congress remained one of the dominant coalition partners in the government formation, in the era of coalition politics in the 1990s, the Congress hardly remained a political force.

The experience of having a coalition government in the state in the second phase was not long in Bihar, but the state had a fair degree of experience of having pre-poll alliance between different political parties.

The year 1989 had marked the end of single-party majority rule in India, as it saw the decline of Congress from 412 parliamentary seats to 196 seats in 1989 general elections, while the opposition camp was led by the JD with 143 seats and the BJP with 85 seats. This was broken only in the May 2014 victory of the BJP—under the leadership of Prime Minister Narendra Modi—when the BJP got a majority of its own and secured 282 seats, even as the coalition led by the saffron party notched 336 seats.

With no political party getting a majority during the 1989 Lok Sabha elections, the National Front minority government had assumed power with the support of the BJP on one side and the Left on the other. The two parties, which extended outside support to the government, were dia-metrically opposed in their ideology. The internal difference among the National Front partners as well as due to the withdrawal of support from the BJP, the government had lost the majority support and was thrown out of power, but another minority government led by Chandra Shekhar was formed with outside support of the Congress.

The first grand pre-poll anti-Congress alliance was formed among the JD, the CPI, and the CPM during the 1989 Lok Sabha elections. This was the time when V.P. Singh led the anti-Congress movement in the country. Although the BJP was formally not an ally of the JD, it had worked out seat-sharing formula to prevent splitting of the anti-Congress vote. The experiment worked, and the Congress was badly defeated during the 1989 Lok Sabha elections. The same anti-Congress alliance contested the 1990 assembly elections and opposed the Congress in Bihar. The alliance had continued even during the mid-term Lok Sabha elections, which took place in 1991. The only difference was that the BJP had even moved out of the electoral understanding and decided to contest elections on its own. The JD contested the 1991 Lok Sabha elections in alliance with the two left parties, the CPI and the CPM. Although the Congress formed the government at the center under the leadership of P.V. Narasimha Rao, following the sympathy wave due to the assassina-tion of former Prime Minister Rajiv Gandhi, the anti-Congress alliance had registered an impressive victory in Bihar.

Three general elections (1996, 1998, and 1999) took place in Bihar between two assembly elections of 1995 and 2000, but the RJD-led alliance was outsmarted by the BJP–Samata alliance in all these three general elections. In the next chapter, how the political history of Bihar traversed in these general elections would be taken up in detail.

During the 1991 Lok Sabha elections, no party got a majority and the Congress had fallen short of a majority. This resulted in the forma-tion of a minority government of Congress party with Narasimha Rao as the prime minister. But with few defections and merger, this minority government managed to muster majority in the house. Since then, there had been five national elections (1996, 1998, 1999, 2004, and 2009), but none of these elections could produce a situation where a single-party majority government could take office. No single political party was able to win majority of seats in the house constitutionally required to form the government.

Following the fact that no single party was able to get a majority of its own, it led to the formation of a large number of coalition governments in India during the period 1989–2014, until the BJP won a majority of its own in the May 2014 general elections. While the first few coalition governments were relatively unstable and could not complete its full term, the NDA coalition government led by the BJP after the 1999 Lok Sabha elections had managed to complete its full five-year term. The two Congress-led UPA governments had also completed their full term in 2004–2009 and 2009–2014, and could be termed as stable dispensation.

References

Ahluwalia, M.S. (2000). Economic performance of states in post-reform period. *Economic & Political Weekly*, *35*(19). Retrieved October 9, 2017, from http://www.epw.in/special-articles/economic-performance-states-post-reforms-period.html

Ansari, J.M., Farz, & Ahmed. (1994). Requiem for a doomed party. *India Today*. Retrieved November 17, 2017, from http://indiatoday.intoday.in/story/latest-split-ends-the-janata-dals-national-relevance-and-may-prove-to-be-Lalus-waterloo/1/293690.html

Choudhary, S.N. (1999). *Power-dependence Relations: Struggle for Hegemony in Rural Bihar.* New Delhi: Har-Anand Publications.

National Crime Records Bureau. (1990 & 1999). Crime in India. New Delhi: National Crime Records Bureau, Ministry of Home Affairs, Government of India.

The Economic Times. (2014). Nitish Kumar demands Bharat Ratna for Karpoori Thakur. Retrieved November 17, 2017, from http://articles.economictimes.indiatimes.com/2014-01-24/news/46562907_1_karpoori-thakur-nitish-kumar-rival-lalu-prasad

Frankel, F. (1989). Caste, land and dominance in Bihar. In F. Frankel and M.S.A. Rao (Eds.), *Dominance and State Power in Modern India: Decline of a Social Order.* Princeton, NJ: Princeton University Press.

Gaikwad, R. (2013). Together they ended Lalu's reign in Bihar. *The Hindu.* Retrieved November 17, 2017, from http://www.thehindu.com/todays-paper/tp-national/together-they-ended-lalus-reign-in-bihar/article4821513.ece

Hauser, W. (1997). General elections 1996 in Bihar: Politics, administrative atrophy and anarchy. *Economic & Political Weekly*, *32*(41). Retrieved October 9, 2017, from http://www.epw.in/special-articles/general-elections-1996-bihar-politics-administrative-atrophy-and-anarchy.html

Jaffrelot, C. (2003). *India's Silent Revolution: The Rise of the Lower Castes in North India.* London: C. Hurst & Co.

Mishra, S. (1995). The scam that destroyed Lalu Prasad Yadav. Sify Finance. Retrieved November 17, 2017, from http://www.sify.com/finance/the-scam-that-destroyed-lalu-prasad-yadav-imagegallery-national-nkdqrMdgigjsi.html

Robin, C. (2009). The new stronghold of OBC politics. In C. Jaffrelot & S. Kumar (Eds.), *Rise of the Plebeians? The Changing Face of Indian Legislative Assemblies* (pp. 85–86). New Delhi: Routledge India.

Sinha, A. (2011). *Nitish Kumar and the Rise of Bihar.* Delhi: Penguin India.

The Times of India. (2008). RJD defends Lalu for admitting he made a mistake. *The Times of India.* Retrieved November 17, 2017, from http://timesofindia.indiatimes.com/city/patna/RJD-defends-Lalu-for-admitting-he-made-a-mistake/articleshow/3745506.cms?

Yadav, Y. (1999). Electoral politics in the time of change: India's third electoral system 1989–99. *Economic & Political Weekly, 34*(34/35), 2393–2399.

4

Beginning of a Phase of New Political Alliances: Elections During 1996–1999

The 1995 assembly elections saw a further rise of JD under the leadership of Chief Minister Lalu Prasad Yadav who returned to power with a thumping majority. The consolidation of backward caste was virtually complete and despite Nitish Kumar breaking away from Lalu Prasad Yadav, the JD romped home primarily due to a fragmented opposition and second due to consolidation of Dalits, Yadavs, and Muslims among others in its favor.

The result of the 1995 assembly elections in Bihar had simultaneously also set the trend for backward caste politics. It was the first time the backwards fought against backwards, and the upper castes, at best, remained at the margins of the political struggle. The backwards managed to have a firm control over political power. It was the type of political struggle that Bihar witnessed then that set the trend for backward caste politics for the next few years.

Nitish Kumar, after receiving a severe drubbing in the 1995 assembly elections, had realized that by maintaining political distance from the BJP, he cannot dethrone Lalu Prasad Yadav from the helm of Bihar. Subsequently for the 1996 assembly elections, his Samata Party struck an alliance with the saffron party under a common minimum program. Thus, the leader powered by Kurmi–Koeri support base aligned with the BJP which by now was being identified as an upper caste party.

> In 1994, (Nitish) Mr. Kumar broke away from the erstwhile ruling Janata Dal (JD) party, taking his OBC Kurmi and Koeri caste supporters with him. He went on to form, with George Fernandes, the Samata Party, which

forged an alliance with the BJP for the 1996 general elections. In 1996, ties between the former socialists (Mr. Kumar participated in the Bihar JP movement) and the Hindutva party deepened, when the BJP emerged as the single largest party in the country and the second largest party in Bihar. (Gaikwad, 2013)

This alliance became a symbol of anti-Lalu Prasad Yadav mobilizations in Bihar. It was very successful in the next three general elections—1996, 1998, and 1999. This could be gauged from the number of seats the BJP–Samata alliance won in these three successive elections (see Table 4.1).

> Formed in 1996, the Samata–BJP alliance achieved a fair degree of suc-
> cess in the 1996 and 1998 Lok Sabha elections, securing 24 and 30 seats
> out of a total of 54 from Bihar. In 1999, the alliance hit the jackpot with
> 41 seats. (Subrahmaniam, 2010)

Nitish Kumar consolidated non-Yadav OBC votes, section of EBCs along with upper castes, and the alliance was winning Bihar, elections after elections. In general, people who even vote for a regional party in the state assembly elections tend to vote for a national party during the parliamentary elections. The fortunes of Congress as a party had already declined in Bihar, be it assembly or Lok Sabha elections, and the BJP was emerging as a credible force after the rise in support of the upper castes. In the 1996 assembly elections, the JD emerged as the single largest party from the state, sending 22 parliamentarians to the Lok Sabha, while the BJP emerged as the second largest party with 18 MPs from the state.

Table 4.1

Party-wise performance in 1996, 1998, and 1999 Lok Sabha elections

Years/Parties	1996	1998	1999
BJP	18	20	23
Samata/JD(U)	6	10	18
JD/RJD	22	17	7
INC (Congress)	2	5	4
CPI/CPM	3	0	1

Source: Election Commission of India.

The Lok Sabha Election, 1996: New Trends in Coalition

Among the major landmarks and transformations, the 1996 Lok Sabha election was where the Dalits were virtually allowed to vote for the first time in large numbers and make a political choice after the 1995 assembly elections in which a chunk of them voted for the JD under Lalu Yadav. Although the Yadavs took the driver's seat in the matter of governing the state, the other backwards and the Dalits had remained aligned with the JD. They felt that they did have a share in the political power in the state. During the Congress regime, political and social power had remained monopolized by the upper castes and no serious attempt was made to incorporate the aspirations and demands of the Dalits and backwards within the general governance of the state.

This long period of Congress rule from 1952 to 1989 may be categorized as the era of single-party majority rule, with relatively greater political stability. It may also not be incorrect to categorize the era of 1996–1999 as the period of coalition politics with a relatively high degree of instability. It is true that there had been few experiments of coalition politics first in the year 1967 at the state level and then in the years 1977 and 1989 at the national level, but the year 1996 could be seen as the real beginning of the era of coalition politics at the national level. No political party was able to get a majority in any of the four national elections held since 1984. In 1989, the Congress had emerged as the single largest party and JD formed the government with support of the BJP and the Left parties. In 1991 general elections, again, the Congress emerged as the single largest party and it formed a minority government.

> The Narasimha Rao government had survived from June 1991 to July 1993 without enjoying a majority in the Lok Sabha. The Congress had won 232 seats in the 1991 Lok Sabha polls and its ally the AIADMK, had won 11, rendering the coalition well short of a majority. It was only when a no-confidence motion was moved against the government in July 1993 that they assembled new allies like Ajit Singh's Rashtriya Lok Dal and the JMM, remembered more for the infamous "JMM bribery case." (Chowdhury, 2012)

In a decade the BJP has been able to become the first major opposition party in parliament (in 1991) and then it became the largest single party in the Lok Sabha in 1996. In three consequent elections in 1996, 1998, and 1999, the BJP has emerged as the largest single party in the

Table 4.2

Seats won by the BJP in national elections

Year	Seats Won by the BJP Nationally	Seats Won in Bihar
1984	2	Nil
1989	86	8
1991	120	5
1996	161	18
1998	182	20
1999	182	23

Source: Election Commission of India.

Lok Sabha (Table 4.2). It is true that the BJP cannot get a majority on its own and has been successful by forging a broad alliance; the strength of the BJP should not be underestimated. The communist party of India (Marxist) observed after the elections that "[while] it is true that the BJP cannot get a majority on its own and has been successful by forming a broad alliance, but the strength of the BJP cannot be underestimated."

Although the country had seen a long spell of coalition politics since 1996 and a couple of experiments earlier as well, there was a great change in its nature. The first two experiments (1977 and 1989) of coalition government were largely driven by the anti-Congress mood, when parties other than the Congress joined together to form the government. But in later years, since the 1996 Lok Sabha elections, the coalition government at the center was marked by the anti-BJP political mood. The politics in different states as well as at the national level seemed to have been divided into the anti-BJP and pro-BJP camps.

The pattern of coalition also saw transformation. While the first few coalition governments were primarily based on the post-elections understanding of sharing power, the coalition in the latter phase took place in the form of pre-election alliances.

This had resulted in greater stability of the coalition governments. Although coalition governments, as an idea, had not been popular among leaders of political parties, mainly national parties, and even among the electorate due to the 1977 Janata experience, both the voters and the electorates had gradually realized that coalition would be the mainstay of governance both at the central and state levels in the coming years. The changing mood of public had been instrumental in providing stability to the coalition governments.

In Bihar, the JD was consolidating its support base among the newly emerging OBC castes, but simultaneously cracks had also started creeping in the Lalu Yadav-led party. The first split in the party took place just before the 1995 assembly elections, when Nitish Kumar left JD and formed the Samata Party. The JD had witnessed another split before the 1998 Lok Sabha, when Sharad Yadav left the party and formed JD(U), while Lalu Yadav named his party the RJD. So, while the early 1990s can be considered the phase of consolidation of primarily anti-Congress parties, the late 1990s can be considered the new phase marked with splitting of the anti-Congress alliance parties. This was the phase when anti-Congress mood shifted to anti-Lalu Yadav mood, which also saw the emergence of the BJP as an important political force in the state. So all these mergers and splits led to a situation where the support base of different political parties remained confined to their different, respective social groups and there was hardly any party which could appeal across the cross-section of voters. This was the time when a new political alignment took place in Bihar and a new coalition between the JD(U) and BJP had emerged as part of alignment of anti-Lalu Yadav mood; since the Yadav strongman had virtually appropriated the entire political process, for himself.

In many ways, the Lok Sabha elections of 1996 could be seen as the real beginning of alliances in Bihar. This was precisely because ever since the 1996 Lok Sabha elections, the anti-Lalu forces, the BJP–JD(U) alliance, had contested all the elections as allies opposing the dominance of the RJD. At the beginning of this phase of alliance in Bihar, while the RJD stood on one side, the BJP–JD(U) stood on the other, and the Congress seemed to be a bit confused.

At times the Congress stitched an alliance with the RJD, but in the very next elections, the Congress decided to contest elections independently. So in the bipolar alliance, while the BJP and JD(U) stood firm in opposing the RJD, the Congress never had a clear policy whether to oppose the RJD or to contest elections as an ally of the RJD. Due to an unclear policy agenda, the Congress experienced a further decline.

From the various shifts in alliances among the political parties in Bihar, what seemed to have emerged was that there had been a bipolar alliance in the state, mainly on anti- and pro-Lalu lines. While the BJP and the JD(U) had been consistent in having an anti-Lalu alliance in the state for Lok Sabha elections held since 1996, the Congress party's position on the issue always remained too flexible. At times it tried to identify with anti-Lalu politics but soon it aligned with the Yadav strongman to defeat the communal forces led by the BJP.

During this phase of alliance, the Congress had formed a stable alliance with the RJD to oppose the BJP–JD(U) ruling coalition at the center, but at the state level, it moved out of the RJD alliance and opposed the ruling RJD in all the assembly elections since 1995. But during the October 2005 elections, the Congress decided to contest assembly elections in alliance with the RJD. The confusion within the Congress on whether to form an alliance or not had continued until the 2010 assembly elections when it eventually opposed both the RJD and the BJP–JD(U) alliance and contested the election alone.

The pattern of alliances in Bihar, by this time, had also changed in respect of the Left parties. While in the early 1990s both the Left parties—the CPI and the CPM—had been an ally of the JD/RJD, gradually there had not been any clear-cut alliance of these two parties with any of the two dominant alliances. Even though the Left parties were opposed to the ruling BJP–JD(U) coalition at the center, they were also opposed to what they called "misrule of the RJD" in the state. So soon after the 1996 Lok Sabha election, both the Left parties moved out of the RJD alliance in the state and contested Lok Sabha elections independently, opposing both the BJP–JD(U) alliance on the one hand and the RJD and its allies on the other. Unfortunately, regarding the assembly elections, there had been no clear-cut policy on whether to have an alliance with the RJD or not. This becomes visible if the alliance pattern of the Left parties is looked at during the various assembly elections they had contested. The CPM had remained with the RJD as an ally for opposing the BJP–JD(U) combine, but the CPI at times had moved out of the alliance too.

The electorate's support for coalition governments was very low before the 1996 Lok Sabha election, when voters hardly had any experience of parties forming alliances and coalitions. Only 18% people were in favor of coalition government during this phase; while 31% were opposed to the idea of coalition government, 46% expressed no opinion on this issue. But the real beginning of coalition era in Bihar was from the 1996 Lok Sabha elections, when for the first time various political parties contested the elections as alliance partners. The two dominant alliances were the BJP–Samata alliance and the JD–CPI–CPM alliance. This was the election when the Congress did not enter into any alliance and contested alone.

The Lok Sabha Election, 1996: BJP on the Rise

In the 1996 Lok Sabha polls, the BJP emerged as the second largest party in Bihar, winning 18 seats. The JD won 22 seats, a loss of 10 seats in comparison to 1991 general elections. As stated earlier, the rapid de-alignment of electoral forces had led to a major shift in the politics of the state. The results of the 1996 Lok Sabha election had demonstrated that a new beginning was made in the politics of Bihar. The JD and its allies had suffered a major setback in this election, which provided more than one signal. First and foremost, the election results had clearly pointed out the limits of sectional politics in a multicultural society. Further, they had demonstrated the constraints of the ruling party in a multiparty democracy, when most of the opposition parties unite against the ruling party while contesting elections. In a multiparty democracy, where a political party captures political power with barely 30% votes, it is exposed to severe limitations when the divided opposition unites against it.

The results of these elections clearly followed from such a scenario. During the Vidhan Sabha election held in 1995, the JD and its allies, CPI, CPM, and JMM(S), had fought a badly divided opposition. Although the Samata Party had some understanding with the CPML, it was mainly the BJP, the Bihar People's Party (BPP), the Congress, and a few other smaller parties that had opposed the JD and its allies separately. The net result was that with just 28% votes, the JD managed to get an absolute majority with 167 seats, and its allies CPI, CPM, and JMM(S) won 26, 6, and 16 seats, respectively, with merely 4.8%, 1.3%, and 3.7% votes, respectively. Many people had great faith in the Samata Party formed on the eve of election and thought that it may provide an alternative to the ruling JD. A party formed mainly by the defectors of the JD and with Nitish Kumar as its leader, it was expected to draw large support from the Kurmis and the Koeris. But the party did not perform well, winning only seven seats with merely 6.9% votes. The Congress, with the support of just the upper castes, went down to a mere 29 seats with 16.4% votes. The BJP, though it managed to improve its tally winning 41 seats with 12.9% votes, however, did not come any closer to realizing its dream of calling the shots in Bihar.

After the success in the Vidhan Sabha election, it seemed as if the JD had become an invincible party in Bihar. The political parties opposing the JD realized their weaknesses and shortly after the Vidhan Sabha election and several rounds of talks, the Samata Party and the BJP entered into an alliance, where the BJP contested 32 seats leaving 22 seats for the Samata Party. The leaders of both parties welcomed this alliance. However, the leaders of the Samata Party, particularly George Fernandes and Nitish Kumar who swore by the socialist tradition, came under severe criticism on account of their alliance with a communal party. These leaders termed it a special arrangement needed for a special time in a special state, "the need of the hour," to put up a challenge to the casteist politics of Lalu Yadav. Earlier, the BPP of Anand Mohan Singh, which had been completely routed in the Vidhan Sabha election, merged with the Samata Party. Since it drew some support from the upper caste Rajputs, it was believed that this alliance may broaden the base of the Samata Party much beyond the support of only the backward caste. Entering into an alliance with the BJP certainly was a step toward forming a front against the JD. The other opposition party, the Congress, marginalized to a great extent, contested the election alone, like the splinter groups of the JMM parties. The JD, on the other hand, contested along with its traditional partners CPI and CPM. But as compared to earlier elections, the only change was in terms of seat sharing as Lalu Yadav had completely dominated over his alliance partners, the CPI and the CPM. The JD had contested in 44 seats, leaving only 8 for the CPI and 2 for the CPM.

Although Lalu Yadav seemed confident of winning most of the seats in Bihar, he was put on the defensive by the opposition parties, which launched a virulent campaign against the fodder scam unearthed during the JD government. On the other hand, the JD championed the cause of the upliftment of the backward castes and the poor from the platform of social justice. It called upon the people to vote for the JD and its allies and to save Bihar from the threat of the communal party, namely the BJP. On the other hand, the BJP and the Samata combined and attacked Lalu Yadav for perpetuating casteist politics in Bihar in the name of social justice. They blamed the government for the fodder and other scams that occurred during Lalu's regime. Although this could not make a dent as an election issue among the poor rural masses of Bihar, the fodder scam, popularly termed *Gawala* scam or "Chara ghotala," got wide publicity. In the beginning, it seemed as if this scam would have little bearing on public opinion and may not affect the electoral prospects of the parties. Two rounds of pre-election surveys conducted by CSDS made it amply clear that the JD still remained the most popular party. Of the total respondents, 33% and 40% intended voting for the JD in the first and second rounds respectively, whereas the support base for the BJP was 8% and 10% only.

Things started to change rapidly as the election drew closer. The virulent attack on the JD and its policies by the BJP and its alliance parties led to a last minute change in the mood of the people at large. The Kurmis and Koeris had already reposed full faith in the BJP–Samata alliance; but now the Brahmins and other upper castes, which had traditionally voted for the Congress, shifted their support to the BJP–Samata alliance as well. This shift had led to some surprising results.

The party which had won an absolute majority in the Vidhan Sabha election barely a year ago was cut down to size, even though its leaders had been confident it would win all the seats. The JD managed to win only 22 seats as compared to 33 seats in the 1991 Lok Sabha election. Its vote went down by nearly 2.2% as it could manage to get just 31.9% votes as compared to 34.1% in the 1991 Lok Sabha election. Its alliance partners, the CPI and CPM, also suffered major losses. The CPI lost more than half of the seats and won only three Lok Sabha seats as compared to eight during the 1991 Lok Sabha election. Its votes were drastically reduced from 7.6% to 5.1% in 1996. The CPM could not even retain its lone Lok Sabha seat won in the 1991 Lok Sabha election.

The BJP, in alliance with the Samata Party, became the major gainer. It won 18 Lok Sabha seats with 20.5% votes as compared to 5 in the 1991 Lok Sabha election with 15.9% votes. In reality, the increase in the votes of the BJP was much higher than it appeared in the 1996 Lok Sabha election, as it had contested on only 32 seats as compared to 51 seats in the 1991 Lok Sabha election. The Samata Party won 6 Lok Sabha seats—they were only contesting on 22 seats—and its vote went up by nearly 7.6% as compared to its votes in the 1995 assembly elections. Although the Congress doubled its tally from one to two, its votes went down from 24.2% in 1991 to 13% in 1996. The JMM which won six seats during the 1991 Lok Sabha election suffered a major loss. The party not only lost much ground in its traditional tribal belt of south Bihar, now Jharkhand, but it also had suffered a loss because its various factions fought amongst each other, which resulted in the split of tribal votes. The JMM(S) managed to win only one Lok Sabha seat and that too by a slender margin of 5,000 votes.

The Lok Sabha Election, 1998

The premature dissolution of the Lok Sabha pushed the country toward another Lok Sabha election much sooner than expected. Even in this short duration, the political scenario in Bihar had taken a major turn. There was mounting pressure on Lalu Yadav from the Left parties and even from within his own party to step down from the posts of party president and chief minister of the state. This resulted in a split in the JD and the formation of the RJD by Lalu Yadav before the 1998 Lok Sabha election. The formation of the new party opened up the possibility of a fresh realignment among various competing political parties.

Although there had been no major shift in the already existing alliance among the dominant political parties, the BJP maintained its alliance with the Samata Party, and the Left-over JD still retained its alliance with the CPI and the CPM. The Congress, which had performed badly in the past few elections, was desperately looking for ways of its revival. Three major factors seemed to be working against the overtly confident Lalu Yadav who was aware of the challenges he was facing electorally. First, he feared possible division in the Yadav votes, which may indirectly help the BJP in winning more seats. Second, he knew it would not be easy to make people familiar with the new symbol of the "lamp" (kerosene lantern) allotted to the RJD. Finally, he realized that the absence of a party organization at the local level may add to the problems for his new party. In view of these constraints, Lalu Yadav was looking for an alliance to at least minimize the split of vote. He naturally found the desperate Congress, which was also in search of an alliance partner. The JMM, a party that was strong in south Bihar in the 1991 Lok Sabha election but performed badly during the 1996 elections because of division in the party, was also searching for an alliance. Lalu Yadav knew that his party had very little presence in south Bihar and so he wisely entered into an alliance with the JMM.

With this alliance pattern, Bihar seemed to be heading toward a three-cornered contest. With the split in the party, the JD was put to a severe test. It was widely believed that the split in the JD would lead to division of votes between the JD and the RJD, resulting in a major loss for the party. It was primarily Lalu Yadav, the leader of the RJD, who was to be tested for his personal charisma. Many believed that the RJD may not be successful as Lalu Yadav, after his involvement in the fodder scam, had become a spent force in the state's politics and it would be hard for the party to win seats. Following the alliances with the Congress and the JMM, Lalu Yadav hoped to put up a contest in north Bihar on account of the shift of the traditional Congress voters still with the party toward the RJD. With 12.2% votes polled by the JMM and 16% by the Congress in south Bihar in the 1996 Lok Sabha election, the alliance hoped to put up a formidable contest there. The BJP–Samata combine hoped to hold together and gain most from the three-cornered contest resulting in a split in the anti-BJP vote.

The results came as a major surprise for many political speculators. Expected to be a three-cornered contest, the Bihar election actually turned out to be a direct contest between the RJD and the BJP–Samata combine, with the JD and its allies putting up no contest at all. The results, however, revealed that the 1998 Lok Sabha election was a more keenly contested election than the past few elections. The previous three Lok Sabha elections in the state had witnessed a narrowing of the victory margin in a large number of constituencies. As compared to only 6 and 10 constituencies where the victory margin was less than 5% in 1991 and 1996 respectively, in the 1998 Lok Sabha election, the victory margin was less than 5% in as many as 18 constituencies and between 5% and 10% in another 16. The narrowing of the victory margin in the 1998 Lok Sabha election had clearly indicated that Bihar was in the middle of more competitive politics as compared to the earlier few elections.

The 1998 Lok Sabha election virtually saw the end of the JD in the state. Ram Vilas Paswan was the only JD candidate who won from the Hajipur Lok Sabha constituency. The party had managed to get only 8% votes as compared to the 32% it polled during the 1996 Lok Sabha election. Its alliance partners—the CPI and the CPM—could not win a single seat and polled as low as 3.1% and 2.1% votes, respectively. Belying popular expectations, the RJD won 17 seats, and polling 25.2% votes, it still emerged as the largest party in terms of vote share and mass base. Although the Congress got only 7.2% votes, nearly 6% less than it polled in the 1996 Lok Sabha election, it managed to win five seats and regain some lost ground. The fewer votes for the party were largely attributed to its contesting fewer seats on account of the alliance with the RJD. In spite of the triangular alliance, the JMM could not open its account and polled 3% votes. As an alliance, the BJP–Samata combine turned out to be the major gainer in the 1998 Lok Sabha election with the BJP getting 19 seats with 23.1% votes and Samata winning 10 seats with 15.8% votes; the alliance won 29 seats, improving its tally of 24 in the 1996 Lok Sabha election.

The Lok Sabha Election, 1999

The coming together of the anti-Lalu Yadav forces, a process which began just before the 1996 Lok Sabha election, got a boost when the Samata Party merged with the JD to form the JD(U), which decided to contest the 1999 Lok Sabha election in alliance with the BJP. The BPP also decided to contest the election in alliance with the BJP–JD(U) combine. So with Congress forming an alliance with the RJD, it was going to be a straight bipolar contest.

In this contest, the BJP and its ally the JD(U) won 41 seats and polled 45.5% of the votes, while the RJD–Congress combine won only 11 seats and polled 37.1% votes. One seat each was won by the CPI and the BPP. If winning seats were the only indicator of a party's success, then one can assume that the BJP–JD(U) registered a massive victory over the RJD–Congress combine, in what was like a one-sided affair. The 1999 Lok Sabha victory established the BJP–JD(U) combine as the dominant political force in the state and virtually overthrew Lalu Yadav out of the political map of Bihar. It appeared that Lalu Yadav was politically finished, but that was not true.

If one looks at the margins of victory, there were indications of a somewhat keener contest. The difference in vote share between the two alliances was 8.4%. Of the 54 seats, the results in 23 Lok Sabha constituencies were decided by less than a 5% margin, while in 1998 there were only 17 constituencies where the victory margin was this small. Of the last three Lok Sabha elections, this was certainly the most keenly contested.

Compared to its tally in 1998, the RJD–Congress alliance had suffered a major loss by dropping 11 seats. However, it is worth noting that in terms of votes, the RJD remained the single largest party in the state. In fact, the vote share of the RJD increased by a little over three percentage points in the 1998 Lok Sabha election.

The success of the BJP–Samata alliance cannot be credited to the rise of the BJP in the state. Although it had increased its seat tally by three seats, it lost nearly one percentage point in vote share; this, of course, might be due to it contesting fewer seats. To a greater extent, the success of the alliance can be credited to the merger of the Samata Party and the JD into the JD(U) and the working out of a formidable alliance between the BJP, the JD(U), and BPP. This had led to a strong consolidation of the anti-Lalu Yadav votes in the state. Although the JD(U)'s vote share fell by nearly three percentage points (if compared with the combined vote for the Samata Party and JD in 1998), it had managed to increase its joint tally by six seats.

Lok Sabha Elections: Region-wise Analysis

The overall results of the three Lok Sabha elections held in 1996, 1998, and 1999 indicate that the JD (RJD since the 1998 Lok Sabha election) which had witnessed a decline over the past few elections was nearly wiped out in the 1999 Lok Sabha polls. The BJP–Samata alliance (BJP–JD(U) in 1999, after the merger of the JD) had grown from strength to strength during the Lok Sabha elections of 1998 and 1999. In order to assess the strength of these parties, it would be better to look at the performance of different parties in the three distinct geographical regions of Bihar, that is, north, central, and south.

The poverty-stricken, flood-prone terrain of north Bihar, accounting for 26 Lok Sabha seats, is politically the most important region of Bihar. It had been a stronghold of the JD during the earlier few elections held after 1990. During the 1991 election, the JD won 22 seats from this region with 48.3% votes, with CPI winning three seats; the combined tally for the alliance was 25 seats. But in the 1996 election, the JD had suffered a loss of six seats in this region. It won only 16 seats and 40.3% votes. The CPI won two seats, bringing the combined tally to a total of 18 seats. The BJP, which had drawn a blank in the 1991 election, managed to win six seats and 33.8% votes along with its alliance partner, the Samata Party. The 1998 Lok Sabha election witnessed further gain for the BJP–Samata combine in the region where it managed to win eight seats and polled 35% votes. The JD and allies had performed badly in the state, but could still manage to save face in the north Bihar region as it polled 18.3% votes and won its lone seat from this region. The RJD had virtually swept the polls in this region by winning 14 seats and polling 29.4% votes (see Table 4.3).

In the 1999 Lok Sabha election, the BJP and its allies had registered an impressive victory in north Bihar. The allies won 20 seats and polled 46.2% votes. The RJD had suffered a major loss of 10 seats as compared to its tally in the 1998 election. This loss does not indicate that the party was losing support in this region. In terms of votes polled, the RJD increased its votes by nearly 5.4% as compared to the 1998 Lok Sabha election. However, despite the increased support base, the party lost a large number of seats mainly due to the consolidation of the anti-Lalu votes. With the merger of the JD and the Samata Party, a large number of the anti-Lalu votes polled by the JD in the 1998 election consolidated with the BJP and its allies (see Table 4.3).

This gives a clear indication that Lalu Yadav remained a major force in the politics of the state. The RJD had a strong presence in north Bihar, and a minor division among the anti-Lalu vote in this region may lead to a thumping victory for the party in this region.

Table 4.3

Electoral performance in North Bihar: Lok Sabha elections, 1991–1999

Year	Turnout (%)	Congress			BJP+			Janata Dal+			RJD		
		Contested	Won	Vote (%)	Contested	Won	Vote (%)	Contested	Won	Vote (%)	Contested	Won	Vote (%)
1991	64.4	25	0	22.8	24	0	13.0	25	25	53.9	—	—	—
1996	61.0	26	1	12.1	24	6	33.8	27	18	45.4	—	—	—
1998	66.6	10	2	5.5	25	8	35.0	28	1	18.3	20	14	29.4
1999	66.1	3	0	3.9	26	20	46.2	—	—	—	21	4	34.8

Source: CSDS Data Unit.

Note: Total seats: 28.

The BJP had a strong presence in the mineral-rich hilly terrain of south Bihar or Jharkhand region, accounting for 14 Lok Sabha seats. It not only remained the most dominant party in south Bihar but also virtually swept the polls in the entire region in the three Lok Sabha elections held in 1996, 1998, and 1999. As compared to the five seats it won in 1991 election, the BJP managed to win 12 of the 14 seats from this region in both 1996 and 1998 and 11 seats in 1999. An equal number of seats for the party in the three Lok Sabha elections (1996, 1998, and 1999) may not indicate that there was no change for BJP in south Bihar. Although the vote for the party remained more or less the same in the two Lok Sabha elections held in 1998 and 1999, the BJP increased its support base enormously in this region between 1996 and 1998. As compared to 34% votes in the 1996 Lok Sabha election, the party polled 45.5% votes in the 1998 election (see Table 4.4).

The JD had registered some success in this region in the early 1990s. The party had won three seats in the 1991 Lok Sabha election. In the 1996 Lok Sabha election, the JD had polled 24.5% votes, though it failed to win a seat. But after the two Lok Sabha elections held in 1991 and 1996, the JD (read RJD since 1998) had never been a strong party of popular support in this region. Besides the BJP, the Congress and the JMM had some presence in this region. Just before the 1998 Lok Sabha election, the RJD entered into an alliance with the Congress and the JMM. Although expected to spring a few surprises in this region, the alliance could hardly make its presence felt. The JMM, which had won the lone Dumka seat in 1996 where the party president Shibu Soren had won by a slender margin of about 5,000 votes, drew a blank both in the 1998 and 1999 elections and its votes also went down from 12.2% in 1996 to 10.5% in 1998 and further down to 9.2% in 1999. It was the Congress that registered some gain in this region. The Congress had contested on all 14 seats but won only 1 seat and polled 16% votes in 1996 Lok Sabha election. The Congress had contested for only seven seats in 1998 Lok Sabha election but managed to win two seats and polled 15.7% votes. In 1999, though the Congress could not increase its tally of seats, it still polled nearly 8% more votes as compared to the 1998 Lok Sabha election (see Table 4.4).

The agriculturally rich central Bihar, accounting for 14 Lok Sabha seats, had witnessed numerous agrarian struggles during the post-independence period. These struggles of the poor and the landless farmers had mainly been led by various factions of the Left parties. The JD and other Left parties were particularly strong in this region. Although the JD

Table 4.4

Electoral performance in South Bihar (Jharkhand): Lok Sabha elections, 1991–1999

Year	Turnout	Congress			BJP+			JD+			JMM		
		Contested	Won	Vote (%)	Contested	Won	Vote (%)	Contested	Won	Vote (%)	Contested	Won	Vote (%)
1991	49.9	14	0	17.9	14	5	32.9	7	3	12.5	8	6	21.4
1996	54.8	14	1	16.0	14	12	34.0	14	0	24.3	14	1	12.2
1998	59.7	7	2	15.7	14	12	45.5	10	0	6.2	8	0	10.5
1999	48.5	11	2	23.8	14	11	45.5	—	—	—	12	0	9.2

Source: CSDS Data Unit.

Note: Total seats: 14.

had remained the dominant party in this region, it faced a stiff challenge from the BJP–Samata combine during the 1996 Lok Sabha election.

The JD and its allies had won 13 of the total 14 seats from this region during the 1991 election but had suffered a major loss as the alliance got only 7 seats (JD—6, CPI—1) in 1996 with the JD getting 25.1% and the Left party 10.6% votes. In the 1998 election, the JD and its allies had lost heavily even in the traditional stronghold of the Left. The alliance not only drew a blank but even its votes went down to only 8%.

The newly formed RJD had failed to perform well in this region and won only three seats but polled 35.9% votes. The RJD did, however, put up a strong contest in this region and polled 32.4% votes in the 1999 election, but managed to win only two seats. The BJP–Samata alliance remained the biggest gainer even in this region during the last three Lok Sabha elections. The BJP, which had drawn a blank in 1991, in alliance with the Samata Party had managed to win six seats with 37.9% votes in 1996.

The alliance had further improved its tally to nine seats, and its votes increased to 42.8% in the 1998 elections. With the merger of the JD and the Samata Party in 1999, the BJP and its allies further consolidated their position in this region. The allies won 10 seats and polled 44.2% votes. The Congress won both the seats it contested from this region (see Table 4.5).

Changing Social Base of Political Parties 1996 Onward

The elections held in the state since 1989 clearly indicate that the JD (read RJD since 1998) which had remained the most dominant party until the 1996 Lok Sabha election had started witnessing a decline after the 1998 Lok Sabha election. The party had suffered a humiliating defeat in the 1999 Lok Sabha election. The BJP which had polled 15.9% votes in the 1991 Lok Sabha election made heavy inroads into Bihar politics during and after the 1996 Lok Sabha election, after entering into an alliance with the Samata Party. The party polled 20.5% and 23.1% votes during the 1996 and 1998 elections respectively. In the 1999 Lok Sabha election, the formation of the JD(U) with the merger of the Samata party and the JD added to the success of the BJP.

Thanks to the new alliance, the BJP had managed to make inroads among the Yadav and Dalit voters in the state who constitute a big section

Table 4.5

Electoral performance in Central Bihar: Lok Sabha elections, 1991–1999

Year	Turnout	Congress			BJP+			JD+			RJD		
		Contested	Won	Vote (%)	Contested	Won	Vote (%)	Contested	Won	Vote (%)	Contested	Won	Vote (%)
1991	62.9	13	1	31.5	13	0	8.4	14	13	46.5	—	—	—
1996	61.1	14	0	12.1	14	6	37.9	13	7	35.8	—	—	—
1998	68.1	4	1	3.5	13	9	42.8	15	0	8.0	12	3	35.9
1999	63.6	2	2	6.4	15	10	44.2	—	—	—	11	2	32.4

Source: CSDS Data Unit.

Note: Total seats: 15.

of the electorate and were primarily voters of JD/RJD. The increase in support, in terms of votes polled, may not look very impressive, but it should be noted that the votes for the party had increased even if it contested fewer seats in subsequent elections on account of the seat-sharing arrangement with its partners.

The survey had revealed that the JD (read RJD since 1998) drew greater support from the backward castes, the Dalits, and the Muslims as compared to other sections of society, while the BJP drew greater support from the upper caste voters. The BJP and Samata Party alliance also made the party a popular choice of two backward castes, the Kurmi and the Koeri. The coming together of the JD and the Samata Party also witnessed a movement of sections of Dalits toward the BJP–JD(U) alliance in the 1999 Lok Sabha election. During the past few years, the popularity of the Congress had declined among all sections of the society. The CSDS surveys clearly show that the social groups which had formed the solid support for the JD (read RJD since 1998) started deserting the party after the 1998 Lok Sabha election, though there were still sections among whom the party seems to be very popular. The majority of the RJD's votes came from Yadav and Muslim voters. The survey also explained the nuances of the changing social base of different political parties in Bihar. The increasing presence of the BJP in Bihar was largely attributed to its growing popularity among upper caste voters. Traditionally, Congress supporters had moved in a big way toward the BJP and its alliance partner, the Samata Party, since the 1996 Lok Sabha election. The survey revealed that the BJP which got only 29% of the upper caste votes in 1995 had got more than 75% votes in the Lok Sabha elections of 1998 and 1999, though the alliance suffered some setback among the upper caste voters during the assembly election in the year 2000.

The JD (read RJD since 1998) did manage to get some support from the upper castes until the 1996 Lok Sabha election, but after that, the party's popularity among the upper castes declined enormously due to assertive backward caste politics pursued by Lalu Yadav, who was in no mood to share power with the upper caste. Over 77% of upper caste voters voted for BJP–Samata alliance in 1998 and 1999 Lok Sabha elections (see Table 4.6). The emergence of Samata Party and its keenness to pursue alliance with the BJP was what revived the sagging political fortune of the upper castes in Bihar.

Table 4.6

Upper caste voting pattern: 1995–2000

Party	1995	1996	1998	1999	2000
Congress	39.1	10.1	8.7	8.3	15.0
BJP+	28.7	59.5	77.6	76.7	60.7
JD+	20.9	29.1	11.6	—	—
RJD	—	—	Negligible	Negligible	10.5

Sources: Bihar Survey 1995; National Election Study 1996, 1998, and 1999; Assembly Survey 1995 and 2000.

Table 4.7

OBC voting pattern: 1995–2000

Party	1995	1996	1998	1999	2000
Congress	13.7	9.9	7.9	14.9	5.0
BJP+	26.2	36.2	42.5	50.3	38.7
JD+	49.8	50.3	17.3	—	—
RJD	—	—	28.0	22.0	40.8

Sources: Bihar Survey 1995; National Election Study 1996, 1998, and 1999; Assembly Election 2000.

The OBCs had come to play an important role in the politics of the state, at least after the 1985 Bihar assembly elections under the banner of Lok Dal. The Congress was not very popular among OBC voters who had traditionally largely supported socialist formations. The formation of the JD before the 1989 Lok Sabha election saw a large section of OBC voters moving toward the party. Surveys indicate that the OBCs had voted for the JD in large numbers in the 1995 Vidhan Sabha and the 1996 Lok Sabha elections (see Table 4.7). The BJP and Samata Party alliance drew OBC voters. In the 1998 election, 43% of OBC voters voted for the BJP alliance, while support for the JD alliance went down from 50% in 1996 to 17% in 1998. The RJD had managed to poll 28% of the OBC vote, but in the 1999 Lok Sabha election, with the merger of the Samata Party and the JD, the OBC support for the RJD went further down to 22%. With the parting of the two parties just before the assembly election, a section of the OBC again moved toward the RJD. Support for the Congress among OBC voters, which was just 14% in

Table 4.8

Muslim voting pattern: 1995–2000

Party	1995	1996	1998	1999	2000
Congress	21.9	23.3	14.9	33.9	6.6
BJP+	7.5	5.6	4.2	13.4	7.9
JD+	57.3	68.9	19.0	—	—
RJD	—	—	59.6	48.2	61.4

Sources: Bihar Survey 1995; National Election Study 1996, 1998, and 1999; Assembly Election 2000.

1995, went down to 8% in 1998; however, in alliance with the RJD, the Congress managed to get 15% of the OBC vote, which went down to just 5% in the assembly election in February 2000. This was an indication that the alliance of the Congress with the RJD did help the party get OBC votes.

The past decade had witnessed a decline of support for Congress among the Muslims. The alienation of Muslims from the Congress had begun soon after the Bhagalpur riots and continued after the demolition of the Babri Masjid. Disenchanted with the Congress, the JD and its allies became the natural choice of Muslim voters in the state. Survey figures indicate enormous support for the alliance in the 1995 Vidhan Sabha and 1996 Lok Sabha elections among Muslim voters. But the split in the JD has led to the erosion of this support. From 69% votes from Muslims in the 1996 Lok Sabha election, the alliance got only 19% with 60% Muslims voting for the RJD. The Samata–BJP alliance barely attracted Muslim voters until the 1998 Lok Sabha election, but with the formation of the JD(U), the BJP allies did manage to get some Muslim votes in the 1999 election (see Table 4.8). However, the Samata Party and JD parted ways just before the recent assembly election and a large number of Muslim voters went back to the RJD.

Over the past few elections, there had been a shift among the upper caste voters toward the BJP, while the majority of OBC and Muslim voters had favored the JD until 1996 and RJD since the 1998 Lok Sabha election. But did it mean that the various jatis within these caste groups vote in a similar pattern? In later years, the backward Muslims or *pasmandas* started leaning more toward Nitish Kumar-led JD(U), while the upper castes were with the RJD.

Effects of the Fodder Scam on Lalu Yadav, Voter Identity, and Loss of JD Popularity in the Late 1990s

In 1996, Lalu Yadav's name had figured in the multi-million dollar fodder scam case. This had led political watchers to believe that his messianic image, which he had earned many years ago, was denuded. His populist caste and social justice rhetoric had reached its limit. The stage was set where his status would be reduced to just yet another Yadav leader from being the messiah of the poor and downtrodden.

General elections to Lok Sabha held in 1996 and 1999 seemed to reflect the declining popularity of Lalu Yadav and his party. The vote share of the RJD declined in successive elections, while that of the BJP and Samata/JD(U) (NDA) increased substantially (see Table 4.9). The RJD had suffered major loss even in terms of seat. At this stage, it may, though tentatively, be argued that Lalu Yadav's messianic image was fast losing its charisma and was bound to be outlived shortly, unless some miracles happen. The political watchers were partially true, because, though his party continued to lose votes and seats in parliamentary polls, it remained relevant in state politics as the results of 2000 assembly elections showed but certainly he was a declining force. But again in 2004 general elections, the RJD alliance bounced back and his party notched 22 seats, pushing the BJP–JD(U) combine to fringe (see Table 4.9).

As there was a widely held perception across Bihar that Lalu Yadav had failed to keep his promises to the vast masses of the poor, who by and large constituted his core support base, and also failed even badly to take the agenda of development forward; political observers felt that the 2000 assembly election was going to be a litmus test for his popularity as a messiah of the poor and the downtrodden and his politics of poverty and social justice.

Before we delve deep into the discussion of caste versus development as major political issues that kept the RJD in power and led to its ouster respectively, let us first briefly examine the social basis of voting in the 1990s. As discussed earlier, the Mandal/Mandir issues in the late 1980s had brought about significant changes in electoral politics of the Hindi heartland. The prevailing understanding of politics in the post-Mandal era was that politics in this part of the country was all about castes, reflecting deep-rooted social and political inequalities and competing interests. There was no gain in saying the fact that there was social and

Table 4.9

Electoral performance of political parties in Bihar, 1996–2004

Major Political Parties	Lok Sabha (1996)		Lok Sabha (1999)		Assembly (2000)		Lok Sabha (2004)	
	Vote (%)	Seats Won	Vote (%)	Seats Won	Vote (%)	Seats Won	Vote (%)	Seats Won
BJP	20.5	18	23.1	23	14.6	67	14.6	5
Congress	12.9	2	8.8	4	11.0	23	4.5	3
RJD (JD in 1996)	31.8	22	28.2	7	28.3	124	30.7	22
Samata (JD(U) in 2000 onward)	14.4	3	20.7	18	8.5	34	22.4	6
Others	20.6	9	19.2	2	37.6	92	27.8	4
Total	100.0	54	100.0	54	100.0	324	100.0	40

Source: Election Commission of India.

economic disparity between different caste groups, which at one level had acted as cleavages in politics and at another level also determined the share in political power. However, these claims had often remained unsubstantiated and, therefore, needed to be examined empirically.

Tables 4.10 and 4.11 provide social bases of support in the 1990s.[1] Reading both the tables together, it would be clear that while the popularity of the RJD had declined in 1996, it continued to draw large support from its core constituency, that is, Yadavs, Muslims, and other lower socioeconomic strata. In the 1999 Lok Sabha election, the vote share of the RJD had further declined which could be attributed to shift of other OBCs and very poor people in general from the RJD to the NDA, and it was because the support of Yadavs and Muslims to the RJD had remained almost intact (see Table 4.10). Similarly, while the RJD had lost its support in rural areas, it managed to increase its support base in the urban areas. It is possible to argue that, having consolidated its support base in rural areas, the RJD had reached out to the urban voters. It can be explained the other way round too. Having seen that the RJD was deeply entrenched in power, the urban voters, including the rich, began leaning toward the RJD, though at a slower pace.

From this analysis, it appears that the political parties in Bihar had their well-defined voting constituency that formed their social bases. While the RJD largely drew its support from Yadavs, Muslims, and to some extent from Dalits and poorer segments as a whole, the NDA's support base constituted forward castes, non-Yadav backward castes, educated, and middle and upper-middle strata of society. The RJD seemed to have lost due to the glaring shift in its core constituency in 2005. On the other hand, the NDA not only managed to consolidate its core constituency but also gained, though marginally, among other voters.

However, this analysis fails to clarify which of the several social identities had been crucial for the mobilization of voters. In the context of Bihar, though caste and class overlap each other to a large extent, the

---

[1] Lokniti has survey data since 1991. However, we concentrate on post-1996 Lok Sabha elections. The reason is that the government of Lalu Prasad Yadav had replaced the Congress only recently, that is, in 1990, and it was the rejection of the Congress rather than the charismatic leadership of Lalu that worked in that election. One of the arguments here is that Lalu created an image among voters, symbolic though it was, during his first stint as a chief minister and as the messiah of backward castes and minorities as well. Whether he was or he was not could be assessed only in the context of post-1991 elections and we, therefore, selected the 1996 Lok Sabha election as our starting point. As far as post-poll of Bihar assembly elections are concerned, we do not have datasets for 1990 and 1995.

Table 4.10

Social bases of voting in Bihar: Lok Sabha elections, 1996–2004

Categories	RJD			NDA			Others		
	1996	*1999*	*2004*	*1996*	*1999*	*2004*	*1996*	*1999*	*2004*
All	32	29	31	35	43	36	33	28	33
Locality									
Rural	33	27	32	34	46	35	33	27	33
Urban	26	39	24	51	29	47	23	32	29
Gender									
Male	31	28	31	33	44	36	36	28	33
Female	33	29	31	37	42	38	30	29	31
Education									
Illiterate	32	30	36	33	40	28	35	30	36
Up to primary	43	28	33	30	46	35	27	26	32
Up to matric	27	25	26	40	52	42	33	23	32
Graduate and above	22	25	26	50	45	46	28	30	28
Caste/Community									
Upper castes	5	2	17	85	75	64	10	23	19
Yadav	59	55	52	24	21	14	17	24	34
Koeri–Kurmi	20	10	10	60	75	68	20	15	22
Other OBCs	37	19	25	37	48	36	26	33	39
Dalits	27	35	36	22	41	45	51	33	19
Muslims	58	64	52	4	13	8	38	23	40
Economic Class									
Very poor	34	29	32	30	37	33	36	34	35
Poor	33	31	34	32	52	34	35	17	32
Middle	28	25	26	40	58	43	32	17	31
Rich	22	25	25	41	45	47	37	30	28

Source: CSDS Data Unit.

Notes: 1. Figures are as percentages of those who voted in the elections.
2. NDA includes BJP and Samata in 1996; BJP and JD(U) in 1999 and 2004.
3. JD in 1996.

Table 4.11

Social bases of voting in Bihar: Assembly elections, 2000–2005

Categories	RJD			NDA			LJNSP			Others		
	2000	2005 February	2005 October	2000	2005 February	2005 October	2000	2005 February	2005 October	2000	2005 February	2005 October
All	28	25	24	21	25	36	—	13	11	51	37	29
Locality												
Rural	28	24	25	22	26	36	—	13	12	50	38	27
Urban	30	33	13	38	25	40	—	7	5	32	35	42
Gender												
Men	28	24	23	21	28	37	—	13	11	11	35	29
Women	29	27	24	22	22	36	—	12	12	11	39	28
Education												
Illiterate	30	33	28	21	23	28	—	13	13	49	31	31
Up to primary	29	25	26	18	26	33	—	13	13	53	36	28
Up to matric	26	19	22	25	29	41	—	12	10	49	40	27
Graduate and above	22	18	13	38	30	51	—	11	6	40	41	30
Caste/Community												
Upper castes	10	7	5	42	51	64	—	12	6	48	30	25
Koeri–Kurmi	21	9	12	39	49	61	—	21	6	40	21	21

(Continued)

Table 4.11

(Continued)

Categories	RJD			NDA			LJNSP			Others		
	2000	2005 February	2005 October	2000	2005 February	2005 October	2000	2005 February	2005 October	2000	2005 February	2005 October
Yadavs	75	79	61	6	3	12	—	3	4	19	15	23
Other OBCs	24	22	17	27	24	47	—	14	8	49	40	28
Dalits	27	23	17	24	20	17	—	14	28	49	43	38
Muslims	48	35	36	3	5	8	—	10	15	49	50	41
Economic Class												
Rich	—	14	17	—	48	54	—	14	5	—	24	24
Middle	—	23	22	—	27	40	—	12	9	—	38	29
Poor	—	30	25	—	18	34	—	14	12	—	38	29
Very poor	—	26	27	—	25	24	—	14	16	—	35	33

Source: Bihar Election Studies, relevant years, CSDS, Delhi.

Notes: 1. Figures are as percentages of those who voted in the elections.

2. NDA includes BJP and Samata Party for 2000 and BJP and JD(U) for 2005.

popular impression was that it was rather the caste identity that influences and informs political choice. Simply put, it was not known as to how likely an illiterate and poor voter was to vote for the RJD regardless of his/her caste affiliation and locality among others. In order to test this question, we use binary logistic regressions[2] for a number of elections (both parliamentary and assembly) and identify the key determinants of voting for the RJD and the NDA. We focused on voting for the RJD

---

[2] Logistic regression, in brief, estimates the probability of an event to occur. It is a generalized linear model used for binomial regression. It makes use of several predictor variables, which may be either numerical or categorical. For example, the probability that a person will vote for "*X*" or "*Y*" party might be predicted from knowing his caste, religion, educational, and occupational background.

Logistic regression predicts the log odds of the dependent variable which could be written in the following form:

$$z = b_0 + b_1 X_1 + b_2 X_2 + \ldots + b_k X_k,$$

where z is the log odds of dependent variable; b_0 is the constant; and there are k independent (X) variables, in the present instance giving the characteristics of the ith voter. If X_1 is a binary (0,1) variable, as is the present case, then $z = X_0$ (i.e., the constant) for the "0" group on X_1 and equals the constant plus the b coefficient for the "1" group. To convert the log odds (which is z, which is the logit) back into an odds ratio, the natural logarithmic base e is raised to the zth power: odds (event) = exp(z) = odds the binary dependent is 1 rather than 0. Thus, if b_1 is statistically significantly different from zero, then the odds ratio for voters with characteristic X_1 ($X_1 = 1$) is statistically significantly different from the odds ratio for the reference category.

To illustrate, the dependent variable in the present analysis is dichotomous and coded 1, if voted, say for RJD and 0 otherwise. The exp(z) is the odds ratio. Odds or the odds ratio is the ratio of the probability an event occurs (e.g., the vote is for RJD) divided by the probability of the corresponding non-event (the vote is not for RJD). When odds are 1.0 for a group, a person in that group is equally likely to experience the event (voting for RJD, in the present case) as to experience the non-event (voting for other parties, in the present case). In other words, an odds ratio of 1.0 means the independent variable has no effect on the dependent variable; that is, to say, the two variables are statistically independent. If odds ratio is greater than 1.0, it indicates that the independent variable increases the probability of the event (probability of voting for RJD or party of interest in the analysis). Larger the positive difference between observed odds ratio and 1.0, stronger the relationship. When an odds ratio is below 1.0, it indicates that the independent variable decreases the probability of the event (in the present case, probability of voting for, say, RJD).

We also reiterate the following points here. The selected sample is representative as mentioned elsewhere in the paper. The responses are for those who actually voted for the party. Further, we believe that the information is reliable because we had used dummy ballot box to ensure that the investigator does not know the preference of the respondent and the respondent does not need to hesitate. In the footnote on page 1, we have already mentioned how we got the respondents to be interviewed.

alone and not its allies because the party had not been consistent in its coalitions. On the other hand, the NDA had been a consistent alliance; therefore, the ensuing analysis was for the NDA rather than different constituents of it. Our list of independent variables includes castes/communities, education, gender, locality, and economic class.[3]

A look at the results of logistic regression presented in Tables 4.10 and 4.11 suggests that the impact of variables on the propensity to vote for JD/RJD varied in the three elections taken for analysis. Education and class help very much in explaining the vote for JD/RJD (except that the poor have shown a preference for the RJD in the 2000 assembly election). It is probably due to very high correlation between caste, class, and educational attainment in Bihar, while the impact of gender and locality seems to be volatile and not consistent across three elections. However, caste–community and voting choice nexus appears to be consistent in the three elections chosen for analysis. As expected, controlling for other background variables, Yadavs were far more likely to have voted for the RJD/JD than other castes.[4] Similarly, Muslims continued to show strong preference for the RJD/JD compared to other castes during these elections. As expected, forward castes and Koeri–Kurmis were least likely to have voted for the RJD/JD compared to other castes.

From this discussion, it would be clear that despite the claims of failure of Lalu Yadav's regime on developmental fronts toward the end of the 1990s, political mobilization based on caste–community identities did take place and propped various political alliances. The solid support of Muslims and Yadavs (popularly known as MY alliance) and to some extent the support of Dalits kept Lalu Yadav and his party in power. If this were not to be the case, the RJD would have been wiped out way back in 2000 as it had apparently failed on all counts, ranging from law and order to development of state, which political observers had always made the basis for predicting the RJD's ouster and each time they failed.

---

[3] Economic class is defined by using a composite index of monthly household income, household assets, and the type of house the respondent resides in. Scores were assigned (in accordance of the precedence of the variable in the scheme of construction of class) to each individual variable related to income/household assets. The scores were summed up for each respondent. Then the entire sample was divided in quintiles and designated as lowest, lower, middle, upper middle, and highest corresponding with very poor, poor, middle, upper middle, and rich. The index for all the elections is based on the same criteria.

[4] Other castes are those other than forward castes: Koeri–Kurmi, Yadav, other OBCs, and Dalits, and taken as reference category for comparing the likelihood of voting of castes/communities reported in the table.

References

Chowdhury, K. (2012). Minority govt precedence under Narasimha Rao. *Business Standard.* Retrieved November 20, 2017, from http://www.business-standard.com/article/economy-policy/minority-govt-precedence-under-narasimha-rao-112092003007_1.html

Gaikwad, R. (2013). Together they ended Lalu's reign in Bihar. *The Hindu.* Retrieved November 20, 2017, from http://www.thehindu.com/todays-paper/tp-national/together-they-ended-lalus-reign-in-bihar/article4821513.ece

Subrahmaniam, V. (2010). Nitish Kumar's elusive "Patnaik" movement. *The Hindu.* Retrieved November 20, 2017, from http://www.thehindu.com/opinion/lead/nitish-kumars-elusive-patnaik-moment/article496997.ece

5

Re-emergence of RJD: Elections of 2000

In the 1999 Lok Sabha election, the RJD had received a drubbing at the hands of the NDA comprising the BJP and JD(U), and it was widely believed that days of Lalu–Rabri raj would be over after the 2000 Bihar assembly election. The NDA had notched 41 out of 54 seats in Bihar, comprising Jharkhand, and led in 199 of the 324 assembly segments. The RJD and Congress had fought the parliamentary polls in alliance, but the results were dismal. The state unit of the grand old party was not in favor of alliance with the Lalu Prasad Yadav-led dispensation, but apparently under the pressure of central leadership they had buckled. Thus, in the 2000 assembly election, Congress decided to go alone, forcing the RJD to strike a chord with CPM and MCC.

On the other side of the fence too, the situation was not rosy as cracks had appeared on the issue of ticket distribution between the BJP and JD(U). Differences emerged also between the Samata Party and JD(U) which led to these three parties contesting elections against each other in many constituencies.

There were reasons for the crumbling of the fortress of Lalu Yadav. The reason had been the realization among a section of Muslims and Yadavs that lumpen elements among their communities were enjoying privileged positions while they were left out. The backward Muslims or pasmandas were finding themselves left out from the political process, as they felt that Lalu Yadav had only empowered Sheikhs, Syeds, and Pathans.

The backward Muslims felt that Lalu Yadav extracted protection votes from them and empowered only the upper castes among their community. On the other side, with a sure victory, the NDA camp disintegrated on the issue of seats. The JD(U) had split after Nitish Kumar walked away with the Samata Party. Sharad Yadav and Ram Vilas Paswan wanted more seats for their people, while Nitish Kumar and George Fernandes were reluctant for the same. The JD(U) vote during the 1999 parliamentary polls was primarily the support base of the Samata Party under the leadership of Nitish Kumar, and Paswan wanted to be projected as Bihar's chief minister but the BJP was not in favor.

This led to the three parties fighting polls against one another in many constituencies, leading to an advantage to Lalu Yadav and his party. The BJP had put up candidates in 168 seats, BPP in 23, JD(U) in 87, and Nitish Kumar-led Samata Party in 120 seats.

> During the election campaign, Nitish presented himself as a man of today and Lalu as a man of yesterday.... Lalu relied with twin mantras: social justice and secularism. Nitish told people that these two ideals were also very dear to his heart but he placed Bihar's development at the top of his agenda, arguing that true social justice and true secularism could be achieved through economic progress.... The Lalu camp again portrayed Nitish as a puppet of the forwards who were bent upon regaining power under the camouflage of development.... He (Nitish) had to convince the poor that development and social justice were complimentary to each other. (Sinha, 2011, p. 181)

The electoral outcome of the 2000 Bihar assembly election was a setback for both the NDA and the RJD. The setback was more apparent for the NDA, for its central and state leadership had built high hopes of a decisive and runaway victory. The NDA failed to capitalize on the massive runaway win it registered in the 1999 general elections due to internal bickering among the BJP, Samata Party, and JD(U); and, hence, the division of votes and an unorganized campaign led to emergence of the Lalu Yadav-led RJD as the single largest party in the state. A united NDA would have won in at least 170–180 seats as they had led in 199 of the 324 assembly segments during the 1999 Lok Sabha polls and won 41 out of 54 parliamentary seats.

The NDA was able to win only 125 seats (including four unofficial candidates who won elections outside the NDA seat-sharing arrangement) and fell way below the expectations, but even worse was that it fell behind the final tally of 126 for the RJD and the CPM. With 124 seats and 28.2% of the popular vote, the RJD emerged as the single largest party in the state, while the BJP finished way behind with 67 seats and 14.5% of votes (see Table 5.1). The NDA needed 41 more MLAs and the RJD–CPM alliance 37 for proving simple absolute majority in the

Table 5.1

Seats and vote share of parties: Bihar assembly elections, 2000–2005

Year/Parties	2000	February 2005	October 2005
Congress	23 (11.06%)	10 (5%)	9 (6.09%)
BJP	67 (14.64%)	37 (10.97%)	55 (15.65%)
SAP/JD(U)	34+21=55 (15.12%)	55 (14.55%)	88 (20.46%)
CPI–CPM	7 (4.51%)	4 (2.22%)	4 (2.77%)
RJD	124 (28.43%)	75 (25.07%)	54 (23.45%)
LJNSP	—	29 (12.62%)	10 (11.1%)

Source: Election Commission of India.

Notes: All figures are in percent. Figures in brackets indicate the vote share.

house. Eventually, Lalu Yadav outmaneuvered Nitish Kumar and other NDA partners and got the support of Congress and CPI, notably though, both these parties had fought the polls on an anti-Lalu platform. The Congress had chosen to weaken NDA nationally than to strengthen itself in Bihar. Thus, Lalu Yadav was back in power with Rabri Devi as the chief minister of the state.

"Even a donkey could have seen a clear NDA victory on the horizon. Lalu would not have come back to power if we had stuck together on seat sharing. Instead we ended up having a hung assembly," Nitish Kumar was quoted as saying in a media report (Sinha, 2011, p. 182).

On the other hand, there can be no doubt about one thing that the upper caste media was always anti-Lalu and it was either not aware of ground-level polarizations in Bihar or deliberately ignored it. If the election results did not appear as a setback for the RJD, it was largely because of the bleak picture painted by the media. Against this background, the RJD's defeat had appeared like a victory. Lalu Yadav presided over a historic shift in the social balance of political power in 1990, a shift that was reaffirmed in the subsequent verdicts of the Lok Sabha election in 1991 and Vidhan Sabha election in 1995. But the 2000 assembly election and the two Lok Sabha elections held in 1999 and 1998 showed his inability to consolidate the social shift into an enduring political regime of the kind the Left Front had once established in West Bengal.

The loss of 43 seats in the 2000 assembly election, as compared to the 1995 assembly election, was a verdict against his non-governance and non-performance. The loss was also the result of realization among the upper backwards that Yadavs would not give space to them under any circumstances, and Lalu Yadav, since assuming office in 1990, had openly sidelined other upper backward leaders such as Nitish Kumar and others. Lalu Yadav, after the arrest of Lal Krishna Advani, had become the darling of the Muslim masses and could grasp that minorities would be polarizing in his favor. This gave him the confidence to sideline Kurmis and Koeris and build up a tactical MY alliance, because Muslims would be happy with protection during communal riots, while Kurmis and Koeris would demand share in power.

There was also a strange coincidence that had led to the victory of the RJD in number of seats and, in fact, the RJD could have ended up behind the NDA's combined strength. The Lalu Yadav-led party had won 5 out of the 7 seats, which were decided by less than 500 votes, and another 4 of 12 seats, which were decided by a margin of between 500 and 1,000 votes.

Bihar Economy and Development

The people of Bihar hoped that at least in this term Lalu Yadav will take development of the state on a serious note, but the RJD leader and his wife Rabri Devi were happy being only a symbol of social change and they lacked the capability of taking the agenda of development forward.

Bihar suffered from a massive underutilization of central funds. Chief Minister Rabri Devi was just a puppet in the hands of her husband Lalu Yadav who wanted to retain power within the family after he was forced to resign over the fodder scam. During this period, the bureaucracy was deeply demotivated. Rabri was a proxy chief minister and Lalu Yadav the de facto leader who sat by her side in meetings and took all the key decisions, making a virtual mockery of the Indian constitutional system. The attitude of Rabri Devi was indifferent, and it bred general apathy in the administration.

> In road construction and rural engineering—the two departments respon-
> sible for providing Bihar urban and rural connectivity—all the posts of
> engineers-in-chief and chief engineers were vacant in the second half of
> Rabri's post-2000 tenure. Of the 91 posts of superintending engineers in
> the two departments 81 had no occupants. (Sinha, 2011, p. 194)

Positive Features of Bihar Economy During Lalu–Rabri Regime

The positive developments in the economic sector during this phase indicate that government is not the only driver of growth. Despite the apathetic attitude of the government and poor implementation of development strategies, the economy of the state did not crumble. Lalu Yadav never sold the positives of Bihar's economy during his electoral and political campaigns, and he virtually succumbed to the propaganda of Nitish Kumar and the BJP on the status of Bihar's alleged crumbling economy. Bihar's average annual growth rate between 1993–1994 and 2004–2005 was over 5%, which was lower than the national growth rate of 6.5%, but it did not suggest that Bihar's economy was not performing or it had collapsed. The agriculture sector of Bihar grew at the rate of 4% which was 1% more than India's national growth rate. The construction sector grew at a rate of 11.63%, trade–hotels at 7.62%, communication by 21.64%, and insurance sector by 10%. Although the growth rate in these sectors was lesser than the national average, all the indices indicate that it was growing at a decent rate. The issue of poor law and order, apparently, spoiled media projections of the growth story of the state achieved during this period.

> Beating the stereotypes of gross rural poverty, the rural deposits of the scheduled commercial banks (SCBs) in Bihar were much higher during Rabri's 2000–05 tenure than those of the Congress-ruled Maharashtra. From 9,067 crore in 2000–01 the rural deposits of SCBs in Bihar rose to Rs.13,328 crore in 2004–05 (making 6.3 per cent of the total national rural deposits), whereas in Maharashtra the figure made about 3.9 per cent of the national deposits. The total deposits of SCBs in Bihar rose from Rs.26,800 crore in 2000–01 to Rs.41,007 crore in 2004–05, nearly 65 per cent higher than neighbouring West Bengal and Uttar Pradesh. In terms of percentage share in total deposits, Bihar ranked very low, yet an average of 16 per cent growth in SCB deposits did not suggest complete collapse. (Sinha, 2011)

Status of Credit–Deposit Ratio

This phenomenon is an indicator of the level of economic activity and credit absorption capacity of a state or region. During the early 1990s, it rose marginally, but during Rabri Devi's regime of 2001–2005, it grew from 20.7% in 2001 to 31.4% in 2004–2005. The five regional rural banks and their 1,466 branches registered a credit deposit ratio of 44.7%, which was much higher than that of commercial banks.

These positive stories which were the results of free market economy and rise of middle class in Bihar virtually did not appear in the media. But in comparison to the rest of India, the states' picture looked bleak due to lack of industrial growth, poor roads, poor conditions of state-run hospitals, and virtual collapse of law and order among others. The public delivery system was also dismal.

This apathetic attitude of the political leadership led to the gradual rise of Nitish Kumar because even a section of Muslims, Yadavs, and backwards now wanted their leader (Lalu Yadav) to take the agenda of social justice toward development and economic emancipation, unlike mere slogans of symbolism. Nitish Kumar had gradually weaned away a chunk of backward or pasmanda Muslims to his side and built up a successful coalition of lower backward castes barring Yadavs, upper castes, section of Muslims, and Kurmi–Koeri. This combination threw out the RJD-led alliance in 2005 polls.

Region-wise Analysis

The region-wise analysis of election results gives a clear picture of the relative strength of different parties in Bihar's three regions—north, central, and south Bihar. In terms of broad strength of the parties, the stronghold of RJD–Samata and JD(U) were in north and central Bihar, while the BJP was more influential in Jharkhand region along with the Congress party. The BJP and the Samata Party had contested the 1995 assembly election against each other. As compared to the assembly election held in 1995, the NDA made gains in all the three regions of the state, in terms of both votes and seats in the 2000 assembly polls.

The gain in terms of seats was more or less proportional to the total number of seats in the region, but in terms of vote share, the alliance had performed much better in south Bihar or Jharkhand region as compared to central and north Bihar. Yet it had failed to sweep the Jharkhand region. By now it was clear that if a separate legislature were to be carved out for Jharkhand region from the present assembly, the new house would also be a "hung" house, like its parent assembly.

The RJD, which had practically swept all but the eastern pocket of north Bihar in 1995 polls, lost the maximum number of seats from this region in the 2000 elections. But such was its dominance then that despite losing heavily, it performed best in the region, winning 74 of its 124 seats. In central Bihar, though the RJD lost seven seats, it increased its vote by nearly 6%. This was largely due to the reason that it did not strike a poll pact with the CPI and contested most of the seats on its own. It came as no surprise that the party had not performed well in south Bihar or Jharkhand region, which was dominated by the BJP, JMM, and the Congress (see Table 5.2).

The local Bihar unit of the Congress had always tried to maintain a distance from the RJD owing to issues of poor law and order or non-governance, but it was the central leadership which always pushed for alliance, taking on the larger picture of defeating the BJP-led NDA in the country. Thus, Congress went to the polls alone in the 2000 assembly election and was hoping for a recovery similar to Uttar Pradesh, but the final results were disappointing. The party could not stage a comeback and won only 23 and polled 11.1% votes. In the 1995 assembly polls, the party had won 29 seats, so the grand old party was losing its vote base, elections after elections, in Bihar.

The Congress did not lose seats in north Bihar, but its vote share went down by 7% despite contesting a much larger number of seats, while in the south Bihar or Jharkhand region, the party lost two seats as compared to the 1995 assembly election but increased its vote marginally. The Congress remained a force in the Jharkhand region, but clearly no more in north Bihar.

The 2000 assembly elections were not only a setback for the RJD and Lalu Yadav, though he was able to form a government due to Congress support, but also for the Left parties—CPI, CPM, CPML, and MCC. The rise of the three socialist parties—RJD, JD(U), and Samata—had led to the weaning away of a chunk of lower backwards and Dalit votes from the Left parties to these three parties. The rise of Lalu Prasad Yadav and later Nitish Kumar—two backward caste leaders in the political horizon of Bihar—virtually took the sail out of wind of the Left parties who now remained active in certain pockets of central Bihar. In the 1995 polls, the Left parties had won 40 seats out of 324, while in 2000, they were reduced to a marginal player winning only 13 seats. The CPI had won 23 seats in the 1990 polls, 26 seats in the 1995 polls, and only 5 seats in the 2000 assembly polls. So, the decline was very steep between 1995 and 2000 polls. This was the period when Lalu Yadav's social justice slogan

Table 5-2

Assembly election, 2000: Region-wise analysis

Region	Seats	Turnout Change		RJD				BJP + Samata Party				INC				Left				Others			
		2000	over 1995	Won	Gain/ loss	Vote share	Swing	Won	Gain/ Loss	Vote Share	Swing	Won	Gain/ Loss	Vote Share	Swing	Won	Gain/ Loss	Vote Share	Swing	Won	Gain/ Loss	Vote Share	Swing
North Bihar	156	66.8	+5.3	74	−31	32.8	−2.4	53	+39	29.9	+11.6	10	0	9.6	−7.0	3	−15	4.4	−1.2	16	+7	23.3	−1.0
South Bihar	84	52.5	−10.1	10	−5	12.2	−3.2	41	+18	32.1	+10.3	11	−2	19.1	+1.4	3	−1	4.7	−1.2	19	−10	31.9	−7.3
Central Bihar	84	65.1	+3.7	40	−7	32.5	+5.5	27	+16	27.6	+6.2	3	−3	7.6	−6.8	1	−9	4.1	−3.3	13	+3	28.1	−1.6
Total	324	61.1	+0.8	124	−43	28.2	0.2	121	+73	29.8	+9.8	24	−5	11.1	−5.1	7	−25	4.4	−1.8	48	0	26.5	−3.0

Source: CSDS Data Unit.

was at its optimum, and the upper castes, who were the main exploiters of Dalits and lower backward farmers, saw opportunity for upward social mobility.

Both the CPI and CPM faced an overall decline in the 2000 assembly election. It was a long time since the CPI had contested elections without a mainstream party as its ally. The invisible decline of the party in this period came to the surface, as it finished behind the CPML. The CPI, following the poll results of 2000 elections, had lost its position as the dominant Left party in the state, with the CPML one seat ahead of it despite contesting fewer seats. Although the CPM contested the 2000 assembly election in alliance with the RJD, it also suffered a loss of four seats as compared to the 1995 assembly election. Still, its support base remained intact in terms of percentage of votes polled. A.K. Roy's MCC, a party based in and around Dhanbad district of Jharkhand, which had won two seats in the 1995 assembly election, could not even open its account in the 2000 polls.

Comparative Performance of Three Alliance Partners—BJP, Samata, and JD(U)

The crux of the 2000 assembly polls was that the BJP was steadily rising and the upper caste had now fully supported the party in Bihar, completely shunning the Congress party. Among the three party alliance of NDA, Samata, BJP, and JD(U), the strike rate of the BJP was the best in the three regions of Bihar—north, central, and south.

The saffron party won 39% of the seats it had contested and polled an average of 29% votes in these seats. The Samata Party won 28% seats and polled an average of 23% votes in the seats it contested. The JD(U) performed badly, won only 24% of the seats contested, and polled an average of only 13% votes in the seats it contested. Both the alliance partners, the BJP and the Samata Party, had a setback in their traditional strongholds, south and central. Although the BJP had polled the maximum number of votes in south Bihar, it failed to win a sizeable number of seats from the region. Similarly, the Samata Party which had contested the largest number of seats in its traditional stronghold of central Bihar won only one-fourth of these. The JD(U) had its presence only in north Bihar (see Table 5.3).

Table 5.3

Comparative performance of political parties: Assembly election, 2000

Region	BJP			Samata Party			JD(U)		
	Seats Contested	*Seats Won*	*Vote (%)*	*Seats Contested*	*Seats Won*	*Vote (%)*	*Seats Contested*	*Seats Won*	*Vote (%)*
North	55	23	11.9	48	14	8.2	52	16	9.9
South	73	31	24.5	20	7	5.5	14	3	2.1
Central	39	12	11.4	52	13	12.5	21	2	3.8
Total	167	66	14.5	120	34	8.8	87	21	6.5

Source: CSDS Data Unit.

Did the multiplicity of NDA candidates in a large number of seats account for the setback to the BJP and its allies in the 2000 assembly election? The NDA leaders would prefer this argument, but a careful look and analysis at the constituency-level results indicated that this factor did not contribute much. The alliance partners had contested against each other in 37 assembly constituencies. In 11 of these constituencies, 1 of the alliance partners won the election, and in 15, 1 was runner; but a united NDA would have made a difference to the electoral outcome only in 2 assembly constituencies (Mohiuddinnagar and Kurtha) which were won by the RJD by a narrow margin. In other constituencies, the victory margin of the winning party was too big to be overcome even if the votes of all the alliance partners were combined. So, a joint NDA seat-sharing arrangement would not have made much difference, if the statistics and figures are to be believed.

Change of Seats Between Parties

A number of seats changed hands between the 1995 assembly election and the 2000 polls. Looking at the pattern, we find that a lot of churning of seats took place from one party to the other. Out of the total 324 seats, 182 seats changed hands between the 1995 and 2000 elections. Although in the 2000 assembly election the NDA won more than double the number of seats won by its various partners in the 1995 assembly election, it did not retain even half of its own seats. So, the seats that the NDA won were new seats that may not be its stronghold, while it lost seats which it had won in earlier election. In the 2000 assembly election, the Congress had managed to retain only 7 of the 29 seats won in the 1995 assembly election and lost 10 seats to the NDA and 6 to the RJD. On the other hand, the Left parties had not only lost a large number of seats, but their retention rate was also very poor. The RJD successfully retained 94 of the seats that it had won during the 1995 assembly election and lost 57 seats to the NDA.

Evaluation of the MLAs

As number of seats changed hands between the RJD-led alliance and the NDA partners, it indicated that there was an element of growing dissatisfaction with the sitting MLAs of respective parties. As NDA won double the number of seats, it did not retain even half of the seats it had won in the previous elections.

The post-poll survey conducted after the 2000 assembly election tried to measure the people's satisfaction and dissatisfaction with the performance of their MLAs who completed their term after being elected in the 1995 assembly elections. Nearly one-third were dissatisfied with their MLAs, while only 15% were very satisfied with them. This trend was more or less even across all sections of the people. The literate were more dissatisfied than the non-literate. Dissatisfaction with the MLAs was higher among the upper caste and the Dalits as well. The majority of the women did not hold any opinion on the issue (see Figure 5.1).

Vote Bank of the RJD

Lalu Yadav was the symbol of backward class politics and gradually since 1990 the Yadav strongman had built up a solid support base among the electorates of Bihar. He was hailed as leader of mass base and despite not performing on development front was voted back to power at least twice owing to this phenomenon. He was successful in carving a committed support base among the majority of Yadav and Muslim (MY) electorates that saw him floating in the political landscape of Bihar. In the 2000 assembly elections, the RJD performed badly in terms of winning seat, but it polled the highest number of votes. The party had seen ups and down in the elections held during the period 1990–2000 in terms

Figure 5.1

Level of satisfaction of people with the MLA

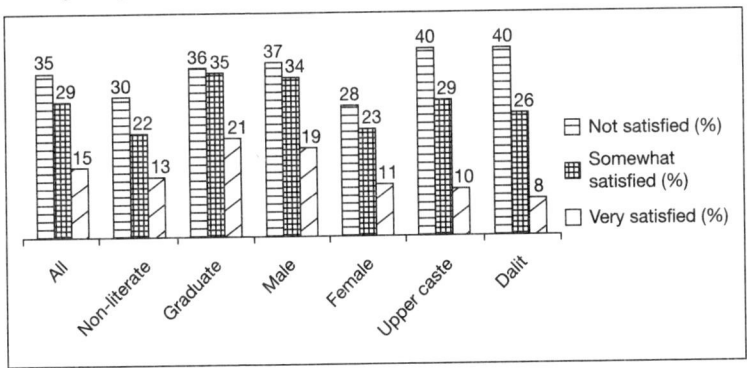

Source: CSDS Data Unit.

Note: Rest no opinion.

of seats, but it had polled more or less the same share of votes. This gives an indication of a solid support base for the party, which had remained static over the past few elections. But does it mean that the same group of people had voted for the party over the years? The survey conducted during the 2000 assembly elections tried to find out the social profile of the RJD vote (see Table 5.4).

There is a sharp contrast between the profile of those who had always voted for the RJD and those who had never voted for the party. While more than 50% of RJD votes came from the Yadavs and the Muslims, of those who had never voted for the RJD, only 6% belonged to these two social groups. There was a divided loyalty for the RJD among the OBCs. If on the one hand party's nearly 21% votes came from them, at the same time, of those who had never voted for the RJD, as much as 26% constituted the people of OBCs. There was practically no change in the composition of the RJD vote, and the opposition parties had failed to make any inroads among the strong Lalu Yadav supporters. He commanded virtual absolute loyalty over his voters. The firm opposition for the RJD came from the upper castes as they constituted half of those voters who had never voted for the RJD during the past 10 years. Forty-five percent who never voted for the RJD constituted the upper caste (see Table 5.4). There were sections among Dalits and Adivasis too that had never voted for the party.

Table 5.4

RJD's vote bank during the past few elections

Caste	Never Voted for RJD	Always Voted for RJD	Voted for RJD in 1999 Lok Sabha Election	Voted for RJD in 2000 Assembly Election
All	28	20	26	27
Upper caste	45	7	9	11
Yadav	2	32	28	27
Muslim	4	26	21	23
Other OBCs	26	21	22	20
Dalit	11	13	19	18
Adivasi	12	1	1	1

Source: CSDS Data Unit.

In the election held in 2000, the RJD had suffered a setback. It lost 43 seats compared to the 1995 election. However, the RJD had emerged as the single largest party, though falling short of the number of seats required for formation of the government. Major support for the RJD again came from Lalu's captive vote bank, namely Muslims and Yadavs. As per the findings of the CSDS Bihar Assembly Election Study—2000, the MY alliance accounted for 60% of the total votes secured by the RJD. A significant proportion of Dalits and other OBCs also voted for the RJD, though the wide social base of the party had somewhat shrunk (see Table 5.4). One obvious reason for this loss or relatively shrunk support base was the drifting away of Koeris and Kurmis under the leadership of Nitish Kumar who had differences with Lalu Yadav and eventually separated to form his own party.

Nitish Kumar's Samata Party, though failed to make a deeper impact in the 1995 assembly election, had already begun to break the ground in Lok Sabha election held in 1996 by winning six seats and continued to improve its seat tallies in the subsequent Lok Sabha elections held in 1998 and 1999. By forging an alliance with the BJP, which had gradually emerged as a bastion of upper castes—Bhumihars, Rajputs, Brahmins, and Kayasthas—after sinking of the Congress party no more a formidable force, Nitish Kumar was gradually emerging as the undisputed leader of anti-Lalu forces in the state, elections after elections.

It forged a pre-poll alliance with the BJP in the wake of the assembly election of 2000. The NDA alliance bagged 121 seats. Major support for the Samata–BJP alliance came from the upper castes and Koeri–Kurmi.

Upper castes had alone contributed one-third of the total votes polled by the Samata–BJP alliance (Bihar Election Study 2000). Although the alliance fell short of the majority mark, taking advantage of the NDA in power at the center, Nitish Kumar was sworn in as the chief minister of Bihar. Not surprisingly, his government survived only for a week, as he could not prove majority on the floor of the house. Following the exit of Nitish Kumar due to his failure to muster support from smaller parties and independents, Lalu Yadav was given a chance to form the government. The Yadav strongman had managed to secure support from the Congress, the Left, and a few independents and eventually proved majority on the floor of the House. However, soon after he became the chief minister of Bihar for the third time, he was charged with being one of the accused in the "fodder scam," the biggest ever scam in the history of the state. Under mounting pressure, he resigned and got his wife Rabri Devi appointed as the chief minister of Bihar, a classical example of familialism—the idea of promoting the family as an institution.

Many Interpretations of the 2000 Assembly Elections

In most general formulations, the results were not only expected but also surprising. Expected in a sense that the mood of people, as explained by experts, political commentators, and media, was against Lalu Yadav and he was sure to pay for his negligence toward development and maintenance of law and order in the state, which, among other things, he had promised when he became the chief minister second time in a row. The results were surprising because though Lalu was down, he was not yet completely out. His RJD emerged as the single largest party after elections and had a stake in the formation of a new government.

Prior to the election results of 2000 assembly elections, as always, the media had painted a very tardy picture of Lalu Yadav and his rule and repeatedly predicted that he will be losing the next polls, but every time the Yadav strongman proved the pundits wrong.

Were the media and political pundits biased? Did they wrongly assess the mood of people? Or the "mood of people" as described in media was the mood of those people who actually did not constitute the support base of Lalu Yadav? Metropolitan media and arm-chair impressionist political commentators might have gone wrong; but why did a large section of voters vote for Lalu Yadav? Was it that while he failed on several counts, he did something substantial for his core constituency of support or was it that the symbolism of self-respect or political power still matter for the neglected lot? We attempt to explore the possible answers to these puzzles.

Lok Sabha Election 2004

Although the RJD did not have a majority in the legislative assembly, it formed the government with the support of the Congress, the Left Front, and others. In a sense, it was a rare occasion for the RJD-led government to learn from the mistakes and improve its image and poll prospects by paying heed to administration, deteriorating law and order, and developmental issues. But reports of kidnapping and atrocities against Dalits perpetrated by upper backward castes including Yadavs and landlord senas, and dismal records of economic and infrastructure conditions dominated the newspaper headlines. However, despite the alleged ills of the RJD regime, the party performed well in the Lok Sabha election held in 2004. One of the reasons for the electoral success of the RJD could be attributed to the GA that the party led. Dalit leader Ram Vilas Paswan's breaking away from the NDA in the backdrop of the Gujarat riots of 2002 had weakened the NDA, and Lalu Yadav succeeded in getting Paswan's newly formed LJNSP and the Congress in his fold. The alliance paid dividends in the election battlefield and the RJD–LJNSP–Congress combine swept the state. Muslims and Yadavs had voted en bloc for the alliance and even though the NDA managed to retain its traditional upper caste and Kurmi–Koeri votes, a decisive lead of 19 percentage points among Dalits along with a lead among other caste groups as well gave the RJD-led alliance an edge against NDA. Although coalition calculus brought spectacular success to the RJD, there was simmering consternation within the party, especially keeping in view the upcoming assembly election, for the issues in its political arsenals had already been exhausted.

The Regional Patterns

The results of the Lok Sabha election 2004 were clearly a setback for both the BJP and the JD(U). Compared to the 1999 Lok Sabha elections, both the political parties lost in terms of both number of seats and percentage of votes polled. The net gainer had been the RJD and its alliance partners. Did the BJP and its allies suffer in all the regions across the state or had there been some gains for the NDA alliance in some regions, though they had lost in some other areas?

For a meaningful regional analysis of the results, Bihar has been divided into five different regions—Tirhut, Mithila, Magadh, East, and Bhojpur. While Tirhut and Magadh were the two big regional divisions accounting for 12 and 10 Lok Sabha seats respectively, the other three regions, Mithila (7 Lok Sabha seats), East (7 Lok Sabha seats), and Bhojpur (4 Lok Sabha seats), were relatively small.[1] An analysis of the results from different regions of the state indicates that in terms of the votes polled, both the BJP and the JD(U) suffered a loss across the regions. There was no region where any of these two political parties could improve upon its performance of the 1999 Lok Sabha. In terms of the number of seats won, the BJP did manage to improve its performance in the East, the region with high concentration of Muslim population, where it won four out of the seven Lok Sabha constituencies improving its performance from the 1999 Lok Sabha, when it won only two seats in this region. It was also in this region that the BJP polled the highest percentage of votes (26.96%), nearly double the percent of votes polled by the party throughout the state.

Although the JD(U) won three of the six Lok Sabha seats from the Tirhut region during the 2004 Lok Sabha elections, it was in this region that it suffered a loss of 11.42% votes, the biggest loss amongst all the five regions. The party had won six Lok Sabha seats from this region during the 1999 Lok Sabha elections and had polled nearly 34% votes. In the Mithila region also, the party suffered a loss of 9.31% votes. Of the seven Lok Sabha seats, the JD(U) had won five Lok Sabha seats in this region during the 1999 Lok Sabha elections, but in the 2004 Lok Sabha elections, it drew a blank. The party also suffered in other three regions of the state.

In terms of the number of seats, except for the Bhojpur region where the RJD suffered a loss of one Lok Sabha seat, the RJD gained in all the regions of the state. One would expect that the party might have increased its support base throughout the state, but the results indicate

---

[1] Parliamentary constituencies in Tirhut: Bagha (SC), Bettiah, Motihari, Goplaganj, Siwan, Maharajganj, Chapra, Hajipur (SC), Vaishali, Muzaffarpur, Sitamarhi, and Sheohar.
Mithila: Madhubani, Jhanjharpur, Darbhanga, Rosera (SC), Samastipur, Saharsa, and Madhupura.
Magadh: Barh, Balia, Monghyr, Begusarai, Nalanda, Patna, Aurangabad, Jahanabad, Nawada (SC), and Gaya (SC).
East: Araria (SC), Kishanganj, Purnea, Katihar, Banka, Bhagalpur, and Khagaria.
Bhojpur: Arrah, Buxar, Sasaram (SC), and Bikramganj.

that this was not what seemed to have happened in Bihar. In spite of a gain of 16 Lok Sabha seats (increasing its tally of seats from 6 in the 1999 Lok Sabha to 22 in 2004 Lok Sabha), the RJD had suffered a loss in terms of votes polled in 3 of the 5 regions.

The increase in terms of votes polled for the party had been only 2.17% in Magadh and only marginally 0.42% in the East. Clearly, the victory of the RJD was due to its alliance with other parties such as the Congress and the LJNSP than to its own improved performance. The alliance of the RJD with the LJNSP and the Congress not only prevented the splitting of the anti-NDA vote but also ensured transferability of votes from one party to the other. This contributed to the victory of the RJD and its allies enormously. For example, the two communities—Dalits and Muslims—in Bihar in general never vote for the BJP but with the presence of three parties—RJD, Congress, and LJNSP—their votes were bound to be split. Dalits and Muslims together constitute at least a quarter of Bihar's population. Thus, with an alliance among the three parties, this chunk of vote would never split. This was the reason why the RJD-led alliance was able to garner more seats in the 2004 general elections.

What Led to This Massive Victory for the Congress and Its Allies?

There were unease about the results in Bihar. The RJD had been in power in Patna since last 15 years. The party had won three successive assembly elections held in the years 1990, 1995, and 2000. But the party had not performed so well during the Lok Sabha elections held during this period. The victories of assembly elections were not reflected in the Lok Sabha polls which means pattern of voting differed in the two sets of polls—one pattern for the government in Delhi while another pattern for the government in the state. As the RJD was a regional party of Bihar, a section of people were willing to consider it as an option for assembly elections but not for the Lok Sabha polls. The other factors might be the nature of alliances because the NDA did not fight 2000 assembly elections as a united force which gave an edge to the RJD, while in earlier elections if the RJD failed to strike chord with LJNSP or Congress it failed to secure substantial number of votes.

If the results of the three Lok Sabha elections—1996, 1998, and 1999—are analyzed, it would reveal that the performance of the RJD had gone down in the parliamentary polls. It was believed that people were generally unhappy with the functioning of the state government and the election might seal the fate of the RJD but on the contrary, the RJD with its alliance partners, the Congress, Ram Vilas Paswan's LJNSP, Nationalist Congress Party (NCP), and the CPM had registered an impressive victory in the state. Does this indicate that people were happy with the performance of the state government? Can one assume that this was a positive vote in favor of the state government and the ruling party the RJD? One cannot have a definite answer for this, but certainly the findings of the survey (which will be discussed later) had suggested that people were not happy with the performance of the state government. Then what had contributed to the victory for the RJD and its alliance?

It was the alliance arithmetic, which seemed to have worked in favor of the RJD and its allies. There had been a significant change in the electoral alliance in Bihar between the 1999 Lok Sabha elections and the 2004 Lok Sabha elections. While during the 1999 Lok Sabha elections, Ram Vilas Paswan got elected as a JD(U) candidate, a few months after the formation of the government, he resigned from the government and formed his own party, the LJNSP. Just before the 2004 Lok Sabha elections, he had entered into an alliance with the RJD and contested 8 of the 40 Lok Sabha seats in Bihar. People generally believe that the success story of the RJD lies in the pre-poll alliance, which it formed before the Lok Sabha election of 2004.

The alliance with the LJNSP of Ram Vilas Paswan had brought some new set of voters into the RJD fold. Both the RJD and the LJNSP had managed to transfer a large number of their voters to the alliance. In turn, they mutually benefitted each other. While this alliance had benefitted both, it was equally important to note that more than the RJD it was the LJNSP that had benefitted more. If there were no alliance between these two parties, both the parties would have suffered electoral loss. Even the LJNSP leader Ram Vilas Paswan might have faced a very tough contest. The findings of the National Election Study 2004 (NES 2004) survey confirmed that voters of both the alliance partners managed to transfer their votes to each other's parties. During the survey, the voters were asked which party they would have voted for if there were no alliances between the political parties. Among those who identified themselves as RJD supporters, 89% confirmed voting for the RJD alliance, while among the LJNSP supporters, 88% confirmed voting for the RJD alliance. True, the alliance did contribute to the success of the Congress alliance in Bihar to a great extent.

The New Alliance

The new alliance brought in a new social coalition of voters form different social strata. The RJD had a strong presence among the Yadav and Muslim voters in Bihar. Various surveys conducted in the past had testified that the Yadavs and the Muslims had been voting for the RJD in large numbers during all the elections that have taken place during the past decade. Similarly, Ram Vilas Paswan had enjoyed support among the Dalits and especially among the voters belonging to Dusadh community. There was no official source about the population figures for people belonging to different castes but according to the NES survey in undivided Bihar, the Yadavs were nearly 12% of the population, while in divided Bihar, their proportion in the population has gone up to nearly 14%. Similarly, the Muslims who constituted 16.5% of the population were the deciding factor in a large number of constituencies. Although Dusadh were numerically not very large, still they were about 5% of the total population of the state. The three castes together were nearly one-third of the total population of Bihar. Such an unbeatable social formation certainly had an electoral strength capable of upsetting the calculations of any political opposition. This was what happened during the 2004 Lok Sabha election. The electoral success of the RJD–Congress alliance in Bihar during the 2004 Lok Sabha election was a reflection of this arithmetic which paid rich dividends at the hustings upsetting the applecart of the BJP–JD(U)-led alliance.

Lalu's Charisma Gave Additional Advantage to the RJD

Lalu Yadav was and remains one of the most charismatic personalities of Indian politics, and still remains a big factor in Bihar politics in 2014. The parties still align or oppose in the name of the Yadav strongman and the political formations that break or take place, somewhere or the other, Lalu Yadav is counted in. Journalists and experts had used the term Laluization of Bihar politics during the first 15 years of his reign when he himself ruled the state for the period and later through his wife.

The results of 2004 Lok Sabha elections had indicated that the Congress alliance stood way ahead of the NDA alliance in Bihar in terms of both the number of seats won and percentage of votes polled.

There were indications that the new electoral alliance did the magic for the ruling RJD, but there was something more which contributed to the success of the RJD and its alliance partners. The alliance arithmetic had contributed to the victory of the RJD–Congress alliance, but this did not capture the essence of the whole story. In fact, the results of 2004 Lok Sabha elections indicate that, besides the alliance, it had been the charisma of the RJD leader Lalu Yadav which also contributed to the landslide victory of the alliance. This did not mean that the people of Bihar were ambivalent on the issue of development or were obsessed with the personality of Lalu Yadav. On the issue of development, the Bihar government was too negatively evaluated in the media and the national discourse. There were other burning issues of social justice which dominated the hearts and minds of the Bihari voters.

Although Lalu Yadav did not carry the same image among voters belonging to all social communities (read upper castes), he still holds a somewhat positive image among the voters belonging to Dalit and backward communities even in 2014. The general belief was that no government can ensure food for the poor people, but it was Lalu who had at least provided dignity to the poor people and it was during his tenure that the poor developed the capacity to live with a sense of pride. This social empowerment of the poor and the backward had an overriding impact on all the ills associated with underdevelopment which plagued the state during the first 15 years of Lalu–Rabri regime.

The findings of the NES 2004 survey indicate that Lalu Yadav was and remains one of the most polarizing figures of Indian politics like the former Gujarat Chief Minister Narendra Modi. While large numbers of people, especially from the socially marginalized segments, consider him as the messiah of the poor, only few among the upper castes show similar faith in Lalu Yadav. In spite of his non-performance, a large number of people among the Dalits and the OBCs still consider him to be the sympathizer of the poor. Not surprisingly, a large number of the poor still believe that he was the one who would think of their well-being.

The backward castes constitute a large section of population in Bihar. In spite of numerical minority, the upper caste has had a firm control over political power in Bihar for a long time. When Lalu Yadav became the chief minister, those belonging to the OBC castes saw new hope for themselves. Even though nothing much had changed for the people belonging to the OBC castes, a large number among them still saw him as the leader who would get justice for the poor and the downtrodden.

This opinion was shared more among those belonging to Yadav caste, compared to people belonging to other OBC castes.

What added to the strength of the RJD was the absence of any formidable leader who could have put up a challenge to Lalu Yadav. Having been in power for so long, Lalu was no more considered a leader only of the RJD but had emerged as a strong OBC leader with mass following. It was true that not all OBC caste voters had accepted him as the leader of the backward communities, but he remained the tallest leader among them all. When Nitish Kumar parted ways with him, he was of no match but gradually emerged as a rallying alternative to the maverick Yadav. The leadership of the Congress still remained in the hands of the upper caste leaders who lacked any base among the masses. The BJP was in alliance with the JD(U) in the state, but the party was also plagued by the problem of mainly the upper caste leadership. Although the JD(U) (earlier Samata Party) has portrayed Nitish Kumar, a backward caste, as the leader of the party, different warring groups within the party never allowed this undisputed OBC leadership to emerge. On the other hand, Lalu Yadav had remained the undisputed leader of the RJD for more than 15 years without any significant challenge. No doubt that a majority of the people—especially among those belonging to the OBC castes—saw Lalu Yadav as the undisputed leader. No other leader had been able to challenge the leadership of Lalu Yadav. At least 36% of respondents agreed in a CSDS survey that there was no alternative to Lalu Yadav as so did at least 60% Yadavs, besides 38% of Muslims echoing similar sentiments. It was not that Lalu Yadav enjoyed popularity only among poor OBCs or Muslims but also across the class and caste spectrum he was recognized as a leader, though the opinion of the people and voting pattern for him and his party were split. In terms of providing justice, an overwhelming 63% Yadavs and 40% Muslims believed that it was the Yadav strongman who could provide justice to the poor and downtrodden, even as only 18% upper caste echoed similar sentiments. At least 40% rich and 38% poor believed that there was no alternative to Lalu Yadav.

Talking in terms of class opinion, a mere 33% agreed that only Lalu Yadav could provide justice to the poor and the backwards, while 46% disagreed. At least 68% of the rich disagreed that only Lalu Yadav could provide justice to the backwards and to the poor. It indicates that Lalu Yadav was always a polarizing figure, but on the one parameter about his messiah image, the majority of Dalits, Yadvs, and Muslims gave him a thumbs up. Seventy percent Yadavs, 66% Muslims, and over 50% Dalits agreed that he was the messiah of the poor.

On the question of him being a messiah of the poor, only very poor and poor agreed that he was the messiah, though a little higher percentage (49%) did not agree. So, most of the opinion about him was vertically split across caste and community even as Yadavs, Muslims, poor, and Dalits always showed some preference for him. Among other things, the NES survey also pointed out that by 2005 Lalu Yadav had lost most of the sheen surrounding his personality and the electoral debacle that the RJD suffered in February 2005 polls may be an indication of that. In the CSDS 2004 survey (see Figure 5.2), majority of the people believed that the Yadav strongman was no more a messiah of the poor, for he was corrupt, he perpetuated Yadav rule, and he encouraged criminals.

Big Question Mark on the Performance of State Government

While the victory of the RJD and its alliance in the 2000 assembly elections and 2004 general elections was an indicator of some kind of popular support of the people for the party, it would be too simplistic to conclude that everything was working well in the state. The overall performance of the state government was more or less satisfactory, but people had

Figure 5.2

Popularity graph of Lalu Yadav

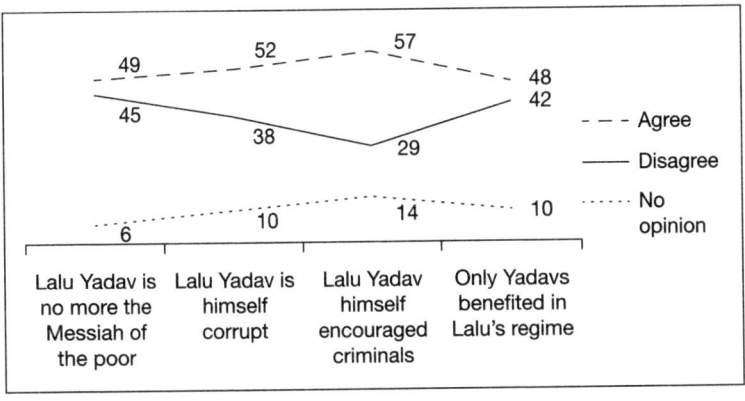

Sources: CSDS Data Unit; NES 2004.

Note: All figures are in percent.

shown a great deal of dissatisfaction on the various civic amenities. There seemed to be no improvement in civic amenities during the last four years. The majority of the people felt that the condition of hospitals and other medical facilities had deteriorated, while only 10% believed the contrary. A section of people always dubbed that the civic amenities, such as maintenance of roads and facilities in the hospitals, were better during the Congress regime of Jagannath Mishra in comparison to Lalu–Rabri years. People of the state said that Patna was better maintained as a state capital during the Congress regimes. Even the supply of electricity was considered better.

When the people of the state were asked regarding civic amenities such as medical facilities, supply of electricity, drinking water, condition of roads, law and order, and employment opportunities, people seemed to be the most dissatisfied with medical facilities, supply of electricity, and condition of the roads. While 55% of the people said that the condition of these things had deteriorated, 43% felt that there was deterioration in employment opportunities. People said that there had been improvement in the Hindu–Muslim brotherhood. Improvement was seen in this field by 44% people (see Figure 5.3).

What explains the victory of the RJD alliance was that the voters in Bihar may not be much concerned about economic development, rather they saw the regime as a symbol of emancipation from the upper caste-led

Figure 5.3

Performance of state government in providing civic amenities

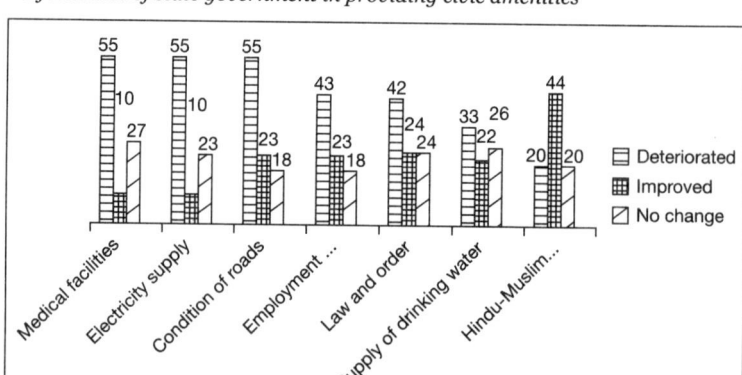

Sources: CSDS Data Unit; NES 2004.

Notes: All figures are in percent; rest no opinion.

Congress governments. With the increasing poverty and immense hard-ships faced by the people, one would have expected the people to be voting against the RJD alliance, but the findings of the survey said that this did not happen in Bihar during the 2004 Lok Sabha elections. During the survey, the voters were asked to express their opinion about the positive changes in their economic condition during the past five years. People's opinion seemed to be greatly divided on the issue of eco-nomic development. It was believed by 48% people that there had been no change in their economic conditions and it had remained stagnant. About a quarter believed that their economic condition had improved, while a similar said that their economic condition had deteriorated. The findings of the survey indicate that voting preferences of the people were hardly influenced by their general economic condition. The RJD voters were hardly concerned about their economic prosperity. Among those who believed that their economic condition had either worsened or that there had been no significant change during the last five years, a large number of people voted for the RJD alliance, while among those who felt that their economic condition had improved, majority voted for the BJP allies. Thus, a conclusion could be drawn that the social justice slogan virtually did not transform into economic emancipation, and that the upper caste groups who virtually never voted for Lalu Yadav contin-ued to enjoy prosperity during the regime.

What added to the success of the RJD alliance was that their support-ers voted for it irrespective of being unhappy about their present eco-nomic conditions, an indication that this issue hardly determined their voting choices. People did not express clearly what they had felt about their present economic condition. Nearly 58% of the people had men-tioned that they were somewhat unhappy with their present economic condition, only 18% were fully satisfied with their present economic condition, while 22% of them were fully dissatisfied. Surprisingly, among those who felt dissatisfied with their present economic condition, a majority voted for the RJD and its allies.

Findings in Table 5.5 and Figure 5.4 suggest that among those whose financial condition had deteriorated and were dissatisfied with their pres-ent financial conditions, a large number of people voted for the RJD alliance. It seemed that the RJD alliance drew large support from the economically poorer section of the society. While for the rich and the middle class people, development meant only economic gains, the poor in the state seemed to have either ignored the notion of development or interpreted it in their own way. But whatever may be the case, the

Table 5.5

Changes in economic condition during the past five years (2004 election)

Economic Condition	Voted for			Proportion in Sample
	Congress +	*BJP +*	*Other Parties*	
Worsened	47	29	24	25
Improved	36	51	13	25
No change	46	34	20	48

Sources: CSDS Data Unit; NES 2004.

Note: All figures are in percent.

Figure 5.4

Level of satisfaction with present economic condition

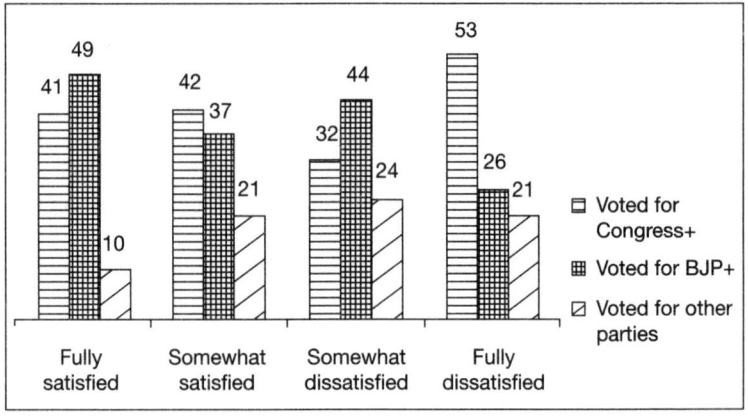

Sources: CSDS Data Unit; NES 2004.

Note: All figures are in percent.

findings of the survey indicate that economic development was hardly a concern among large numbers of voters in Bihar. Another way to look at it would be that for a large majority the Lalu Yadav regime was a symbol of pride and honor under which they lived for 15 years. Later on, this consciousness was taken ahead by Nitish Kumar from where Lalu Yadav left.

Respondents had also raised questions on the performance of the parliamentarians. The level of dissatisfaction with the performance of the MPs was generally high. Nearly one-third of the respondents were fully

Figure 5.5

Level of satisfaction with MPs of different political parties

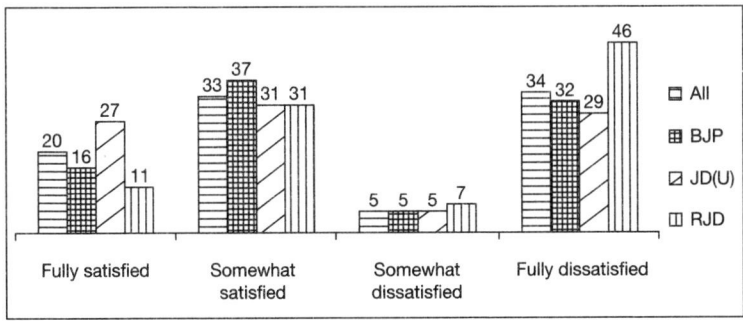

Sources: CSDS Data Unit; NES 2004.

Note: All figures are in percent.

dissatisfied with their members of parliament, while only 20% were fully satisfied. There was also variation in terms of MPs belonging to different political parties. The level of dissatisfaction of the people with the MPs belonging to the RJD was much higher compared to the level of dissatisfaction with the MPs of other political parties such as the BJP and the JD(U) (see Figure 5.5).

Hopes Still Alive

Although the RJD and its allies had registered a big victory, this was in no way any reflection on the performance of the general functioning of the state government. There had been deterioration in the services of a large number of civic amenities; naturally, people cannot feel happy about that. Large numbers of people thought that they had become much poorer during the preceding five years, and not surprisingly, a large number of people were dissatisfied with their present economic condition.

In spite of this, the people of Bihar seemed to be on high spirits and they were hoping for a better tomorrow. Nearly one-third of the people believed that their economic condition would improve in the coming years, while only 9% people thought that it would deteriorate. There were a large number of people who did not express their views on this issue.

Figure 5.6

General image of the country has improved

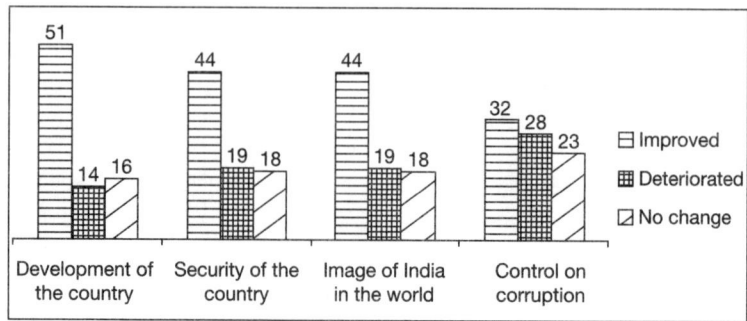

Sources: CSDS Data Unit; NES 2004.

Note: All figures are in percent.

The hope for a better tomorrow might have propelled a large number of the electorate to vote for the RJD-led alliance.

Figure 5.6 indicates that a majority of the people thought that there had been some development in the country and the security situation had improved. This was not surprising that there were large numbers of people who thought that the image of the country in the world also improved. People tended to believe that though there was corruption compared to the previous tenures, now a sound mechanism existed to control it. The findings of the survey also suggested that during the previous five years, there had been improvement in the Hindu–Muslim relationship in Bihar.

The results of the 2004 Lok Sabha elections in Bihar had suggested that while the new alliance made it possible for the RJD to register a thumping victory, it was also Lalu's charisma that added to the victory. It was true that there had been very little infrastructural development in the state, but the findings of the survey suggest that development was hardly an issue for a large number of voters in Bihar. Had development been a prime concern, a large number of voters who confirmed becoming much poorer during the last five years may not have still voted for the RJD and its allies. Some of them even did not see a bright future as far as their economic situation was concerned, still, among such people, a large number voted for the RJD and its allies. For a large chunk of Muslims it was security that came ahead of development because Lalu Yadav, though faced allegations of corruption and poor law and order, ensured zero-tolerance toward communal riots in which the victims mostly belonged to the minority community. It was virtually a "vote for security."

There were very few (only 10%) who believed that their economic condition would deteriorate in the coming years but even among them a large number of people voted in favor of the RJD. Nearly one-third of the people had expected that their economic condition might improve in the coming years but among them a majority had voted for the BJP and its allies, the JD(U) among others. Clearly among those who expected their economic condition to improve, few had faith in the ruling RJD and its allies. Thus, it could be concluded that the poor and downtrodden saw Lalu Yadav as a symbol of social justice and voted for him despite their economic condition not improving, while Muslims voted for the Yadav strongman for security, and his caste-men voted for their social and political emancipation.

Social Patterns of Voting

The results of the 2004 Lok Sabha elections indicate that the BJP–JD(U) combine had suffered a major setback, while the RJD-led alliance made gains. But in spite of a major defeat, the findings of the survey indicate that the BJP remained popular among the voters in the urban areas (45%) compared to the RJD alliance (44%). While the lead for the BJP alliance over the RJD alliance in the cities was very narrow, the RJD alliance remained very popular among the rural voters (45%) and the BJP (36%). What added to the advantage of the RJD was that while nearly 25% of the voters in Bihar lived in urban cluster, towns, and cities, a vast majority of voters lived in villages and sub-urban towns. Merely being popular among the urban voters was not sufficient for the BJP allies to set the stage for the victory and stall the march of the Lalu Yadav-led party.

What added to the success of the RJD alliance were the sharply polarized voters belonging to the Yadav and Muslims communities, who also were numerically the strongest. Muslims and Yadavs constitute over 30% of Bihar's population (see Table 5.6). The findings of the NES 2004 survey indicate that in spite of the poor performance of BJP and its alliance partner, the JD(U), the alliance had still not lost support among the upper caste voters in the state.

Table 5.6

Yadavs and Muslims sharply polarized in favor of the RJD alliance

Caste	Congress+	BJP+	Others	N
Upper caste	25	64	11	214
Yadav	77	16	7	126
Kurmi + Koeri	19	65	17	97
Other OBCs	39	36	25	226
Schedule castes	44	28	28	124
Muslim	79	9	12	150

Sources: CSDS Data Unit; NES 2004.

Note: All figures are in percent.

Due to the alliance with the Congress, the RJD did manage to get some upper caste votes but essentially the upper caste voters stood firmly behind the BJP–JD(U) alliance. The OBC voters seemed to be divided in their support for the two alliances. While a majority among the Yadavs voted for the RJD allies, one could see similar kind of support for the BJP–JD(U) alliance among voters of the other two dominant OBC caste voters—Kurmi and Koeri. Besides the three dominant OBC castes' voters, those belonging to the other OBC castes seemed to be more or less equally divided between the two alliances. One would have expected the voters belonging to the Dalit caste to have voted for the RJD alliance in large numbers, but they seemed to be somewhat divided yet largely tilted in favor of the RJD alliance.

The pattern of support base for the Congress' alliance seemed to continue in similar direction, if the voting patterns of those belonging to different economic classes are looked at. While the RJD–Congress alliance had remained the popular choice of voters belonging to all economic classes (very poor—48%, poor—42%, lower middle—43%, and middle—49%), the support for the BJP alliance was much higher among the rich voters, that is, 43% (very poor—31%, poor—40%, and lower middle—40%).

Similar voting patterns could be seen among voters belonging to different educational levels. Among the large number of non-literate voters, the Congress alliance (49%) remained the popular choice with the BJP at 29%. Among the educated voters, though, the support for the BJP alliance was a little higher (46%) than the support for the Congress alliance (45%).

There had been a very little variation in voting patterns among voters belonging to different age group; still, the survey had suggested that the young voters in Bihar voted more in favor of the RJD–Congress alliance (see Figure 5.7). The support for the Congress alliance was higher compared to the support for the BJP alliance among voters of all age groups. The highest percentage of voters for JD(U)–BJP alliance came from voters in the age group 36–55 years.

Bifurcation of Bihar and Birth of Jharkhand (2000)

The ruling Rashtriya Janata Dal declared that they would oppose the Bihar Reorganisation Bill, 1998. Party supremo Lalu Prasad Yadav's reaction to the demand for a separate state of Jharkhand was dramatic. "Over my dead body!" he said. The RJD legislature, true to this feeling, would oppose the Bill. They also launched "Bihar Bachao Andolan," an agitation to save Bihar, from September 15. Yadavs called on the people to lend support to this completely. (UNI, 1998)

The reduced seat count in Bihar assembly in the 2000 assembly polls made Lalu Yadav do a U-turn to secure Rabri Devi government's

Figure 5.7

Young voters more in favor of the Congress alliance

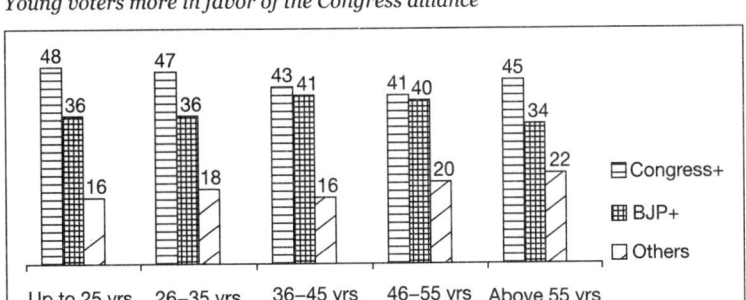

Sources: CSDS Data Unit; NES 2004.

Note: All figures are in percent.

political survival. The Congress had extended support to the Rabri Devi government in Bihar post 2000 assembly polls on the condition that the RJD would support the Bihar Reorganisation Bill for the creation of Jharkhand which the NDA government—led by Atal Bihari Vajpayee—had proposed for the creation of the state. At least 11 of the 23 Congress MLAs belonged to the Jharkhand region of Bihar. The bifurcation led to diminishing of the Congress and BJP's influence in Bihar as most of their MLAs came from Jharkhand. The division led to the RJD virtually touching the majority mark in the thus reduced Bihar assembly. The 324-member Bihar assembly was reduced to 243, and the RJD's strength increased from 38% to 47%. It also led to formation of the first BJP government in Bihar. Earlier, the RJD was 39 short of majority, but after the bifurcation of the state, the gap was reduced to 7. The Samata Party–JD(U) also grew in strength in Bihar, and the BJP virtually became a junior partner as a chunk of its MLAs also came from Jharkhand. It was 55 versus 67 (BJP) in the undivided Bihar house. Now the BJP was reduced to 35, prompting Nitish Kumar to set priorities and determine the political course of action for the NDA.

On April 25, 2000, the RJD members in both the houses of parliament voted along with the NDA, JMM, and other parties for the ratification of the bill. The Lok Sabha gave the nod on August 11, 2000 and the Rajya Sabha on August 25, 2000. Jharkhand officially came into existence on November 15, 2000.

Massive Economic Loss to Bihar

Bihar suffered massive loss after the creation of the new state. The entire mineral wealth, heavy industries, steel plant, and three-fourths of the forest wealth went to the new state, making Bihar a purely agrarian state with its total revenue reduced to one-third, as nearly 70% of the revenue used to come from coal royalties and other such remittances. Most of the top urban centers including Ranchi, Jamshedpur, Dhanbad, Bokaro, and Hazaribagh went to the new state. Bihar was reduced to an agrarian economy, and that also was in poor shape. Most of the major power plants—thermal and hydro—also went to the new state, throwing a fresh challenge for Bihar to survive and it sank deeper. The political parties had promised that bifurcation of the state would be entwined with a big financial package that never came.

Analysis of Political Impact of Bihar's Division

The support base of the RJD had increased in Bihar after the birth of Jharkhand. The performance of the RJD during the 2004 Lok Sabha elections, post division of the state, considerably improved. Of the 26 Lok Sabha seats which the party contested, it won in 22 and polled 30.7% votes. Its alliance partner, the LJNSP, managed to win four of the eight Lok Sabha seats which it contested and polled 8.2% votes. The Congress contesting the 2004 Lok Sabha in alliance with the RJD won three of the four seats it was allotted and polled 4.5% votes.

Comparison of RJD's Performance in Two Lok Sabha Polls—1998 (Undivided Bihar) and 2004 (Divided Bihar)

If the electoral performance of the RJD is compared between the two Lok Sabha polls—1998 (united Bihar) and 2004 (divided Bihar)—it would come out that the RJD was mostly concentrated in Bihar minus Jharkhand. The Jharkhand region of the state was never a forte for the Lalu Yadav-led party. Thus, once Jharkhand was created, it led to rise in strength of the RJD in Bihar with substantial increase in its vote share.

The RJD had polled 26.6% votes in the undivided Bihar, and its vote share in the 2004 election went up by nearly 5.3%. Similarly, during the 1999 Lok Sabha elections, while the RJD polled 28.3% votes in undivided Bihar, its votes went up by 5.6% in the present-day Bihar. The trend continued even during the 2000 assembly elections. While in the undivided Bihar the party had polled 28.2% votes, its vote share in the state had gone up to 32.7%, an increase of 4.5%. Thus, the 2004 Lok Sabha polls were the first elections after Bihar's bifurcation, and the division actually helped Lalu Yadav and his party-led alliance.

The question was: Whether the vote share of all the political parties increased in Bihar after the division of the state? All the important political parties in undivided Bihar had relatively strong presence in different regions of the state. While the RJD had the strongest presence in north Bihar, the Samata/JD(U) had strong support base in central Bihar, the BJP, the Congress, and the JMM had presence in the south Bihar region which is now Jharkhand. If the division of Bihar had resulted in increasing vote share for the RJD in present-day Bihar, it had weakened the electoral prospects of the main opposition party, the BJP. While during the 1998 Lok Sabha elections the BJP polled 24% votes in the undivided Bihar, its vote share went down to 17.5% in the present-day Bihar. Similarly, during the 1999 Lok Sabha elections, the vote share of the BJP went down from 23% in undivided Bihar to 16.9% in present-day Bihar (see Table 5.7). The trend had continued even during the 2000 assembly elections when the BJP's vote share in the present-day Bihar went down by nearly 3%. This had happened mainly because the BJP had not polled much vote in this region, which is the present-day Bihar, and its support base had remained localized only in the south Bihar region or Jharkhand region.

The BJP's alliance partner—the Samata/JD(U)—had benefitted marginally from the division of the state. The JD(U) had witnessed an increase in the vote share by 1.8% in 1998, 6.3% in 1999 Lok Sabha elections, and 1.2% in 2000 assembly elections. Similarly, the vote share for the Samata Party had increased by 4.8% during the 1998 Lok Sabha and only 1.9% during the 2000 assembly elections. Since the Congress also had the support base concentrated mainly in south Bihar region, the vote share of the party had also gone down in the present-day Bihar compared to its vote share in the undivided Bihar (see Table 5.7). So the division of Bihar had at once resulted in much stronger support for some political parties while resulting in a relatively weaker support base for the other parties. The question was, how could this happen?

The findings of the series of post-poll survey conducted by the CSDS had indicated different support bases of different political parties. Voters

Table 5.7

Vote share of different political parties: Present and undivided Bihar

Political Parties	Lok Sabha Elections 1998		Lok Sabha Elections 1999		Assembly Elections 2000	
	Old Bihar	New Bihar	Old Bihar	New Bihar	Old Bihar	New Bihar
RJD	26.58	31.88	28.29	33.92	28.17	32.70
BJP	24.03	17.49	23.01	16.92	14.53	11.59
Samata	15.74	20.54	—	—	8.08	10.04
JD(U)	8.72	10.53	20.07	26.39	6.45	7.64
Congress	7.27	4.69	8.81	4.77	11.14	8.75

Source: CSDS Data Unit.

Note: All figures are in percent.

belonging to different castes had been sharply polarized in favor of different political parties. While the Yadavs and the Muslims had remained polarized in favor of the RJD, the Samata/JD(U) was extremely popular among voters belonging to the OBCs, the Kurmis, and the Koeris (see Figure 5.8). The BJP had strong presence among the upper castes and the Adivasis. The Congress also had presence among the upper castes, the Adivasis, and the Dalit voters. The findings of the CSDS survey had indicated that between 65% and 75% of the Yadavs and the Muslims had voted for the RJD for all the elections held in the state during the last decade. In these elections, similar proportion among the Kurmis and the Koeris voters had voted for the Samata/JD(U), and about 60–70% among the upper castes had voted for the BJP. The BJP had replaced the Congress as the first choice of upper caste voters since the rise of Lalu Yadav in Bihar. The Dalit voters had showed their divided loyalty between the RJD, the BJP, and the Congress from time to time. The influence of Ram Vilas Paswan among the Dalit voters especially among the *Dusadhas* had an impact in changing their voting preferences from one party to the other. A majority of the Adivasis had been voting for the JMM in these elections.

The settlement pattern of people belonging to different castes had been somewhat different. While south Bihar (now Jharkhand) had the largest concentration of the Adivasis, the Yadavs and the Muslims were largely concentrated in the north Bihar region. The central region of the undivided Bihar, especially the districts of Nalanda, Gaya, Nawada, Barh, and Munger, had seen the concentration of large number of Kurmis and Koeris. Post division, the proportion of Yadavs surged in Bihar. As per the census, the proportion of the Muslims and the Dalits in Bihar had gone up from 14.8% and 14% in 1991 to 16.5% and 17.1%, respectively in 2001. Although there were no official figures for the proportion of the Yadavs, the estimates based on the surveys had suggested that their share in the population of Bihar had increased by about 4%. Against about 13% of the total population, now Yadavs constituted about 17% in present-day Bihar. The Muslims and the Yadavs combined constitute nearly 33.5% of the population of present-day Bihar. With these two sharply polarized in favor of the RJD and Lalu Yadav, the stake of the party-led alliance would always be boosted.

The findings of the NES 2004 had indicated that on development issues, the performance of the state had been rated negatively. The survey had indicated 54% voters mentioning deteriorating condition of roads, medical facilities, and electricity supply (see Table 5.8). On other

Figure 5.8

Sharp polarization of voters of different social communities for different political parties

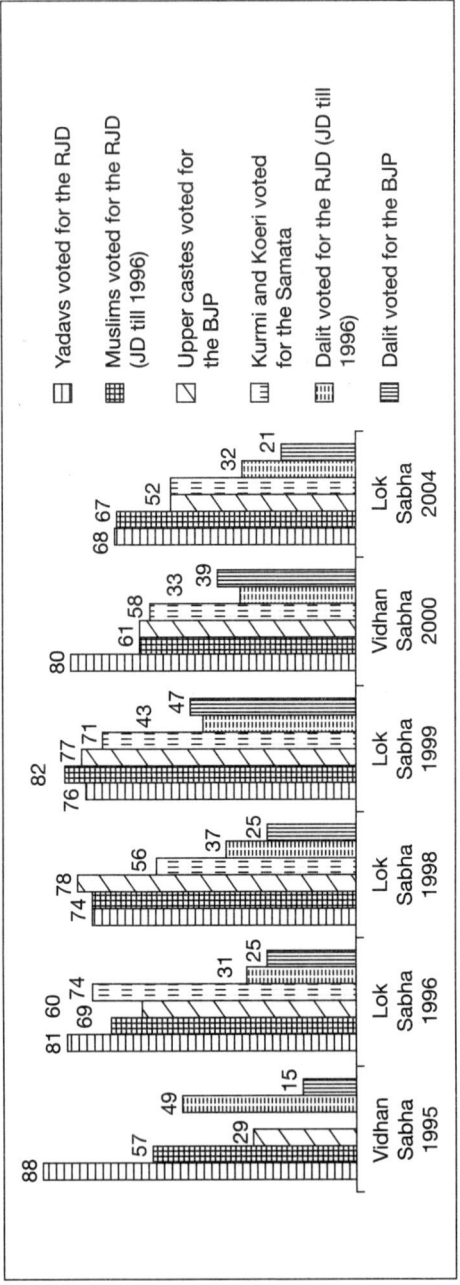

Yadavs voted for the RJD

Muslims voted for the RJD (JD till 1996)

Upper castes voted for the BJP

Kurmi and Koeri voted for the Samata

Dalit voted for the RJD (JD till 1996)

Dalit voted for the BJP

Source: Various surveys conducted by CSDS-lokniti.

Notes: All figures are in percent; the RJD contested the 1998, 1999, and 2004 Lok Sabha elections in alliance with the Congress; figures for Muslims, Yadavs, and Dalits voted for the RJD are for the RJD–Congress alliance; the BJP contested all the four Lok Sabha elections (1996, 1998, 1999, and 2004) for which the data had been presented and the assembly elections 2000, in alliance with the Samata/JD(U); figures for the BJP support among different social communities were for the alliance; similarly, figures for the Kurmi–Koeri support for the Samata were for the Samata + BJP alliance.

Table 5.8

Deterioration in condition of supply of civic amenities

Civic Issues	Deteriorated	Improved	Same as Before	No Opinion
Condition of roads	54	24	18	4
Medical facilities	54	11	28	7
Supply of electricity	54	11	24	11
Security of life and property	41	26	25	8
Supply of drinking water	33	23	27	17

Sources: CSDS Data Unit; NES 2004.

Note: All figures are in percent.

issues such as security of life and property (41%) and supply of drinking water (33%), the performance of the RJD government had again been rated negatively. Lalu Yadav apparently did not allow development of the state to become an issue. He carried his entire political career on rhetoric of secularism and social justice.

It was true that in spite of its non-performance, the RJD had managed to win all the three assembly elections in the state held in the years 1990, 1995, and 2000. People often believe that it was the *charisma* of Lalu Yadav who was considered the *messiah* of the poor which had won elections for the RJD. This was somewhat true since people often believed that though Lalu Yadav had not carried out development, he had actually given izzat (prestige) especially to the poor and the downtrodden that formed the support base for the RJD.

By 2004, Lalu Yadav was losing sheen from his personality because the poor were at the receiving end of negligence in governance and now question marks were being raised about the leader being a messiah of the poor and downtrodden.

The findings of the NES 2004 survey had suggested that Lalu Yadav was no more considered a messiah for poor. Nearly 49% people did not consider him as the messiah of the poor, instead 57% blamed him for encouraging criminals in politics. A large number of people also believed that it was only the Yadavs who had benefitted during the 15 years of the RJD rule and no one else. In the survey, the people were also asked to express their opinion about different leaders of the state. Despite Lalu Yadav being rated negatively by a majority of people, he remained the most popular leader amongst his generation during that phase. Nearly 33% had rated him to be a bad leader, while another 23% had considered him to be so-so. On the contrary, only 21% people rated him to be a very good leader. Lalu Yadav, despite being rated negatively, remained the most famous leader of his generation. BJP leaders such as Ravi Shankar Prasad, Rajiv Pratap Rudi, C.P. Thakur, and Shahnawaz Hussain were neither well-known among electorates nor were they popular, though more or less their image were not negative. Lalu Yadav's contemporaries such as Nitish Kumar, Ram Vilas Paswan, and Sushil Kumar Modi carried much better image than the Yadav strongman but were nowhere near his stature of being a mass leader. The RJD, thus, relied on the personal charisma and popularity of Lalu Yadav, and if the star falls, the entire party would sink with him.

Large numbers of people—primarily Yadavs and Muslims—had believed that there was no alternative to Lalu Yadav in Bihar.

Similarly, large numbers of people also were of the firm belief that in Bihar only Lalu Yadav could give justice to the poor and to those belonging to the backward castes. Again, this opinion was shared more among the Yadavs and the Muslims compared to voters of other communities. The poor also tend to show greater faith in Lalu Yadav, compared to the people belonging to other classes.

It was true that majority of people no more saw Lalu Yadav as the messiah of the poor during 2004 polls, but this positive opinion was still popular for nearly 45% voters. Among Yadavs, nearly 70% had considered him as the messiah of the poor, and among the Muslims nearly 66% shared a similar opinion. The majority of the Dalits and large numbers among those who belonged to the very poor economic class also considered Lalu Yadav as the messiah of the poor. But opinions had changed when it came to the upper castes as only 25% had favored the leader and described him as a messiah of poor, while 71% rejected the idea.

Despite Lalu Yadav losing his iconic image among the majority of people, he still commanded the same respect among the majority of Yadavs, Muslims, Dalits, and the poor. The findings of the CSDS surveys had indicated that these were the social communities that had voted for the RJD in large numbers during most of the elections held in the state post 1990.

The impressive victory of RJD–Congress–LJNSP alliance in 2004 general election could be assigned to the popularity of Lalu Yadav and Ram Vilas Paswan among the Yadav, Muslim, poor, and Dalit voters of Bihar, whose consolidation in the favor of the alliance led to resounding victory. Had these three parties contested elections separately, results in the state might have gone in favor of the NDA. The findings of the survey had indicated that the alliance partners did manage to transfer sizeable section of votes to their alliance partners. Among those who had mentioned voting for the Congress in case of party contesting elections separately, 66% had voted for the alliance, among the RJD voters, 89% voted for the alliance, and among the LJNSP voters, 84% voted for the alliance. This indicates that the RJD and the LJNSP had managed to transfer the votes for the alliance much more effectively compared to the Congress. This transfer of votes by different political parties for the alliance did contribute to the success of the tripartite alliance.

2005 Assembly Elections Analyses: End of Lalu's 15-year Rule

Even as the political processes that had begun in 1990 offered a window for studying political reconfiguration marked by the end of hegemonic politics in Bihar, there did not appear any serious studies capturing the dynamics underlying this long-awaited political change. Nor did there appear any scholarly work explaining how far the political change or political reconfiguration beginning in 1990 kept its promises; its impact on corresponding changes in other aspects of life, and why even the newly reconfigured politics was giving way to yet another political reconfiguration. However, these issues were occasionally debated in electronic and print media. There were many explanations, some using empirical evidence and others simply based on impression or personal acquaintance with the state affairs. However, broadly two explanations had appeared to be more important than others. One hypothesis was that Lalu Yadav, the leading light of political upsurge that took place in 1990, could fruitfully mobilize hitherto neglected, marginalized, and not-so-marginalized communities. The politics of symbolism combined with Lalu's rhetoric skill gave these masses a sense of pride and dignity, though in reality they remained on the same social and economic terrain where they were. But politics of symbolism has its own limitations and could not last long. Along with dignity (izzat), people wanted *roti* (bread) and *dhoti* (cloth) too. Deteriorating law and order, threadbare economic and infrastructure conditions over a decade, and other issues of governance weaned away the voters from the RJD. As a result, the so-called caste–community combination, particularly the MYD (Muslim,

Yadav, and Dalit) who voted for the RJD, weakened in the assembly election of 2000 and finally disintegrated in the assembly election held in 2005. Thus, the issues of governance and development rather than politics of symbolism were the crucial factors that led to the fall of RJD's 15-year rule.

The other explanation was that the caste–community factor had continued to play a crucial role in the voting and expression of political preferences. The RJD was voted out of power not because of pre-eminence of concerns for development but because of shift in caste alliances. Yadavs and Muslims still overwhelmingly voted for the RJD, and the upper castes for the NDA. The 2005 elections were no different from previous elections in the 1990s, except that Ram Vilas Paswan, the most popular Dalit leader, was no longer on Lalu's side but fighting against him. He took away a large section of Dalits with him. The RJD failed to strike a compromise and to form a strategic alliance with Paswan that cost the RJD the loss of power. Had the RJD and LJNSP come together, an RJD-led government might have been in place and hence yet another extension of RJD rule in the state.

Amidst the hope and despair, confidence and consternation in the rival camps, came the assembly election in the month of February 2005. A crucial political event between May 2004 and February 2005 was the tussle between Lalu Yadav and Ram Vilas Paswan over the Railway Ministry at the center. This, along with a general personality clash on who was the popular leader of Dalits and other marginalized sections in Bihar led to the drift in the popular alliance of the 2004 Lok Sabha election. Ram Vilas Paswan had decided to go alone in the electoral battlefield. This created a complicated situation both for the political parties and the voters, for Paswan was banking on the same voters who constituted the support base of the RJD and to some extent of the JD(U).

As expected, the poll results created a complicated situation as the verdict was even further splintered compared to that in 2000. The seat tally of the RJD came down to 75, from 115 in 2000. On the other hand, while the BJP increased only 2 seats compared to what it had won in 2000 (35), the JD(U) made a spectacular success—a gain of 37 seats by improving its seat tally from 18 in 2000 to 55 in February 2005. However, even putting together their seats, both the JD(U) and BJP were far from the majority mark. The RJD and Congress combine too was unable to form the government, for the two parties together had only 85 seats. The key to power, however, was in the hands of Paswan, even though his party had won only 29 seats.

Thus, the undisputed gainer from this election was Ram Vilas Paswan and his party, the LJNSP, which had succeeded in creating a niche in the state's electoral space by pushing the party above the threshold of viability. The Paswan factor made a deeper impact on the electoral outcomes as his LJNSP had played spoiler for all its former allies and caused a huge loss to the RJD. Without the support of the LJNSP, no party or alliance could have proved a majority on the floor of the house. Although the election results had put the major actors in the dock, the situation was even more difficult for Ram Vilas Paswan. If he wanted to see a popular government in place, he had to join either the NDA or the RJD-led alliance. The dilemma of Ram Vilas Paswan emanated much more from his personal relationship with the chieftains of the two grand coalitions and his self-interest, rather than his ideological stand for which he was regarded by people. While on the one hand, he had to settle personal scores with Lalu Yadav, he had embittered his relationship with the NDA before the 2004 Lok Sabha election. Further, he was a cabinet minister in the UPA government at the center. Being part of the government of the rival coalition at the center, he could not have supported the NDA in the state to form the government at the same time. However, he argued that he would not support the RJD to form the government because the party had led the state to darkness and people wanted to get rid of it. It was, therefore, his duty not to alter people's verdict. With regard to support to the NDA, the argument invoked was: since the NDA-led government was a mute spectator of Gujarat massacre and for which he had deserted the NDA, it would be a joke and go against his principled political stand if he supported the NDA.

Due to the fact that no party/coalition was able to prove majority in the assembly, President's rule was imposed. Even during the President's rule, no compromise between the RJD and LJNSP became feasible, nor could the NDA manage the requisite number of MLAs to stake claim to form a popular government. It implied that only fresh election, due in October, could solve the crisis. It certainly did when the election results were out. Although political equations remained intact, the results of October 2005 assembly elections were decisive and did give a clear mandate to the JD(U)–BJP coalition. With this, the 15-year rule of the RJD finally came to an end. Out of the 243 seats, the JD(U) and BJP bagged 88 and 55 seats, respectively, while the RJD with 54 seats was placed third. The LJNSP was punished and its seat tally reduced to 10, from 29 in the February election. In short, the political landscape in the state underwent remarkable modifications.

Let us now examine the popular explanations for the RJD's ouster in the October 2005 assembly elections. At the outset of this section, two hypotheses seeking to explain regime change in Bihar after 15 years were discussed. The first hypothesis was that in the 2005 elections, development and related issues of governance such as law and order were the major concern for the voter and as a consequence, caste–community alliance did not work for the RJD. The ultimate result was the dislodgement of the RJD from power. Was development an issue in this election? Did the caste–community alliance disintegrate?

It is evident from Table 5.9 that, overall, the people now had negative opinions on issues of development. Only a few were of the opinion that security of common people, condition of roads, and supply of electricity had improved during Lalu–Rabri regime. Majority of the voters across the board felt that the situation had worsened.

However, it was significant to note that the opinion of people on the issue of dignity (izzat) of the poor was not as polarized as on other issues

Table 5.9

Voters' opinion on different issues: Assembly election, 2005 (February)

	Those saying...		
Issues	*Worsened*	*Did not change*	*Improved*
a. Security of common people			
All	45	28	20
Rural	45	27	20
Urban	43	36	21
b. Condition of roads			
All	63	20	11
Rural	64	18	11
Urban	56	29	14
c. Supply of electricity			
All	63	22	7
Rural	62	23	7
Urban	69	22	7

Source: Bihar Election Studies, post-poll, 2005 (February), CSDS, Delhi.

Notes: Figures indicate percentages of the response to respective question; row figures do not add up to 100 because "no opinion" has not been reported.

Question wording: Now I will read out a few issues. For each one, tell me whether it has improved, worsened, or remained the same as before under JD/RJD government during the last 15 years?

Table 5.10

Voters' opinion on different issues: Assembly election, 2005 (February)

Issues/social groups	Those saying…		
	Declined	*Did not change*	*Improved*
a. Dignity of poor			
All	25	32	37
Very poor	25	38	37
Poor	24	33	39
Middle	25	34	37
Rich	44	28	26
b. Strength of backward			
All	22	24	46
Yadavs	7	24	60
Koeri–Kurmis	27	23	44
Other OBCs	18	27	46
Dalits	19	32	40
Muslims	26	22	46
Upper castes	32	17	46

Source: Bihar Election Studies, Post-poll, 2005 (February), CSDS, Delhi.

Notes: Figures are percentages of the response to respective question; row figures do not add up to 100 because "no opinion" has not been reported.

Question wording: Now I will read out a few issues. For each one, tell me whether it has improved, worsened, or remained the same as before under JD/RJD government during last 15 years?

such as condition of roads and security of common people. The proportion of poor people themselves who held that dignity of the poor worsened was significantly lesser than those who thought otherwise (see Table 5.10).[2] What was even more significant to note was that though people discounted RJD regime on developmental fronts, most of them had accepted that the strength (taaqat) of backward castes had increased. Not surprisingly, Yadavs were more likely to feel the strength than others.

---

[2] A question may be raised about interpreting the response "did not change." It refers to a situation of status quo with reference to what existed before regardless of what it was (good or bad). In a sense, "did not change" is a reference point for the assessment of a prevailing situation compared to past.

How these issues mediated with propensity of voters along with their caste and other identities to accept/reject the RJD as their political choice is difficult to measure directly. A direct question was asked: What was the main consideration while voting for a candidate or a party as well? Again, it appears that a majority of voters across caste–communities were driven by issues of development when they did cast their vote (see Table 5.11). Taking the two tables (Tables 5.9 and 5.11) together, following observations could be made. First, a good majority of voters poorly rated RJD's rule on issues of security and safety, and development. Second, development was the most powerful driving force for majority of voters in terms of selection of party to vote for in the assembly elections held in the month of February 2005. The logical corollary is that development was an important factor that had caused the downfall of the RJD government in that election.

If development was really an issue that mobilized people to vote against the RJD, it can be surmised then that caste–community coalition that used to vote for the RJD either must have fallen apart and charted out an independent course or even if the bond of coalition was there, it was not as compact as it used to be earlier. The results of logistic regression presented in Table 5.11 enable us to examine the proposition at hand.

Table 5.11

Issues that influenced the voters for selection of party

Social Groups	Issues			
	Development of State	*Employment*	*Good Candidate*	*Dignity of Caste–Community*
All	58	19	11	5
Upper castes	66	13	12	4
Yadavs	55	16	14	6
Koeri–Kurmis	56	21	10	6
OBCs	58	16	13	5
Dalits	62	22	4	6
Muslims	52	24	10	3

Source: Bihar Election Studies, 2005 (February), CSDS, Delhi.

Notes: Figures are percentages of those who responded to the respective question; row figures do not add up to 100 because other considerations have not been responded.

Question wording: Out of the issues mentioned to you, which was the most important for you while casting your vote?

It can be seen that predictor variables such as gender and location of voters in terms of rural/urban do not appear to be statistically significant as far as their propensity to vote for the RJD is concerned. However, caste variables demonstrate stronger association.

In the assembly elections held in 2000, there was a further decline by one percentage point in the vote share of the RJD. The pattern of support to the RJD remained more or less same as in general elections to Lok Sabha held in 1996 and 1999, except that it lost significant portion of Muslim votes. However, the RJD improved its electoral performance in terms of both vote share and seats in the general elections to Lok Sabha held in 2004. The RJD won back Muslims and Dalits as well as illiterate masses. It can be explained, though tentatively, by its striking an alliance with the Congress and LJNSP of Ram Vilas Paswan, and the Gujarat communal riots in 2002, that the RJD was able to gain in strength. While the alliance with LJNSP helped the RJD to get Dalit votes, Gujarat communal riots and its aftermath might have forced the Muslims to vote for the RJD as Lalu Yadav always maintained the anti-Modi and anti-BJP rhetoric during his political communication with Muslim electorates.

Nevertheless, the electoral conditions had changed in less than a year. The vote share of the RJD again had declined in the assembly elections that were held within months in February 2005 so much so that it lost the electoral edge to remain in power. It lost support among all sections of society but more spectacularly in its own core constituency. The Yadavs still supported the RJD overwhelmingly, but it lost significantly among Muslims, Dalits, and poor sections as a whole. At the slight risk of repetition, it must be noted here that the coalition crystallized in 2004 but fell apart in 2005. Ram Vilas Paswan had fallen out with Lalu Yadav reportedly over ministerial birth at the center and he went to the polls on his own. It cost the RJD Dalit and Muslim votes. However, there were growing dissatisfactions among Muslims in general. While during the RJD regime, Bihar was free from communal riots, it was felt that nothing substantial was done to improve socioeconomic conditions of the community. Added to this, Nitish Kumar was able to make a dent into pasmanda (backward) Muslims by taking along with him pasmanda Muslim leaders such as Ali Anwar, Manazir Hasan and Aijazul Haq. The RJD further lost its traditional constituency in the assembly election held after six months, that is, in the month of October 2005.

In the assembly elections held in February 2005, Yadavs stood solidly behind the RJD regardless of their education, residence, and class location and were more likely to have voted for the RJD than for other parties. However, Muslims and Dalits did no longer constitute the core support base of the RJD as they used to. They were likely to vote for the RJD with more or less same propensity as other castes (the referent category) did, when controlling for other variables. Hence, the RJD lost its formidable Muslim–Yadav alliance. Why the Yadavs still voted for the RJD when the electoral tide was against Lalu Yadav is understandable. Lalu Yadav was still a symbol of power for Yadavs, and it was natural in a situation where caste identity was linked with access to scarce resource. Also, as political observers commented, there was a phenomenon of "Yadavization" whereby Lalu Yadav delivered to the interests of his fellow castes by giving important administrative posts and contracts (Das, 1997; Hauser, 1997). But the others had no choice other than sulking or going against him. This could be one of the reasons why Muslims and Dalits drifted away from the RJD. In short, the caste–community combination that kept the RJD in power for 15 long years did not work in the assembly election held in February 2005.

The Yadavs as a whole or some sections among them might still be willing to invest in symbolism, but how did a large majority of voters see this election? What might have loosened the social coalition (Muslim–Yadav) as it appeared to be the case in preceding section? Was development an issue that drove a large majority of RJD supporters, leave alone others?

Development of the state, including employment, was the most preferred consideration for casting their votes. In order to examine how the electorate voted for development was an important issue to cast their vote, we clubbed the preferred considerations of voting such as the issues of corruption, employment, and development of state together and entered the same in the regression. When controlling for all other variables, it appears that compared to those for whom dignity of caste–community was the most important consideration, voters for whom development was an issue were much less likely to vote for the RJD and more likely to vote for the NDA. The impact of this issue was further crystallized in the election held six months later and finally led to the exit of the RJD from power. Thus, it can be reasonably argued that the issues of development mattered in the election and many of the core supporters of the RJD would have drifted apart.

Now, let us examine what contributed to the rise of the NDA. In a sense, what works against a position might be favoring the opposition straightaway. In other words, what acted against RJD's electoral prospect must have favored the NDA, the largest opposition political formation.

But in competitive electoral politics where there were more than one opposition party, it was possible that the dividends of anti-incumbency waves may get divided among several actors and also may not harm the incumbent party in terms of seat tally as it would seem to appear.

Broadly speaking, the NDA had kept its core constituency (i.e., forward castes, Koeri–Kurmi, and highly educated section) intact in the assembly elections held in 2005. Those concerned about governance and development of state were more likely to have voted for the NDA when all other variables are controlled for. This relationship emerged stronger in the October 2005 election and it added to relative advantage of the NDA other than split in MY alliance of the RJD. In sum, it can be stated that the defeat of the RJD was due to the combined effects of split of MY alliance and development of state emerging as major issue rather than effect of either alone. Had development been the driving factor, large sections of those who drifted from the RJD (namely Muslims and Dalits) would have voted for the JD(U), but this did not seem to be the case.

Now let us take up the "alliance hypothesis." There was hardly any doubt that the breakup of the Lok Sabha alliance had damaged the prospects of both the RJD and the Congress. The RJD allies (UPA) in the Lok Sabha elections had polled 44.3% of votes. In the 2005 assembly elections, the combined vote share of all these parties that now fought the elections separately was about the same at 43.7%. In simple arithmetic terms, had the UPA contested the February 2005 assembly elections while maintaining the alliance of 2004 Lok Sabha elections, the alliance could have been in majority in the 243-member Bihar state assembly. Even an alliance between the RJD and the Congress would have brought some dividends and the combine could have won about 102 seats. In the 31 seats won by the NDA, the Congress and the LJNSP emerged as the spoiler and directly harmed the RJD, as their vote share in these seats was larger than the difference between the NDA and the RJD's votes. Although the splitting of the UPA votes caused some harm to the RJD, it would not be correct to say that this election verdict was the reflection of the making or unmaking of alliances. If Ram Vilas Paswan's LJNSP secured 12% votes and won 29 seats, it probably could be because he had fought against the RJD and provided an alternative window to a large section of voters who would not like either the RJD or NDA. In other words, even if Paswan were with the RJD, it could have done marginally better in the polls, for part of Paswan's votes might have gone to parties other than the RJD.

The UPA Split

The Congress–LJNSP–RJD had fought the 2004 Lok Sabha alliance winning 29 out of 40 Lok Sabha seats. But in the assembly elections, the alliance split, with the three parties fighting the polls separately and thus directly handing out advantage to the BJP and JD(U). But the LJNSP did not only harm the RJD and Congress but also the JD(U) and BJP because it did cut into their traditional vote banks too. If the figures are to be believed, the LJNSP which secured 12.6% of votes in February 2005 assembly elections that it fought alone, had more share of upper caste and Kurmi–Koeri vote than the traditional Yadav and Muslim vote of the RJD. Among all the voters of LJNSP, 12% were upper caste, 22% Kurmi–Koeri, 16% other OBCs, only 3% Yadavs, and 9% Muslims (see Figure 5.9). But on the other side, those who voted for the LJNSP were more Congress and RJD supporters than JD(U) and BJP supporters. Of the voters who voted for LJNSP, 17% were traditional Congress voters, 21% from the RJD, 12% from the BJP, and 10% from the JD(U). So, the LJNSP did impact the NDA considerably along with the RJD and Congress.

Figure 5.9

LJNSP vote by caste–community, 2004–2005

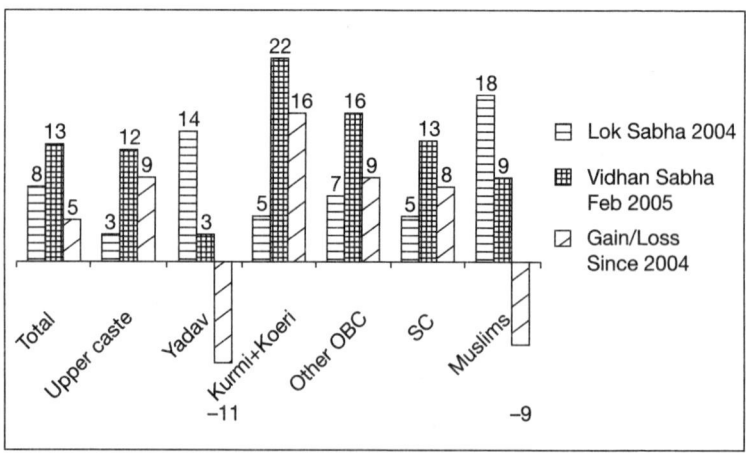

Sources: CSDS Data Unit; National Election Study 2004—Sample size, 1,191; Bihar Assembly Election Study 2005—Sample size, 887.

Note: All figures are in percent.

Analysis of February 2005 Assembly Elections and the Effect of Turnout

First, if a comparison is made on the turnout during the February 2005 assembly elections in Bihar with the 2000 assembly elections, it would be found that the turnout dropped by as much as 18 percentage points, from 64.9% during the 2000 assembly elections to only 46.5% during the February 2005 polls. Not only that, in the three-phased elections, the turnout kept dropping from one round to another. In the first phase, the turnout went down by 14.5%, in the second phase by 18.4%, and in the third phase by 21.2%. The decline in the turnout also links to the electoral outcome. Compared to the 2000 assembly elections, the vote share of the RJD went down in each phase of elections from 6.6% in first phase to 9.8% in second phase and finally 10.5% in the third phase. There was some evidence to link this decline to the electoral outcome. The three regions of the state—Magadh, Mithila, and Tirhut—that witnessed more than 20 points drop in turnout levels were also the regions where the RJD suffered its heaviest electoral debacle and where the BJP–JD(U) alliance actually improved its tally. The other two regions on the eastern and the western borders—East and Bhojpur respectively—saw a much lower drop in turnout. In both these regions, the RJD did not suffer much loss. The analysis of voter's turnout, both regions-wise as well as phase-wise, had suggested that the drop in the turnout affected the RJD more than any other party.

There seemed to be some evidence to suggest that communities that had been more enthusiastic to vote for the RJD experienced a steep fall in turnout than the rest. The survey had indicated that compared to the 2000 assembly elections, the turnout among the Dalits increased even as it dropped significantly among the Muslims. During the 2000 assembly elections, the turnout among Dalits was 6.5% points lower than the state average and among Muslims it was 3.5% points above the average turnout. This pattern was reversed in February 2005 election, which had witnessed 5.3% points above average turnout among the Dalits and 5% points below average turnout among the Muslims. Also, there was evidence that the traditional BJP–JD(U) voters came out to vote in greater numbers compared to the traditional supporters of the Congress or the RJD.

The story will become clearer when the turnout during the February 2005 assembly elections is compared with that of the 2004 Lok Sabha elections. Besides other factors, what explained the defeat of the RJD during the February polls, just after its impressive victory during the 2004 Lok Sabha election, was also the fall in the voter's turnout by 11.6% compared to the 2004 Lok Sabha elections. The findings of the CSDS suggest that the communities who had been more enthusiastic to vote for the RJD experienced a steeper fall in turnout than the rest.

When we look at the turnout patterns among voters of different communities, we see that compared to the 2004 Lok Sabha elections the turnout had increased only among the Dalits by about 3% point, while it dropped among voters of all other communities. The drop in voter's turnout was most significant among Yadavs and the Muslims, the traditional voters of the RJD by about 27%. Findings of the surveys indicate that voters of these two communities had been voting for the RJD in large numbers in various elections held during the last decade. Since large numbers among them did not come out to vote during the February elections, it affected the electoral prospects of the RJD.

It could be concluded that there was a fall in voting percentage across castes and communities between the Lok Sabha polls of 2004 and assembly elections of February 2005. The good performance of the RJD alliance in the 2004 Lok Sabha also stemmed from the fact that Muslims and Yadavs had voted in large numbers, while in 2005 polls their voting percentage had fallen down. Yadav voting percentage fell from 73% to 46%, Muslim voting percentage fell from 62% to 35%, while Kurmi–Koeris and upper castes voted in large numbers. The voting percentage for Yadavs and Muslims fell by 27%. Not only that, but the poor and very poor who too were considered the voters of the RJD also seem to have lost interest in the assembly polls as their voting percentage too saw sharp decline. The middle-income group people who are considered voters of the BJP saw their voting percentage rise by 4%. The other reasons may be that the BJP was more a party of towns and cities while the strength of the RJD was in rural areas which saw sharp decline in voting percentage. The rural areas experienced a fall in voting share by 12%, while in the urban areas it fell by 7% only. The political participation of men in the assembly polls of 2005 saw lower decline than women. Men are in general considered more supportive of the BJP-led alliance. On the other hand, another reason for the defeat of the RJD and Congress in the 2005 assembly polls was that there was sharp decline in their coming to booths to vote. At least a 26% fall was recorded in comparison of Lok Sabha polls of 2004 in case of Congress supporters, while in the case of RJD supporters there was decline of 22% (see Table 5.12). On the other

Table 5.12

Fall in turnout by traditional loyalty, 2004–2005

Traditional Supporter of...	Voted Lok Sabha 2004	Voted in Vidhan Sabha 2005	Fall in Turnout 2004–2005
All	58	46	−12
Congress supporter	72	46	−26
RJD supporter	66	44	−22
BJP supporter	64	57	−7
JD(U) supporter	52	60	+8
Not a supporter of any party	54	55	+1

Sources: CSDS Data Unit; National Election Study 2004—Sample size, 1,191; Bihar Assembly Election Study 2005—Sample size, 887.

Note: All figures are in percent.

hand, at least 8% more JD(U) supporters came out to vote in the assembly polls. So, there was a remarkable fall in the political participation of Congress and RJD supporter, while there was an increase in electoral participation by the JD(U) supporters.

Although the turnout also dropped among upper caste voters, it was not significant. Figures in Table 5.13 indicate that the drop in turnout among voters belonging to the upper caste was only 2%. Similarly, among the Kurmi–Koeri combine, the drop in the turnout was only 4%. The lower turnout among them hardly affected the prospects of the BJP– JD(U). The voters of these communities had been voting for the NDA in Bihar in large numbers during the last few elections. The drop was somewhat significant among the voters of OBCs (11%). Since they had been a divided lot in most of the elections, it would have affected both the RJD and the NDA in a more or less similar manner. In a nutshell, it seemed that the drop in turnout had adversely affected the RJD more than any other party during the February 2005 assembly elections. The evidences suggest that large numbers among the traditional RJD voters did not come out to vote during the polls, which proved too expensive for the RJD. A slight increase in the voter's turnout among the traditional voters of the RJD may have helped the UPA in consolidating its position.

Similarly, if an analysis of the voter's turnout among voters of different economic class was done, it would reflect that the decline in voter's turnout was more among those who were economically very poor or

Table 5.13

Vote by caste–community for all major parties: Assembly election, 2005

	RJD+	Congress	LJNSP	BJP + JD(U)	Others
All	25.8	5.0	12.6	25.4	31.1
Upper caste	7.0	5.0	12.0	49.0	28.0
Yadav	81.0	4.0	3.0	1.0	11.0
Kurmi + Koeri	9.0	Negligible	22.0	46.0	23.0
Other OBCs	25.0	3.0	16.0	24.0	32.0
SCs	23.0	5.0	13.0	19.0	40.0
Muslims	35.0	14.0	9.0	3.0	40.0

Sources: CSDS Data Unit; Bihar Assembly Election Study 2005—Sample size, 887.

Note: All figures are in percent; RJD+ (RJD, CPM, MCC).

poor. The drop in turnout among voters of these two communities was 13% and 19% respectively. Findings of the past surveys had suggested that they had been the vote bank for the RJD, voting for the Lalu Yadav-led party in large numbers during the last decade. Not surprisingly, their lower participation in February 2005 assembly elections had affected the RJD more than any other political party.

The Real Contest

While all these had indicated possible scenarios of electoral outcomes in different perspectives, the electoral history also suggests that in spite of the defeat in February 2005 assembly elections, the RJD still remained one of the strongest forces in Bihar politics. The combined UPA had begun the new electoral race with some advantage over the NDA. An analysis of the strongholds of different alliance suggests that the UPA was very strong in 57 assembly seats; similarly, the NDA had a very strong presence in another 52 assembly seats. These were the seats which had been won by the respective alliances during the last two assembly elections. Besides these constituencies, there were another 51 assembly constituencies which had witnessed straight contest between the UPA and the NDA, but there was always a seesaw battle. The rest of the 83 assembly constituencies had witnessed a multi-cornered contest with different parties winning different seats in different elections.

Of these 83 constituencies, the LJNSP had won 29, independents had won in 17, Samajwadi Party had registered victory in 4, CPML had won in 7, while the BSP was successful in 2 seats. In terms of victory, the 2 alliances—the UPA and the NDA—were neck-to-neck, winning 11 and 10 seats respectively. While in about 160 assembly constituencies, the NDA and the UPA were in keen contest, what made UPA's position stronger was its slightly stronger presence in the remaining 83 assembly constituencies compared to the NDA in terms of vote share of the two alliances. The combined vote of the NDA in these 83 constituencies was slightly less than 15%, but the UPA had about 25% votes in their fold.

Analysis of Broader Trend: 1996–2005

An analysis of the broader trend of politics between 1996 Lok Sabha polls to two assembly elections in 2005 indicates that RJD-led alliance and the JD(U)–BJP alliance were locked in an interesting political battle. The opposition to Lalu Yadav-led RJD was strengthened by the crossing over of Nitish Kumar to the side of the BJP-led alliance. The JD was at its peak of political power in the state in the 1995 assembly polls when it won 167 seats, a simple majority, on its own. As per Table 5.14, the Yadavs and Muslims were the main supporters of the RJD. In the 1996 Lok Sabha polls, 67% Yadavs and 55% of Muslims supported the party. In the 1999 Lok Sabha polls, the Muslim support for the RJD went to the extent of 71%, while 65% Yadavs had supported the alliance. The Yadav support for the RJD further went to 81% and 77% in the 2000 assembly polls and the 2004 Lok Sabha polls respectively (see Table 5.14). The 2005 assembly polls saw the virtual split of the Muslim–Yadav alliance as only 33% Muslims backed Lalu Yadav, while 81% Yadavs sided with it.

The Congress remained in the margins of the polls in this period. At times, it fought polls in alliance with the JMM and at times fought elections in alliance with Lalu Yadav. The upper castes, Dalits, and Muslims who had been traditional supporters of the party had dumped the party in this phase. But still whatever support base it had in that period had been coming from Dalits and Muslims which may be tactical to defeat the BJP. In 1996, out of the total votes the party got, 22% were Dalits and 20% were Muslims (see Table 5.15).

Table 5.14

Vote for RJD/JD by caste–community, 1996–2005

	Lok Sabha 1996	Lok Sabha 1999	Vidhan Sabha 2000	Lok Sabha 2004 (with INC + LJNSP)	Vidhan Sabha 2005
All	34.9	35.3	34.0	46.4	25.8
Upper caste	11.0	2.0	11.0	25.0	7.0
Yadav	67.0	65.0	81.0	77.0	81.0
Kurmi + Koeri	22.0	20.0	19.0	17.0	9.0
Other OBCs	30.0	31.0	25.0	44.0	25.0
SCs	26.0	41.0	31.0	46.0	23.0
Muslims	55.0	71.0	61.0	79.0	33.0

Sources: CSDS Data Unit; National Election Study 1996—Sample size, 880; National Election Study 1999—Sample size, 881; Bihar Assembly Election Study 2005—Sample size, 2,205; National Election Study 2004—Sample size, 1,191; Bihar Assembly Election Study 2005—Sample size, 887.

Note: All figures are in percent.

Table 5.15

Vote for Congress by caste–community, 1996–2005

	Lok Sabha 1996	Vidhan Sabha 2000	Vidhan Sabha February 2005
Total	11.8	8.5	5.0
Upper caste	9.0	16.0	5.0
Yadav	2.0	1.0	4.0
Kurmi + Koeri	6.0	7.0	Negligible
Other OBCs	9.0	4.0	2.0
SCs	22.0	10.0	5.0
Muslims	20.0	8.0	14.0

Sources: CSDS Data Unit; National Election Study 1996—Sample size, 880; Bihar Assembly Election 2000—Sample size, 2,205; Bihar Assembly Election Study 2005—Sample size, 887.

Note: All figures are in percent.

Summary Review of 2004 Lok Sabha Elections, February 2005 Elections, and October 2005 Elections

The three elections which took place in Bihar in the two years (2004–2005) had witnessed three different kinds of results. First, the Lok Sabha elections 2004, when the RJD and its allies had managed to register a convincing victory, though the performance of the government was negatively rated. The results had come as a surprise for many. A year later, the RJD and its allies got defeated during the assembly elections held in February 2005. While this was welcomed by those who were opposed to the ruling RJD government in the state, still a puzzle remained in the minds of many as to what changed in between the two elections that led to the defeat of the ruling RJD which had just registered an emphatic victory in the Lok Sabha elections.

The answers to these two puzzles need little explanation. The decline of the RJD and its allies during February 2005 assembly elections, and subsequently its defeat during the October 2005 assembly elections, could be credited to the poor performance of the RJD government during the last 15 years of its rule. Since the performance of the past 15 years of the RJD government was rated negatively, the voters of Bihar chose to oust the Lalu Yadav-led party. If we look back, the performance of the RJD government was not rated positively even during the 2004 Lok Sabha, but still the RJD with its allies managed to register a massive victory due to it being in alliance with the Congress and LJNSP.

The struggle for political dominance had resulted in total neglect of the issue of development in Bihar. There had been hardly any development in the state during the 15 years of the RJD rule. Realizing that the issue of development could result in the defeat of the ruling party, Lalu Yadav had successfully diverted the attention of the voters from development to "izzat" and security. While he had been able to play his izzat card successfully among the Dalits and the large numbers of the OBC castes, he had been equally clever in reminding the Muslims of security of their lives and property during the 15 years of the RJD rule, which was free of any communal violence in Bihar. This had again worked in favor of Lalu Yadav during the 2004 Lok Sabha elections. What added to the popularity of the party was its solid support base among the numerically dominant Yadav. Although they might also complain of having no development in the state, they still showed support for the RJD as they had become politically and socially empowered.

The partition of Bihar had also resulted in making the political position of the RJD much stronger. The new state of Jharkhand was created separating the Adivasi-dominated districts from Bihar. The settlement pattern of people had been such that the present-day Bihar had the largest concentration of the Yadavs, Muslims, and Dalits. While their numbers had remained the same, due the division of the state their proportion in the population of the parent state Bihar went up by about 2–3%. As per the 2001 census, the proportion of Dalits and the Muslims in present-day Bihar had gone up from 14% and 14.8% to 17.1% and 16.5%. Unofficial estimates put the proportion of Yadavs as nearly 17% of the population in present-day Bihar, an increase of about 4%. This actually added to the political strength of the RJD in the present-day Bihar. This also explained why Lalu Yadav performed much better compared to the 1999 Lok Sabha elections. Lalu Yadav knew that his strength was in Bihar minus Jharkhand; thus, he agreed for the bifurcation, even as in earlier years of his political career he had proclaimed, "Bihar would be divided over my dead body."

In spite of his dominant position, doubts were raised about for how long would the two magic words "izzat" and "security" (for Muslims) get votes for the RJD in Bihar. These doubts turned into reality with the defeat of the RJD in the October 2005 assembly elections. The results of the October 2005 assembly elections clearly indicated that Lalu Yadav's charisma had reached its saturation. People were no more content with only "*Swar* if not *Swarg*" which Lalu had claimed to have given to the poor people of Bihar. After 15 years of the RJD rule, they did want some development to take place in the state, prompting the rise of Nitish Kumar.

Consequentially, did the new JD(U)–BJP government in Bihar indicate the return of the upper caste dominance in Bihar politics? It was true that the coalition of the JD(U) with the BJP did enable the upper caste leadership to play greater role in Bihar politics compared to what was used to be during the Lalu Yadav regime, but it may be an overstatement to say that the new government in Bihar signified the return of the upper castes politics. The new Chief Minister Nitish Kumar represented the other dominant OBC caste, the Kurmi. The mantle of leadership passed from one OBC group to the other; earlier it was the Yadavs under Lalu Yadav but now it was Kurmis in case of Nitish Kumar but yes, the upper castes got space in Bihar politics after a span of 15 years. Still, the OBCs continue to dominate the state of affairs even after the change in government.

The acceptance of Nitish Kumar as the leader of the alliance certainly added to the success of the JD(U)–BJP alliance during the October 2005 assembly elections. The BJP leadership had accepted Nitish Kumar as the leader of the NDA in spite of disliking some upper caste BJP leaders. The social reality was to give adequate share to the OBC leadership in the state if any alliance wanted success in politics of Bihar.

The social churning which had taken place in the state in the 1990s marked a radical shift in Bihar politics from the dominance of the upper caste to the dominance of the OBC. It seemed likely that in the next few decades the government will come and go, political parties would win and lose elections, but the dominance of the people from OBCs in Bihar politics was likely to remain. The key to success for any political party in Bihar would remain in accommodating the aspirations of the people belonging to the numerically dominant OBCs. The party, which would master this art, was destined to rule the state in the coming years.

References

Das, A.N. (1997). Still paying old debts. *The Telegraph*, June 6.

Hauser, W. (1997). General elections 1996 in Bihar: Politics, administrative atrophy and anarchy. *Economic & Political Weekly*, *32*(41). Retrieved December 5, 2017, from http://www.epw.in/special-articles/general-elections-1996-bihar-politics-administra-tive-atrophy-and-anarchy.html

Sinha, A. (2011). *Nitish Kumar and the Rise of Bihar*. Delhi: Penguin India.

UNI. (1998). Laloo pledges life to prevent separate Jharkhand. *Rediff News*. Retrieved November 20, 2017, from http://m.rediff.com/%0D%0Anews/1998/sep/14jhark.htm

6

Change of Guard: Elections of 2005

Overview of 2005 Assembly Elections

In the May 2004 general elections, the NDA was crushed by the mighty coalition that Lalu Prasad Yadav had formed with Ram Vilas Paswan of LJNSP and the Congress party in Bihar, but this coalition withered away before the 2005 assembly elections. The fractured verdict of February 2005 elections gave a fresh lease of life to Nitish Kumar's tune of *Nutan Bihar* (new Bihar) and the BJP–JD(U) won a majority in the November 2005 elections. Lalu Yadav and Paswan remained ministers in the central government until 2009. However, things in Bihar under the leadership of Nitish Kumar underwent change. The language and grammar of politics in the state had changed drastically by this time. Nitish Kumar was stressing on governance with a clean image. The administrative set was revamped and suddenly Bihar seemed a much safer place. Nitish Kumar had sent strong signals on the law and order front by sending his own JD(U) party men to jail. Simultaneously, his government took proactive measures for increasing school enrollment. Distribution of bicycles to school-going girls became the poster image of changing Bihar.

The October 2005 assembly elections had not only resulted in a change in the political trajectory of Bihar, but it had also led to change in the economic trajectory of the state. The elections ended the 15 years of Lalu–Rabri rule in Bihar, as the JD(U)–BJP formed the new government with Nitish Kumar in command and BJP leader Sushil Kumar Modi as his deputy. With support from the people, the JD(U)–BJP alliance won 143 of the total 243 assembly seats in Bihar and polled 35.01% votes (see Table 6.1). Compared to this, the RJD alliance had won only 65

Table 6.1

Results of the two assembly elections in 2005

Party	February 2005		October 2005	
	Seat Share	*Vote Share (%)*	*Seat Share*	*Vote Share (%)*
Congress	10	5.00	9	6.00
BJP	37	10.97	55	14.55
JD(U)	55	14.55	88	20.46
CPI, CPM, and CPML	3+1+7=11	4.71	3+1+5=9	5.14
RJD	75	25.07	54	23.45
LJNSP	29	12.62	10	11.10

Source: Election Commission of India.

Note: Rest are other parties.

assembly seats and polled 31.1% votes. Amongst its allies, the Congress had won nine seats and polled 6.1% votes, while the NCP and the CPM had won one seat each and polled less than 1% vote. The RJD had won 54 assembly seats and polled 23.5% votes. The other important political player in the state, Ram Vilas Paswan-led LJNSP, had managed to win only 10 seats and polled 11.1% votes.

The results of the February 2005 assembly elections were a reversal of the results of the 2004 Lok Sabha elections. The RJD–Congress–LJNSP alliance had registered a massive victory winning 29 of the 42 Lok Sabha seats, while the NDA could win only 11 seats. There may be several reasons for the RJD's debacle during the February assembly elections. The breaking of their alliance contributed to the poor performance of both the RJD and the Congress, but what added to the misery of the RJD was the extremely low voter turnout during the February 2005 assembly elections. Compared to the 2000 assembly elections, the turnout dropped by nearly 18%, and when compared to the 2004 Lok Sabha elections, it dropped by nearly 11.8%. Lesser participation of the voters during the February assembly elections actually affected the RJD much more than any other political party or political alliance.

The October assembly elections sealed the fate to 15 years of the RJD rule in Bihar. The February 2005 assembly elections had indicated that the decline of the RJD had begun, and the October 2005 assembly elections saw the RJD government being thrown out of power. This election witnessed the worst ever performance for the RJD. Not only was the RJD defeated in this election, but even in terms of the tally of seats, it came third (even lost the advantage of being the second largest party) after the JD(U) which won 88 assembly seats and the BJP which won 55 assembly seats. The RJD, which had won 75 seats barely 8 months ago in the February 2005 assembly elections, now managed to win only 54 seats and polled only 23.5% votes.

> In his inimitable style, Lalu called the UPA alliance consisting of the RJD, Congress, NCP, and CPI (M) as "foolproof" and "perfect." The others, he said, were merely "shops" that would down their shutters once the elections were over. (Ahmed & Jha, 2005)

Despite such bold posturing, the RJD-led alliance was badly bruised in the October 2010 assembly elections. Clearly, there had been a decline in the support base of the RJD as well. The results clearly indicated a great degree of disenchantment of the people with the RJD and its supremo— Lalu Yadav.

The Nitish Kumar-led government came to power not only with huge support from the common people of Bihar, but it also carried the responsibility to meet their aspirations and expectations. People had huge expectations from the new government, and large sections of them believed that Bihar would change. The record of developmental work during the last five years of the JD(U)–BJP government seemed to be reasonable. Things seemed to have changed on various fronts. The law and order and the condition of roads had improved.

> The improvement in law and order is no less dramatic. Gone are the days of brazen *rangadaari*, of extortion, loot and kidnappings with open political patronage. These practices have not completely disappeared from the state. Nitish with some of the political dons bought peace before the elections. Yet the contrast with the past is there for everyone to notice, and it matters even to the landless labourer who can now ply his rickshaw without the fear of being dragged for *begaar* (unpaid labour). (Yadav, 2010)

There had been enormous changes in Bihar in terms of condition of roads and bridges, law and order, employment, flood relief, and various other issues which concerned the common man.[1] Besides, the government

---

[1] During little less than five years of rule, more than 6,800 km of roads were built/rebuilt. Similarly, during the same period, more than 2,100 bridges were built. As a result, the turnover of state-run Bihar Pul Nirman Nigam Limited mandated to build bridges had leaped from ₹42.62 crore in 2004–2005 to ₹858 crore in 2008–2009.

launched various schemes mainly for the welfare of the deprived and the marginalized groups in the society, namely, women, Dalits, Muslims, and those belonging to the lower OBCs. When the Nitish Kumar government reserved 50% seats for women in panchayat, Bihar became the first state to do that. The state government also launched various other schemes to address the issue of gender disparity in the state.[2]

The government tried to make distinction between the upper and the lower Dalits so that the government schemes can aim to benefitting those who really need it, which became popular as the *Mahadalit*. Of the total 22 Dalit castes, the government demarcated 21 castes as Mahadalit, those who were economically much lower compared to the Dushadhas. The government worked hard for the welfare of the minority, namely the Muslims, with the aim of uplifting especially the lower class Muslims (the Pasmanda Muslims).[3] Aiming for bringing about land reforms, mainly to guarantee security to the tenant cultivators, the government initiated the process of bringing about Tenancy Reforms popularly known as *Bataaidaar Bill*, but it was shelved due to political reasons. As the CSDS survey indicated during Lok Sabha election held last year, a fairly large section of voters did approve his efforts toward development of the state (Kumar & Ranjan, 2009).

Findings from various surveys conducted by CSDS, Delhi, indicated that the popularity of Nitish Kumar was increasing constantly, especially after 2000. The popularity graph of Nitish Kumar touched new heights during February 2005 assembly elections. Over one-fifth of people preferred him as the chief minister of Bihar. Six months later, he left all others much behind. He was preferred by 42% as the most suitable candidate for the chief minister. His popularity was much higher than any other leader including Ram Vilas Paswan. The decline in Ram Vilas Paswan's popularity was due to the fact that many people held him

---

[2] Other schemes launched by Bihar government to address the issue of gender disparity were Lakshmibai Social Security Pension Scheme, Nari Shakti Yojana, Mukhyamantri Kanya Vivah Yojana, Kanya Suraksha Yojana, Mukhyamantri Balika Poshak Yojana, and Mukhyamantri Balika Cycle Yojana.

[3] Among various schemes which the government launched for the welfare of the Muslim were Mukhyamantri Shram Shakti Scheme for minority, Grant-in-aid for students in Minority hostel with a total strength of 3,800 students, Mahatama Gandhi/Maulana Azad Residential Training School for Minorities boys and girls, Occupational training for minorities, plantation in graveyard, grant-in-aid for minority orphanages, Kasturba Gandhi residential school for Minority girls, Hazrat Fatima skill development program, stipend for minorities, and community irrigation.

responsible for blocking the formation of the government after February 2005 assembly election in which his party had won large number of seats and held the key to formation of the new government (Kumar, Alam, & Joshi, 2008).

Caste/Community, Development, and the Rise of Nitish Kumar

During the assembly elections held in February 2005, both the RJD and the JD(U)–BJP alliance had managed to corner about one-fifth of the Dalit vote, while LJNSP managed to get 14% of the Dalit vote. The assembly elections, held within a gap of few months (October 2005), hardly witnessed any change in the voting patterns amongst the Dalits except for their greater polarization in favor of the LJNSP. During this election, 28% of the Dalits voted for the LJNSP. In 2007, the Bihar government set up the Mahadalit Commission to identify the most deprived of the deprived, ostensibly for better targeting of schemes for their uplift. To begin with, the commission identified 18 of Bihar's 22 Dalit castes as Mahadalit or greater Dalit, that is, all Dalit groups except four: Jatavs and Paswans, the two most numerically dominant groups, and Dhobis and Pasis, the two groups considered relatively better off in terms of development parameters. A year later, Pasis and Dhobis were also included in the list. In 2009, the Jatavs followed them, leaving out only the Paswans. New schemes for Mahadalits were created. Although Mahadalit strategy was criticized for just being an "eyewash," Nitish went on with his strategy of extending targeted benefits to other communities. His government extended significant patronage to Muslims through several minority welfare schemes. By helping two prominent Muslim politicians (Ali Anwar of the All-India Pasmanda Muslim Mahaj and Dr Ejaz Ali of the All India United Muslim Morcha) to become Rajya Sabha MPs, Nitish was carefully designing a catch-all rainbow coalition.

Besides the three dominant OBC castes, there are various other OBC castes which constitutes nearly one-fifth (20%) of the total voters in Bihar. Due to the numerical strength, they are seen as important vote bank by political parties. While the political parties may eye the lower OBC as a vote bank, since the lower OBC constitute of various castes, many of the voters of different lower OBC caste vote differently. While the smaller sample size does not allow us for such a detailed analysis, the

Table 6.2

The 2005 assembly elections' decisive shift in the lower OBC vote from RJD+ to JD(U)–BJP alliance

Year of Election	RJD+	JD(U) + BJP
1996 Lok Sabha	37	36
1998 Lok Sabha	26	41
1999 Lok Sabha	30	45
2000 assembly	35	25
2004 Lok Sabha	38	36
2005 February assembly	24	26
2005 October assembly	22	48
2009 Lok Sabha	12	58

Source: Figures reported in the table are from various surveys conducted by the CSDS, Delhi, in Bihar during various assembly and Lok Sabha elections.

Notes: All figures are in percent; figure for 1996 refers to vote share for the JD since the RJD came into being in 1998; figures reported in the table are vote share for the RJD with its allies amongst Muslims. The RJD contested various elections in alliance with different political parties (1996, RJD+CPI+CPM; 1998, RJD+INC+JMM; 1999, RJD+INC; 2000, RJD+CPM+M-COR; 2004, RJD+INC+LJNSP+NCP; 2005 February, RJD+CPI+CPM+NCP; 2005 October, RJD+INC+CPM+NCP; 2009, RJD+LJNSP; 2010, RJD+LJNSP).

very fact that the votes of the lower OBC had remained divided between the RJD alliance and the JD(U) alliance indicates that various castes within the lower OBC castes had voted differently, election after election. The shift in the vote of the lower OBC castes in favor of the JD(U) alliance began during the October 2005 assembly elections and continued even after that. One can clearly see the decisive shift of the lower OBC voters in favor of the ruling JD(U)–BJP alliance during the 2009 Lok Sabha and the 2010 assembly elections. During 2009 elections, 58% of lower OBC castes voted for the JD(U)–BJP alliance, giving the alliance a decisive lead, while only a very small proportion of the lower OBC caste voted for the RJD alliance (see Table 6.2).

The 2009 Lok Sabha election was a landmark in the sense that it saw the decline of the RJD in the national politics. From 22 seats, the party was reduced to only 4. The Lalu Yadav-led party was decimated beyond redemption (see Table 6.3). The Congress party saw its strength coming down to 2. The BJP improved its performance in comparison to the 2004 Lok Sabha and notched 12 seats, while its alliance partner JD(U) got 20

Table 6.3

Decline of RJD in national elections after 2005 assembly elections

Year/Party	2004 Lok Sabha	2009 Lok Sabha
Congress	3 (4.49%)	2 (10.27%)
BJP	5 (14.57%)	12 (13.94%)
JD(U)	6 (22.36%)	20 (24.05%)
RJD	22 (30.67%)	4 (19.31%)

Source: Election Commission of India.

Note: Figures in parentheses show vote percentage.

seats; so in total the NDA got 32 seats. The drastic fall in the seats for the RJD was due to a negative swing against it, of at least 10 percentage points. From 30.67%, its vote share fell to 19.31% which led to massive loss of seats for it. Although the BJP–JD(U) combine saw a marginal improvement in its vote share, it was the decline in vote share of the RJD and the virtual breakdown of Muslim–Yadav combine that led to the victory of Nitish Kumar-led alliance.

Congress' *ekla chalo* policy had left Lalu Yadav and Paswan high and dry. Lalu Yadav himself lost in one of the two seats he contested, and Paswan's party drew a blank. There was a new wave of hope among Congress workers as the party's vote share reached double digits. Since 2009 general elections, the NDA had faced its own share of troubles and thus while there was near unanimity in predicting the victory of the NDA alliance, few were sure of the magnitude of this win.

Just after the 2009 Lok Sabha elections, there were massive reversals in Bihar as Lalu Yadav made a strong comeback in the by-elections in which the NDA won only 5 out of the 18 seats that went to polls. By-elections usually put the incumbent party on a stronger wicket; however, the results put a question mark to Nitish Kumar's Mahadalit strategy. Several reasons were forwarded for this defeat. It was argued that Nitish enforced the rule that no relatives would get the JD(U) nomination in the by-election and turned down the nominations of relatives of MPs and MLAs. Some JD(U) leaders even worked with rivals to ensure the defeat of the official JD(U) candidate. It seemed that resurgent Congress had got a good chunk of Muslim votes, and a part of the upper-caste social base of the JD(U)–BJP combine had returned to the Congress. This probable shift in upper caste base was due to the fear of introduction of the Bataaidaar Bill. Nitish's government had created a Land Reforms

Commission under D. Bandyopadhyay that proposed a bill which called for legal recognition of bataaidaars or tillers, which the earlier tenancy legislation in Bihar did not recognize. Nitish Kumar had to eventually turn soft on the issue and put it on the back burner but the damage in terms of antagonizing upper caste was already done. Moreover, there were allegations of mismanagement and corruption as far as the relief work on Kosi Floods of 2008 was concerned.

Nitish Kumar was accused by some of his own party men of running a "one-man show" and relying heavily on bureaucrats rather than party members. There were also rebellions in his own party, as leaders such as Prabhunath Singh and Rajiv Ranjan revolted against him. Although there were rebellions in opposition too, Lalu Yadav and Ram Vilas Paswan closed ranks and made public declarations of unity. Lalu Yadav also sent Paswan to the Rajya Sabha with RJD backing, considering Paswan lost his Lok Sabha seat and did not have numbers to elect himself to the Upper House. The RJD–LJNSP alliance hoped their alliance would consolidate Yadav, Muslim, and SC votes and rebels, and a resurgent Congress would dent chances of another NDA government from coming to power in 2010.

Broader Pattern of Electoral Alliance

There were four assembly elections between 1995 and 2005. These polls saw alignment and re-alignment by different political parties. Broadly, two alliances remained—one led by JD/RJD and the other led by JD(U)–BJP. In the 1995 polls, Congress was not a part of JD/RJD-led alliance. In 1995, there were four broad levels of alliances. First was the JD–CPI–CPM–JMM(S), second was Samata–CPML, third was Congress, and fourth was the BJP. In these elections, both the national parties realized that they have to align with one of the aforementioned two if they want to remain floating in the politics of Bihar.

In the 2000 assembly polls, the BJP, the Samata Party, and the JD(U) came together to fight the RJD-led alliance which also had CPM. The Congress fought the state assembly elections separately and was not a part of the Lalu Yadav-led alliance.

The Congress(I) went alone in 2000 polls hoping for a revival of the sort it experienced in Uttar Pradesh, but that was not to be. It won only 24 seats and secured 11.1% of the popular vote. As compared to 1995, the party contested more seats in northern Bihar, and although it did not lose seats, its vote share went down by 7 percentage points. In southern Bihar, although the party lost two seats compared to 1995, it increased its vote share marginally (Kumar, 2000).

In the February 2005 polls, JD(U) and BJP again took on the might of Lalu Yadav-led RJD and virtually displaced it out of power. The Congress was again not present in the Lalu Yadav-led alliance and fought the polls independently. The CPI, CPM, and NCP were part of Lalu Yadav-led alliance. When a government could not be formed due to the hung verdict, another election took place in November 2005 in which the JD(U)–BJP alliance got a majority of its own. In October polls, Congress was part of the Lalu Yadav-led alliance (see Table 6.4).

Voting Pattern Across Caste and Communities

In Bihar, different castes and communities have been voting according to a pattern. Generally, the upper castes had favored the BJP and the JD(U) along with Kurmis and Koeris. The Yadavs and Muslims, along with a section of Dalits, supported the RJD, while the Congress fragmented the votes of Dalits, Muslims, and the upper castes in few pockets. But the caste and community support to the political parties varied election after election. In the 1996 Lok Sabha elections, 81% of Yadavs supported the RJD+ but this percentage dipped to 76% in 1999 Lok Sabha polls, while again in 2000 Vidhan Sabha polls it went up to a whopping 80% because of the Lalu Yadav factor (refer Figure 5.8 in Chapter 5).

The Muslim vote for the RJD varied and was not as stable as the Yadav vote for the RJD. During the early 1990s, the Muslim vote was stable for the JD/RJD but gradually it started fragmenting as Nitish Kumar was able to wean away a substantial part of it during the later period (see Figure 6.1). Again, in the 2014 Lok Sabha elections, it virtually polarized in favor of the RJD. At least 64% Muslims and an equal percentage of Yadavs voted for the RJD alliance.

The Dalit vote fragmented between the RJD and BJP–JD(U)-led alliance since 1996. Both the political alliances garnered substantial chunks of Dalit vote; but in 2014 Lok Sabha elections, the RJD-led alliance virtually lost the Dalit vote to the BJP-led alliance—maybe due to Ram Vilas Paswan fighting the polls in alliance with the saffron party (see Figure 6.2).

Table 6.4

Pattern of electoral alliance: Assembly elections, 1995–2005

	Alliance I		Alliance II		Others	
	Party	*Vote %*	*Party*	*Vote %*	*Party*	*Vote %*
1995	Samata	7.1	JD	28.0	INC	16.3
	CPML	2.4	CPI	4.8	BJP	13.0
			CPM	1.4	JMM	2.3
			JMM (S)	1.3	Other parties[a]	9.6
					IND	13.8
	Total	**9.5**	**Total**	**35.5**	**Total**	**55.0**
2000	BJP	14.6	RJD	28.3	INC	11.1
	Samata	8.7	CPM	0.9	JMM	3.5
	JD(U)	6.6	M-COR	0.3	CPML	2.5
					Other parties[b]	12.2
					IND	11.4
	Total	**29.8**	**Total**	**29.5**	**Total**	**40.7**
2005 (February)	BJP	11.0	RJD	25.1	LJNSP	12.6
	JD(U)	14.6	CPI	1.6	INC	5.0
			CPM	0.6	CPML	2.5
			NCP	1.0	Other parties[c]	9.8
					IND	16.2
	Total	**25.6**	**Total**	**28.3**	**Total**	**46.1**
2005 (October)	BJP	15.7	RJD	23.5	LJNSP	11.1
	JD(U)	20.5	INC	6.1	CPI	2.1
			NCP	0.8	CPML	2.4
			CPM	0.7	Other parties[d]	8.3
					IND	8.8
	Total	**36.2**	**Total**	**31.1**	**Total**	**32.7**

Source: CSDS Data Unit.

Notes: Data for the 2005 assembly elections is for the divided Bihar, referred as "New Bihar", while data for 1995–2000 assembly elections is for undivided Bihar, referred as "Old Bihar."

[a] Includes BSP (2), SP (2), M-COR (2), JPP (2), JKP (1), JMM(M) (3), CVP (1), and BPP (1).

[b] Includes BSP (5), CPI (5), UGDP (2), and KSP (2).

[c] Includes BSP (2) and SP (4).

[d] Includes BSP (4), SP (2), and AJVD (1).

Figure 6.1

How Muslims have voted in Bihar during various elections (1996–2009)

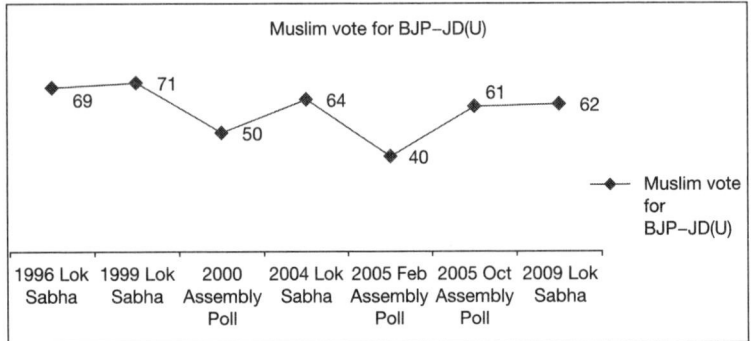

Source: Figures reported here are from various surveys conducted by CSDS, Delhi, in Bihar during various assembly and Lok Sabha elections.

Notes: All figures are in percent; figure for 1996 refers to vote share for the JD since the RJD came into being in 1998; figures reported in the figure are vote share for the RJD with its allies amongst Muslims. The RJD contested various elections in alliance with different political parties (1996, RJD+CPI+CPM; 1998, RJD+INC+JMM; 1999, RJD+INC; 2000, RJD+CPM+M-COR; 2004, RJD+INC+LJNSP+NCP; 2005 February, RJD+CPI+CPM+NCP; 2005 October, RJD+INC+CPM+NCP; 2009, RJD+LJNSP).

Figure 6.2

Fragmentation in the Dalit vote

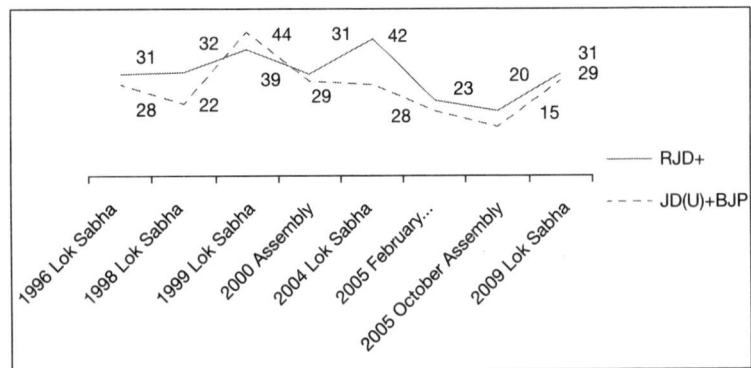

Source: Figures reported here are from various surveys conducted by CSDS, Delhi, in Bihar during various assembly and Lok Sabha elections.

Notes: All figures are in percent; figure for 1996 refers to vote share for the JD since the RJD came into being in 1998.

Figure 6.3

How Kurmi–Koeri have voted in Bihar during various elections (1996–2009)

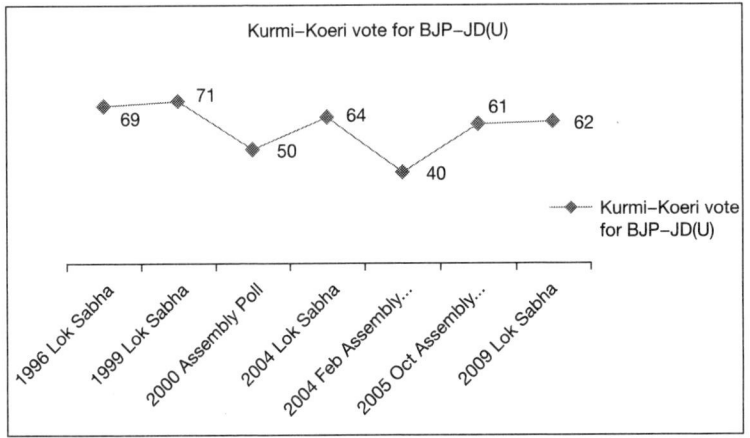

Source: Figures reported here are from various surveys conducted by CSDS, Delhi, in Bihar during various assembly and Lok Sabha elections.

Note: All figures are in percent.

The Kurmi–Koeri vote was always tilted toward the JD(U)–BJP-led alliance in Bihar due to Nitish Kumar factor. In the 1996 and 1998 Lok Sabha polls, the entire vote bank virtually polarized in favor of the JD(U)–BJP alliance with around 70% of them voting in their favor (see Figure 6.3). The same was with the upper castes who are the most ardent votaries of the BJP (see Figure 6.4).

Rise of Nitish Kumar

Nitish Kumar had gradually emerged as a popular leader. In 1995, he was the choice of a mere 7% of the voters but gradually he overtook Lalu Yadav as the most popular Bihar leader. In February 2005, he was the choice of about 22% of voters which surged to 42% in October 2005, while his rivals Lalu Yadav was at 16% and Ram Vilas Paswan a poor third at only 14%. Compared to the other chief ministers of his time, he was reasonably popular and more than Y.S. Rajasekhara Reddy and Sheila Dikshit at

Figure 6.4

How upper castes have voted in Bihar during various elections (1996–2009)

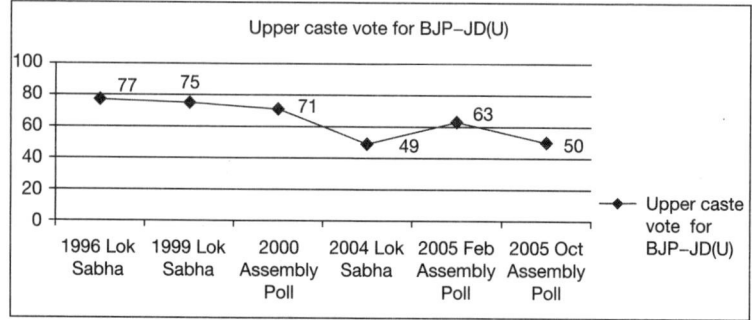

Source: Figures reported here are from various surveys conducted by CSDS, Delhi, in Bihar during various assembly and Lok Sabha elections.

Note: All figures are in percent.

35% and 32%, respectively. He was just below Buddhadeb Bhattacharjee in West Bengal (46%) and Narendra Modi in Gujarat (44%).

The Role of Tension in Coalition Government: Analysis of October 2005

When one talks about political tension, they should talk about two kinds of tension. They should talk more about tension in allocating seats for different alliance partners rather than actual tension between coalition partners in running the government. Let us first talk about tensions in allocating seats for the alliance partners. Apart from October 2005 assembly elections, there has hardly been any tension regarding the allocation of seats between the two alliance partners, that is, the BJP and the JD(U). This was the only election when there had been some confusion regarding the allocation of seats for the two alliance partners. This was primarily created due to defection of some of those LJNSP leaders who had won the February 2005 assembly elections on the LJNSP ticket but had later joined JD(U). Since they had been the winner during the last election, they needed to be given tickets. This ultimately meant cutting into the number of seats allocated for the BJP during the February 2005 assembly elections.

On the other hand, there was greater confusion among the alliance partners, especially among Congress and the RJD regarding allocation of the number of seats. Some issues had ultimately led to breaking of the alliance between Congress and the RJD as they contested the February 2005 assembly elections independently, but at times such confusions were resolved. Needless to mention, similar confusion had arisen with regard to allocation of seats to other alliance partners as well.

The state has had very little experience of having a coalition government. Since the government was not formed on any ideological basis, there has hardly been any instance of a common agenda being planned for the working of the government. There have been tensions with regard to allocation of ministries among the ministers belonging to the RJD and the Congress. Also, since majority of the leaders from the Congress were opposed to the idea of having a coalition with the RJD in the state, there was always a blame game about the prospects of Congress party being harmed by the RJD leaders since the government did not carry a good image among a section of common people. So such tensions were quite frequent during the Rabri-led coalition government in Bihar.

Whenever there were tensions with regard to allocation of seats, it was always resolved by way of discussion and intervention of the senior leaders. All such tensions have been resolved by way of working out some kind of compromise, but one could hardly find any formal mechanism of solving such issues among alliance partners. When it came to tensions regarding seat allocation among the BJP and the JD(U) during the October 2005 assembly elections, it was mainly resolved by way of BJP leaders accepting the demands of the JD(U) leaders. This was mainly because JD(U) was the senior partner in the alliance. But at times, even senior alliance partners had to accept the demands of the junior partners. This is what happened when the RJD tried to enter into an alliance with the Congress for contesting the October 2005 assembly elections. Congress wanted a larger number of seats compared to what RJD leader Lalu Yadav was ready to give. But on the insistence of the senior Congress leaders, Lalu Yadav accepted to give larger number of seats to the Congress. While on the one side there was some pressure from the senior Congress leaders, at the same time, Lalu also had the realization that the RJD needed Congress as an ally if it had to put up a formidable challenge to the BJP–JD(U) combine in the state. This necessity of the RJD drove Lalu to work out a compromise. Such compromise by Lalu could have been unthinkable few years ago.

Action Against Electoral Malpractice in October 2005 Elections

The assembly elections held in Bihar in October 2005 were somewhat different. The Election Commission decided to enforce electoral laws and made it clear that it wanted to conduct a free and fair election so that all registered voters, irrespective of caste, community, or class, should have an equal chance for exercising their franchise. Everyone should have the equal opportunity to vote during the elections without any fear of violence or persuasion. This resulted in enforcing electoral laws, model code of conduct, and deployment of large-scale police and paramilitary forces for smooth conduct of elections. There were various other initiatives like installing camera for getting all the voters turning up at the polling booth to be photographed. The following initiatives were taken by the ECI for conducting free and fair elections in Bihar (*Hindustan Times*, 2005):

- Deployment of about 605 battalions of paramilitary forces. This was much higher compared to 492 battalions deployed during the February 2005 assembly elections.
- Elections to be held in four phases compared to three phases during February 2005 for smooth movement of forces and effective deployment of forces at different polling booths.
- Deletion of names of about 20 lakh forged voters from the electoral roll.
- Issuing voter identity card to many more voters, the estimated figure is that the voter ID had been issued to about 80% of registered voters.
- One central observer for each assembly constituency, compared to one observer for three–four assembly seats during the February 2005 assembly elections.
- Installing digital cameras on all polling booths for voters to be photographed which would help in checking the bogus voters, who vote more than once. This was the first time it was being introduced in Bihar.
- Instruction for video recordings of sensitive and hypersensitive booths during polling.
- Provision for creation of an auxiliary polling booth if the number of registered voters exceeds 1,400 and provision of an extra

polling officer in every polling booth where the number of registered voters is between 1,200 and 1,400.

- Issued instruction to state government for not deputing officers above the rank of sub inspector to election duty in his/her home district. Also, officials who have completed three years of posting in one district during the last four years should not be posted in the same district for election duty.

The efforts of the Election Commission to ensuring a free and fair election were largely applauded by the BJP and the JD(U) for the following reasons:

- Strict enforcement of model code of conduct by the ECI.
- Adequate deployment of security forces for ensuring free and fair elections.
- Minimizing incidences of booth-capturing and rigging.
- Controlling the menace of bogus voters.

It is true that the BJP and JD(U) applauded the efforts of the Election Commission and complimented them for ensuring a free and fair election, but do we have evidences to support the claims of the BJP and JD(U)? Did the Election Commission succeed in holding a free and fair election? Let us first look at the official data.

One can say without any doubt that the 2005 October assembly elections in Bihar were much more peaceful than any election held in the state during recent times. There were hardly any reported instances of violence during the election (see Table 6.5).

While the official data tells us some story, the opinion of the common people also helps us in understanding if the elections were really peaceful. What do the common people think on this issue? All the caste and religious communities shared similar opinion that there were no malpractices in the elections, even as 64% had no opinion.

Looking at the instances of poll-related violence during the October 2005 assembly elections hardly leaves any doubt in the mind of common man that those elections were not only free and fair but were much fairer compared to other elections held in the state in the recent past (see Table 6.6). This gets supported by what common people had to say about freeness and fairness of October assembly elections. From the findings of the survey, it is clear that cutting across caste–communities, people believed that this election was much fair compared to the February elections.

Table 6.5

Incidence of electoral violence in Bihar

Election	Year	No. of Deaths	No. of Injured	Cases of Booth-capturing/Ballot Paper Looting	No. of Incidence of Violence
Assembly Elections	1969	7	150	—	—
	1977	26	309	146	194
	1980	38	788	57	757
	1985	60	91	94	376
	1990	87	291	318	520
	1995	54	163	22	1,270
	2000	61	150	—	633
	2005 February	15	—	—	—
	2005 October	2	—	—	—
Lok Sabha Elections	1996	42	187	—	—
	1998	44	—	—	1,485
	1999	76	147	—	452
	2004	15	78	—	279

Sources: Shrikant (2005); for assembly elections 2005, *Hindustan Times* (2005).

Table 6.6

October 2005 election compared to February 2005 election

October Election Was	(%)
More fair	9
Less fair	1
Same (no difference)	1
Malpractices never take place	24
No opinion	65

Source: CSDS Data Unit, post-poll survey in Bihar, October 2005.

The Dispute over Participation: How Far Are the Charges Valid?

While the Election Commission was applauded for ensuring a free and fair election in Bihar during the October 2005 assembly elections, this was not far from criticism. The RJD, which lost elections, criticized the

Election Commission for being biased and playing a partial role. The party put various kinds of blames on the ECI regarding the low turnout and also for their defeat in these elections. The party went to the extent of saying that the ECI planned the election in connivance with the BJP and the JD(U) in such way that it would ensure the defeat of the RJD. Leaders of the RJD criticized the ECI for restricting the franchise for large number of people as a result of various initiatives of the Election Commission. The criticism was on the following grounds:

- The RJD charged the Election Commission for selective deletion of names during revision of the electoral roll. The selective deletion was aimed at deleting names of voters belonging to those caste communities (Yadavs and Muslims) who had been traditionally voting for the RJD.[4]
- The unreasonable restrictions by the ECI resulted in a very low turnout during the elections. The marginalized sections of society who were the traditional supporters of the RJD were the worst affected.[5]
- Photo identification was must for all the voters at the polling booth. This was especially disadvantageous for the poor and the downtrodden who found it difficult to keep such documents safe in villages prone to devastating floods year after year. The poor had been the traditional voters of the RJD.
- All the voters were to be photographed and for that purpose most of the polling booths were fitted with video camera. This discouraged the women voters, especially the Muslim women, for coming out to vote. The RJD leaders claimed that this adversely affected their party since they had also been traditional supporters of the RJD.
- Large-scale deployment of police and paramilitary forces for ensuring free and fair elections scared many voters when they turned up at the polling booth.

We tried to look at these criticisms one by one and attempted to figure out how valid these charges were and how these initiatives of the ECI affected the diversity in political participation. Were these initiatives of the ECI aimed at any specific community? Did these initiatives in

---

[4] Findings from various surveys conducted by the CSDS suggest that Yadavs and Muslims had been voting for the RJD in large numbers during various elections held in the state during the past couple of decades.

[5] Findings of the CSDS surveys also suggest that the voters belonging to poorer sections of society have been voting for the RJD in large numbers during the past few elections.

any way affect the political participation of voters of any specific caste–communities?

Did Election Commission Indulge in Selective Deletion of Names from Electoral Roll?

Electoral rolls were accompanied by vast discrepancies and inaccuracies. It so happened that in some cases those who were genuine eligible voters found their name missing in the electoral roll, whereas in other cases false/ bogus names of voters were listed on the rolls. These practices were always reported, particularly in the states such as Assam, Bihar, West Bengal, and Uttar Pradesh. Undoubtedly, part of the problem could be attributed to the inefficiency and flawed system, but, as Goswami Committee reported, "some of it is also the result of purposeful tampering which may have happened due to partisan attitude of local officials who may have had their own local affinities or may be brought over by vested interests."[6] Electoral rolls were highly defective either due to the callousness of the officials or deliberately deleting names of some and adding others.

As a routine exercise, revision of electoral roll was undertaken in Bihar before the October assembly elections. It was generally alleged that electoral rolls were particularly bad in Bihar, particularly in respect of additional names. During the revision, while the names of those who attained the age of 18 or those who had moved in to a new locality were generally included, what did not happen was that the names of those who should not be there (for various reasons such as death and permanently shifted) were not deleted and continued to remain in the voters' list. It was alleged that the names of several lakh bogus voters still appeared in the voters' list, which helped the anti-social elements to indulge in bogus voting. During the revision, the ECI decided to delete the names of such bogus voters to the extent as far as possible. But the revision of electoral roll in Bihar during the October elections was marred by lots of controversies. The general allegation by the RJD leaders and others was that ECI indulged in selective deletion of names from the electoral rolls.

---

[6] This was a Consultation Paper on 'Review of Election Law, Processes and Reform Options' that was prepared by the Advisory Panel on Electoral Reforms; Standards in Political Life. It is based on a paper prepared by the Centre for Policy Research (CPR), New Delhi, for the Commission on January 8, 2001.

There were similar such charges from various other people as well against the ECI for showing biased attitude while making revision on electoral rolls. The only way to check the reality was by checking with the voters. A sample check was conducted among a little more than 15,000 voters to check how far these allegations were true. The findings of the study indicated that while some allegations had some substance, other charges seemed to be baseless.

Through the survey, we tried to ascertain how valid had been the revision of electoral rolls in Bihar. Regarding the issue of whether names of voters with valid identity card had been deleted, the findings of the survey suggested that nearly one quarter of the voters whose names were deleted during the revision had a valid voter's identity card. The findings also suggested that among those whose names were deleted, 60% names were wrongly deleted, while 13% voters who were temporarily away from the locality had their names deleted too. Name deletion due to death, permanently away, and other reasons constituted to 8%, 15%, and 5% respectively. There seemed to be valid reasons for deletion of names of other voters whose name had actually been deleted.

So, prima facie, it seems that there had been some discrepancy during the electoral roll revision in Bihar during the October 2005 assembly election. But what is the validity of the claim that the ECI indulged in selective deletion of names of the voters? It was alleged that this subjectivity was guided by the caste and community consideration of the voters. Through the study, we also wanted to check if there is any reasonable evidence to suggest selective deletion of names.

The findings of the survey hardly suggest any bias in deletion of names from the voters list. The instances of wrong deletion of names were more or less evenly spread across voters from different caste–communities. There was hardly anything to suggest that voters from particular caste–community were targeted while revising the electoral rolls. There does not seem to be any substance in the charges levelled against the ECI for selective deletion of names.

There were also cases of deletion of names of such voters who were temporarily away from the locality during the revision of electoral rolls. Findings of the survey suggested that there was hardly any systematic bias against voters from any particular caste–community while deleting names of those voters who had been temporarily away from their place of residence. This shows that the charges against the ECI of systematic deletion of names hardly seemed to have any substance.

Did Strict Regulations Affect the Turnout During October Assembly Elections?

The turnout figure for the October 2005 assembly elections hardly leaves any doubts that it witnessed the lowest turnout of voters in Bihar (see Table 6.7). While in the 1990s when the turnout used to be around 60%, during the October 2005 assembly elections it went down to nearly 45%. There were claims and counter-claims for this extremely low turnout. The ECI offered the following clarifications for low turnout during this election:

- Deletion of names of bogus voters who cast their votes in previous elections resulted in artificial increase in voter's turnout.
- Strict measures that were adopted by the ECI on polling day prevented anti-social elements from capturing the polling booth, which may have resulted in artificial increase in turnout.

Table 6.7

October assembly election's low turnout in year 2005

Year of Elections	Turnout (%)
1951	39.7
1957	40.6
1962	47.0
1967	51.5
1969	52.8
1972	52.8
1977	50.5
1980	57.3
1885	56.3
1990	62.1
1995	61.8
2000	62.6
2005 February	46.5
2005 October	45.9

Source: Election Commission of India.

- Deployment of police, paramilitary, and army in sizeable numbers to ensure free and fair elections prevented the bogus voters from indulging in electoral malpractices.

On the other hand, the ECI was blamed for this extremely low turnout of voters during the October 2005 assembly elections.

Was There Any Caste–Community Pattern to Low Turnout During the October Assembly Elections?

The RJD leaders blamed the Election Commission for low turnout during the February and October assembly elections. The party also blamed the ECI for its defeat, since it alleged that the stringent measure of the ECI regarding the conduct of election resulted in lower turnout of voters of those caste–communities who had been traditionally voting for the party during the past elections. As their supporters did not turn out to vote, it resulted in the loss of the party. The RJD also alleged the ECI of conniving with the BJP while fixing the dates for the election during the month of Ramadan. Later, it was also alleged that large number of Muslim voters, perceived as the traditional supporters of the RJD, did not turn out to vote during the October assembly elections. The CSDS study tried to ascertain how valid these claims of the RJD were.

A comparison of community-wise turnout during the two assembly elections (February and October) in the state suggest that it was not the Yadavs and the Muslims (the traditional supporters of the RJD) whose turn-out had gone down in October elections, rather it had gone down amongst the upper caste (the traditional supporters of the BJP and the JD(U)). This could have adversely affected the BJP–JD(U) combine and not the RJD. In fact, if we compare the turnout amongst the Muslims in October elections to that in February elections, we see that their turnout had increased.

Reasons for Low Turnout

While different people have mentioned different things about the low turnout during the 2005 assembly elections, the findings of the survey helped us in understanding what might have discouraged or prevented people from turning out to vote on the election day. The ECI was blamed for low turnout due to lack of voters identity card. While the ECI worked hard to issue voter's identity card to as many voters as possible, it may be incorrect to claim that all registered voters in Bihar received the voter's identity card. From the estimates of the CSDS survey, one notes that 76% voters were issued voter's identity cards. The ECI worked hard before the October assembly elections which resulted in issuing voter's identity card to about 87% registered voters in Bihar. While the proportion of voters with valid identity card increased before the October assembly elections, still some voters without valid identity card could not vote as many of them did not have any knowledge about other documents that they could use for exercising their franchise. Clearly, this became one of the reasons for some voters for not turning out at the polling booth on the election day. Of those voters who could not vote during the October elections, 15% could not vote due to lack of voter's identity card, while 28% of them could not vote since they were out of station (see Table 6.8). Other stated reasons such as not being well and not interested in elections. The lower turnout was witnessed across communities (see Table 6.9).

If we compare the two assembly elections, one held in February and the other held in October, we notice two important changes. First, the proportion of such voters who could not vote due to fear of violence had gone down considerably from 10% in February to only 1% during October elections. The other important thing to be noted is that the proportion of voters who could not vote because they did not have a

Table 6.8

Reasons for low turnout

Reason for Not Voting	February 2005	October 2005
Out of station	7	28
No identity card	31	15
Not well	16	12
No interest in election	11	9
Fear of violence	10	1
Other reason	16	11
No opinion	9	24

Source: CSDS post-poll surveys in Bihar, February 2005 and October 2005.

Note: All figures are in percent.

Table 6.9

Turnout pattern across communities

Caste–Communities	February 2005	October 2005
Actual turnout	**47**	**45**
Upper castes	59	45
Yadavs	46	45
Kurmi–Koeris	54	48
Other OBCs	42	45
Dalits	50	47
Muslims	35	43

Source: CSDS post-poll surveys in Bihar, February 2005 and October 2005.

Note: All figures are in percent.

valid identity card had gone down from 31% in February to only 15% in October. These findings suggests that though the turnout went down, the efforts of the ECI actually resulted in minimizing fear in the minds of the voters, and this possibly cannot be the reason for lower turnout of the voters.

Was There Any Community Pattern for Those Who Could Not Vote Due to No Identity Proof During October Assembly Elections?

Although the proportion of voters who could not exercise their franchise due to lack of valid voter's identity card went down from 31% in February to 15% in October, from the survey we also tried to figure out if there was any community pattern to it. Was there any variation in proportion of voters not having a valid identity card across caste–communities? Findings of the survey suggest that the proportion of voters without a valid voter's identity card was slightly less among Muslims and Yadavs (traditionally voting for the RJD) during the past few elections (see Table 6.10). The findings of the survey does provide evidence of some discrepancy as far as issuing voter's identity card to the voters is concerned, but it is not clear if this was intentional or it was just a matter of chance.

Table 6.10

Non-voting due to lack of voter identity card

Caste–Community	Figures in %
All	15
Upper castes	13
Yadavs	18
Kurmi–Koeris	10
Other OBCs	13
Dalits	15
Muslims	20

Source: CSDS post-poll surveys in Bihar, October 2005.

Conclusion

Did strict enforcement of electoral laws help in promoting or restricting diversity in political participation in Bihar? One hardly needs any evidence to prove that the level of participation of the people during the October elections was low compared to any other election in Bihar. But from the evidences presented in this chapter, it is difficult to establish any correlation between the low turnout and strict conduct of elections, except that the lack of voter's identity card did affect the voter's turnout to some extent. While it is true that voters could have used any of the 17 other alternative documents for proving their identity, due to lack of awareness among the voters that hardly worked. While one cannot say that there was anything wrong in making voter's photo identity mandatory before voting, it also seems there is a need for issuing voter's photo identity card to all those who are still left out. While the provision of producing any other photo identity instead of the voter's identity card is actually a voter-friendly step of the ECI, voters needed to be educated about that. For a common voter in a rural village, it was still the voter's identity card which they thought was the most valuable for them. So, overall, the ECI was responsible for the lower participation of the people during October assembly elections to some extent.

Although there were allegations that strict conduct of elections resulted in restricting the political participation of voters of particular communities ultimately resulting in restricting diversity in political participation, there was hardly any evidence to suggest that the initiatives of the ECI resulted in that. In fact, compared to the February elections, voters were less fearful during the October elections, which in one way or the other may have promoted the participation of the weaker sections of society. At the same time, there was hardly any evidence to suggest that the strict enforcement of electoral laws and strict conduct of elections ultimately resulted in promoting diversity in political participation.

References

Ahmed, F., & Sanjay, K.J. (2005, October 10). The three musketeers. Bihar polls: It's Lalu Prasad Yadav vs Nitish Kumar, Ram Vilas Paswan. *India Today.* Retrieved November 21, 2017, from http://indiatoday.intoday.in/story/bihar-polls-lalu-prasad-yadav-vs-nitish-kumar-ram-vilas-paswan/1/192839.html

Hindustan Times. (2005, July 23). Election Commission issues directions to Bihar government for forthcoming elections. Retrieved November 21, 2017, from http://www.highbeam.com/doc/1P3-1093507011.html

Kumar, S. (2000, March 18–31). The return of RJD. *Frontline, 17*(6). Retrieved November 21, 2017, from http://www.frontline.in/static/html/fl1706/17060270.htm

Kumar, S., Alam, S., & Joshi, D. (2008). Caste dynamics and political process in Bihar. *Journal of Indian School of Political Economy, 20*(1&2), 1–32.

Kumar, S., & Ranjan, R. (2009). Bihar: Development matters. *Economic & Political Weekly, 44*(39), 141–144.

Shrikant. (2005). *Bihar main Chunao.* New Delhi: Vani Prakashan.

Yadav, Y. (2010, October 31). Bihar election is all about hope, period. *The Times of India.* Retrieved November 21, 2017, from http://timesofindia.indiatimes.com/home/sunday-times/all-that-matters/Bihar-election-is-all-about-hope-period/articleshow/6844452.cms

7

Consolidation of Power by JD(U)– BJP Alliance: Elections of 2010

The Result and the Regional Pattern

The results of both the 2009 Lok Sabha and 2010 assembly elections in Bihar did not surprise many, which were more or less on expected lines. What came as a surprise was the way the RJD–LJNSP alliance got routed in both these elections. The RJD–LJNSP alliance managed to win only 25 of the 243 assembly seats and polled 25.5% votes (RJD 18.8% and LJNSP 6.7%), while the ruling JD(U)–BJP alliance won 206 assembly seats (JD(U) 115 and BJP 91) and polled 39.1% votes (JD(U) 22.6% and BJP 16.5% votes). The Congress had hoped to make its presence felt in state politics by taking a decision not to ally with any regional forces but to contest assembly elections alone. Instead of making any improvement, compared to last assembly elections, the Congress faced further marginalization as it managed to win only four assembly seats and polled 8.4% votes.

The result of the 2010 assembly elections was not only a continuation of the decline of the RJD and LJNSP, which had begun soon after JD(U)–BJP came to power in October 2005, but was also reflected during the electoral battle of 2009 Lok Sabha election. The RJD–LJNSP alliance had managed to win only four Lok Sabha seats (all four won by the RJD) and polled 25.8% votes (RJD 19.3% and LJNSP 6.5%). On the other hand, the JD(U)–BJP alliance registered an impressive victory. The JD(U)–BJP combine won 32 Lok Sabha seats (JD(U) 20 and BJP 12), and the alliance polled 38% votes (JD(U) 24.1% and BJP 13.9%). Although Congress managed to increase its vote share by nearly

6 percentage points, it could win only two Lok Sabha seats, a loss of one seat compared to the 2004 Lok Sabha elections.

More than the continuation of decline in the political support of the RJD–LJNSP, the results of the 2010 assembly elections witnessed further erosion in the support of the alliance. If the RJD–LJNSP could have even managed to repeat its poor electoral performance of 2009 Lok Sabha elections, the alliance would have won 38 assembly segments (they led in 38 assembly segments), while the ruling JD(U)–BJP alliance would have got restricted to winning only 175 assembly seats. The Congress would have been lucky in winning 10 assembly seats since it led in those many seats during the 2009 Lok Sabha elections. But the 2010 assembly elections witnessed further decline of the RJD–LJNSP and rise in the popularity of the JD(U)–BJP alliance in terms of both vote share and seats; there was hardly any region where the ruling alliance lagged behind the RJD–LJNSP alliance (see Table 7.1).

Was There a Regional Story in the Electoral Verdict?

The state of Bihar could be divided into five main regions, namely Tirhut, Mithila, Magadh, Bhojpur, and the East also known as "Seemanchal." These five regions are not merely geographical divisions, but they also exhibit a language and culture somewhat different from the other. Maithali is the dominant language in the Mithila region, while Bhojpuri is the most widely spoken language in the Bhojpur region. Similarly, large proportions of people speak Magahi language in the Magadh region of the state. Historically, the regional diversity also reflected in the diverse political culture, with some political parties having a stronger base in one region compared to other. But the recent elections in Bihar had wiped out the regional difference in the support base of political parties. During the 2009 Lok Sabha elections, the JD(U)–BJP combine swept the polls in Mithila (8 Lok Sabha seats) and Magadh regions (11 Lok Sabha seats), winning all the Lok Sabha seats in these two regions. The story of the 2010 assembly election was hardly different from the story of the previous Lok Sabha election. Even during the 2010 assembly elections, the ruling JD(U)–BJP alliance swept the polls in these two regions, winning 34 of the total 43 assembly seats in Mithila region and 58 of the 65 assembly seats in Magadh. The JD(U) performed particularly well in Magadh region, the party's traditional stronghold.

Table 7.1

Region-wise analysis of results: Assembly election, 2010

Regions	Total Seats	Turnout	BJP		JD(U)		RJD		LJNSP		INC		Other Parties	
			Won	Vote	Won	Vote	Won	Vote	Won	Vote	Won	Vote	Won	Vote
Tirhut	73	53.6	33	18.2	34	20.9	3	18.7	0	5.5	0	7.1	3	29.6
Mithila	43	52.4	12	11.2	22	28.1	9	23.8	0	5.1	0	9.0	0	22.8
Magadh	65	49.6	20	14.9	38	26.9	4	17.0	0	9.6	0	7.4	3	24.2
East	40	56.7	17	21.2	13	16.0	3	15.2	2	6.7	4	12.7	1	28.2
Bhojpur	22	53.1	9	16.9	8	17.6	3	21.7	1	5.6	0	6.0	1	32.2
Total	**243**	**52.7**	**91**	**16.5**	**115**	**22.6**	**22**	**18.8**	**3**	**6.7**	**4**	**8.4**	**8**	**27.0**

Source: CSDS Data Unit.

The East, which has a sizable Muslim population (one-third voters are Muslims in this region), remains a stronghold of the BJP, the ally of the JD(U). During the 2010 assembly elections, the BJP won 17 of the 40 assembly seats in this region and polled 21.2% votes, higher compared to 16.5% vote share in the state. It was a kind of repeat of BJP's performance in this region during the 2009 Lok Sabha election when the party won three of the five Lok Sabha seats, and polled 25.8% votes, higher compared to its average vote share in the state in that election. The BJP seemed to have benefitted from the higher turnout in this region, 56.7% compared to the state's average of 52.7%, as a result of the polarization of voters on religious lines. The shift in the Muslim vote away from the RJD resulted in a decline in the vote share of the RJD in this region both during the 2009 Lok Sabha and the 2010 assembly elections.

Many political commentators who summarized the electoral politics in Bihar in the past, simply in terms of caste-based voting, now concluded that the 2010 assembly elections were only about development and nothing else. People in Bihar, irrespective of their caste, voted for developmental work done by Nitish Kumar-led JD(U)–BJP government. While it is true that things have improved in Bihar during the last five years of JD(U)–BJP rule, especially with regard to condition of roads and law and order situation, it is not clear if this was the only issue which motivated the people to re-elect the government in 2010, which had been in power for the last five years. There is very little empirical evidence in the existing body of literature to support or contest such an argument. This chapter seeks to answer this question based on the results from the 2010 assembly elections, and from the empirical evidence collected from the post-poll survey conducted by CSDS in Bihar during the 2010 assembly elections.

If people in Bihar had voted only on their caste considerations or caste affiliations, the RJD and LJNSP should have done fairly well during the 2009 Lok Sabha as well as the 2010 assembly elections. Going by the voting pattern of various castes for various parties during the past few decades, the simple caste arithmetic should have put the RJD–LJNSP ahead of JD(U)–BJP combine, even though they had broken their alliance with the Congress. The electoral alliance of the RJD and LJNSP, in social terms, meant an alliance of the Yadavs, the Muslims, and the Dalits who constitute nearly 50% of the total electorate. The Muslims and Yadavs together constitute about 33.5% of the population, while Dalits account for 16.5% of state's population. With the Yadavs and

Muslims sharply polarized in favor of the RJD as indicated by studies in the past, the RJD should have performed well in this election (Kumar, 2005). Amongst the Dalit voters, a sizable proportion had voted for LJNSP since the party came into being. On the other hand, the JD(U) has a strong support base amongst the two dominant OBC castes, the Kurmis and the Koeris, and its alliance with the BJP did attract the upper caste voters. In simple arithmetic calculations of castes supporting or voting for the two alliances, the JD(U)–BJP lagged behind the RJD–LJNSP alliance. If people had voted only on caste lines, the RJD–LJNSP alliance should have got more votes compared to the ruling JD(U)–BJP alliance. But during both the 2009 Lok Sabha and 2010 assembly elections, the JD(U)–BJP alliance registered impressive victories, leaving behind the RJD–LJNSP combine by a huge margin. If this was one lone election, one would have even thought it was episodic, but the successive defeats of the RJD–LJNSP alliance do indicate that the caste equations which had helped them in the past were no more working in their favor. The results of the 2009 Lok Sabha elections gave initial indication for possible change in the nature of politics, but the emphatic victory of the ruling JD(U)–BJP alliance almost confirmed that the nature of politics has changed.

Did successive victories of the JD(U)–BJP combine, more so its impressive victory during the 2010 assembly elections, indicate that people in Bihar voted only on developmental issues and the ruling alliance did not mobilize the voters on caste lines? Did the traditional vote bank of different political parties melt down? Does this indicate an end to caste-based voting in Bihar? The chapter seeks to examine if the 2010 elections mark the beginning of a new phase, which may be seen as the fourth phase of politics in Bihar? Was development the real mantra for the electoral success of the ruling JD(U)–BJP coalition? The findings from the Bihar assembly elections study 2010 helped us in explaining what this verdict was all about.

For many, the 2010 assembly elections seemed to be the beginning of a new phase in politics of Bihar. People cited various reasons in favor of putting forward this argument. First, this election witnessed not only a significant increase in voter's participation in electoral process (from 45.9% during 2005 to 52.8% during 2010 assembly election) but also marked women voters outnumbering the men voters by a huge margin, a rare event in the Indian electoral history. While the overall turnout was 52.8%, the turnout amongst women was higher compared to men. Not only did the turnout increase, in popular perception, this election also changed the nature of electoral contest from caste-based voting to a positive vote for development, as the voters were generally happy by the ruling JD(U)–BJP-led state government. Some also believed this election to be historic due to the magnitude of victory and the immense personal popularity of Chief Minister Nitish Kumar.

Was This a Really Historic Victory?

If we compare the votes polled by the ruling JD(U)–BJP combine during the 2010 assembly elections with their vote share during the previous assembly elections (2005), it had increased merely by three percentage points. The vote share of the ruling coalition remained below 40% (39.1%). But if we compare the vote share of JD(U)–BJP during the 2010 assembly elections with all other assembly elections in Bihar, it was remarkable, since there have been only few occasions in the past (four assembly elections) when the ruling party/coalition managed to poll more than 40% votes. These were somewhat unusual elections, the first three assembly elections held at the backdrop of the euphoria of independence and the other was the 1977 assembly elections, when the anti-Indira/Congress wave was sweeping most of the states in North India, Bihar being one of them. Lalu Prasad Yadav, even at the peak of his popularity, managed to poll only 35.5% votes during the 1995 assembly elections. Although the ruling JD(U)–BJP combine did not have the maximum percentage of votes in the electoral history of Bihar, if we see that in terms of percentage of seats won, the ruling JD(U)–BJP alliance created history by winning 85% of the total seats in the state legislative assembly (see Table 7.2). One can hardly dispute that this was one of the biggest victories of the ruling party in the electoral history of Bihar. Not only was this the biggest victory of the ruling JD(U)–BJP alliance compared to past electoral verdict in Bihar, this could also be considered as one of the biggest victories in the electoral history of assembly elections held in various other states until now. Seen in terms of percentage of seats won in the assembly, there are only few other assembly elections where the ruling party/coalition managed to win more seats (in percentage terms) compared to the seats won by the ruling JD(U)–BJP alliance during the 2010 assembly elections. That happened twice in Sikkim, once in Tripura, and recently in the assembly elections held in Tamil Nadu (see Table 7.3).

Table 7.2

Electoral performance of the winning party: Assembly elections, 1952–2010

Year of Assembly Election	Winner Party	Votes Polled (%)	No. of Seats Won	(% of Total Assembly Seats the Winning Party Won)
1952	INC	41.4	239	72
1957	INC	42.1	210	66
1962	INC	41.4	185	58
1967	INC	33.1	128	40
1969	INC	30.5	118	36
1972	INC	33.1	167	51
1977	Janata Party	42.7	214	66
1980	INC	34.2	169	52
1985	INC	39.2	196	60
1990	JD	24.8	122	38
1995	JD+	35.5	205	63
2000	RJD+	29.5	127	52
2005 February	RJD+	28.3	82	34
2005 October	JD(U)+BJP	36.1	143	59
2010	JD(U)+BJP	39.1	206	85

Source: CSDS Data Unit.

Table 7.3

The significant victories: History of assembly elections

State (Year of Election)	Winner Party/ Front	Seats Won/ Total	Seat Share (%)	Vote Share (%)
Sikkim (2009)	SDF	32/32	100	66.0
Sikkim (2004)	SDF	31/32	97	71.1
Tripura (1977)	Left Front	54/60	90	49.7
J&K (1987)	NC–INC	66/76	87	53.2
Bihar (2010)	JD(U)–BJP	206/243	85	39.1
Bengal (2006)	Left Front	235/294	80	49.5
Bengal (2011)	TMRC	227/294	77	48.4
Tamil Nadu (2011)	ADMK+	203/234	87	51.8

Source: CSDS Data Unit.

Was the Electoral Success Only a Result of the Developmental Work of the Government?

The gross state domestic product (GSDP) of Bihar had grown at 11% per year between 2004–2005 and 2008–2009, when the all-India growth rate for the same period was at 8.5%, making Bihar the fastest growing state of the country. The national and the local media more or less jointly applauded the developmental work of the ruling JD(U)–BJP government, the echo of which could be heard nationally and internationally. Many commentators have attributed the state's turnaround to good governance and visible improvement in the road condition, and given the credit to Chief Minister Nitish Kumar for such an impressive performance on development. There were also counter-claims about the issue of development.

> The indexed values of Bihar gross state domestic product (GSDP) by major sectors for the period 1999–2000 to 2007–08 showed acceleration, predominantly in the secondary sector. During the period, the trend growth rate of primary, secondary and tertiary sectors was 0.7 percent, 12.9 percent and 6.9 percent per year respectively. In other words there was practically no growth in the primary sector and less than national average growth rate in the tertiary sector. On further disaggregation, it was seen that the boom in the secondary sector is entirely on account of construction, whose value add up two and half times in three years from Rs. 3100 crores in 2004 to Rs. 7400 crores in 2006–07—an annual growth rate of 46 percent. The mystery of Bihar's superlative growth therefore lies in the three year long construction boom. Bihar's economic growth during the last decade (2000–2010) was marginally lower than the national average, with considerable yearly fluctuations and two years of negative growth. The recent acceleration was narrow and based almost entirely on public works programmes during 2006–07 and 2008–09. Whether the completed work could boost value added in construction to such an extent seemed doubtful, given the infirmities in state domestic product estimation method. Moreover as per the official sources, the completed works was much less than those reported in the popular press and in the official advertisements. They also seem significantly less than the road works sanctioned. (Nagraj & Rahman, 2010)

Other interpretation of Central Statistical Organisation (CSO) data on domestic product for the decade since 1999–2000 also revealed a cyclical move toward a higher growth continuum rather than any structural break under the NDA government led by Nitish Kumar. There has been very little positive impact on agriculture, which is the lifeline of the bulk of the workforce in Bihar (Gupta, 2010). Citing data on various aspects of development, scholars had been able to point the holes in the claims of development by the government.

The findings from the micro-level study conducted by CSDS indicated there was a shared common perception of things having improved in Bihar during the last five years. There is no doubt that people of Bihar had felt that a lot of development had taken place in the state in the last five years (see Figure 7.1). During the survey, special attention was paid to collection of information about how had the situation changed with regard to infrastructural facilities available in primary and middle schools, government hospitals, and primary health centers in all the villages and localities in towns where the survey was conducted. The findings of the survey suggested that there was a shared feeling of a great deal of improvement in infrastructural facilities such as building and boundary wall of the school, facility of toilet and drinking water, and furniture in both primary and middle schools. Not only had the infrastructural facilities improved in primary and middle schools, but the attendance of teachers in schools was much more regular compared to what it used to be five years back (see Figures 7.2 and 7.3). There was a positive

Figure 7.1

Shared perception on Bihar development

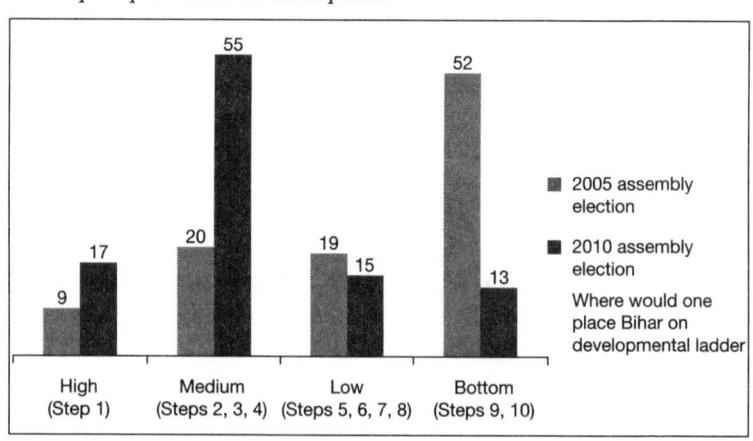

Sources: Bihar Assembly Election Study 2005 and 2010.

Note: All figures are in percent.

Figure 7.2

Improvement in infrastructural facilities in government schools

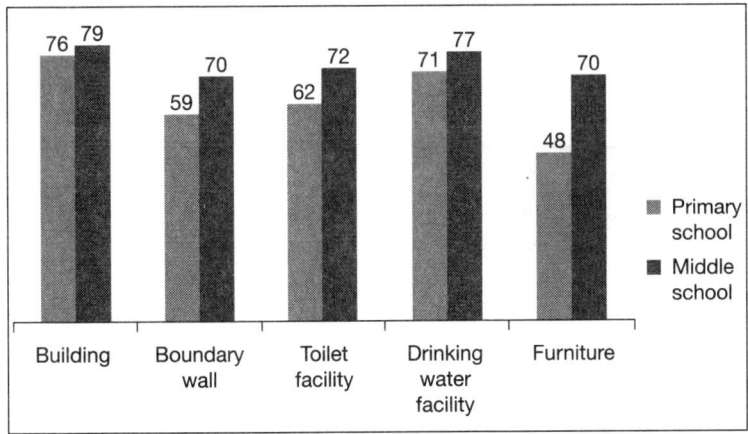

Source: Bihar Assembly Election Study 2010.

Notes: All figures reported here are in percent; figures reported for those who mentioned these facilities have improved during last five years, rest mentioned it remained the same, and very few mentioned deterioration in these facilities.

Figure 7.3

Improved attendance of teachers in government schools

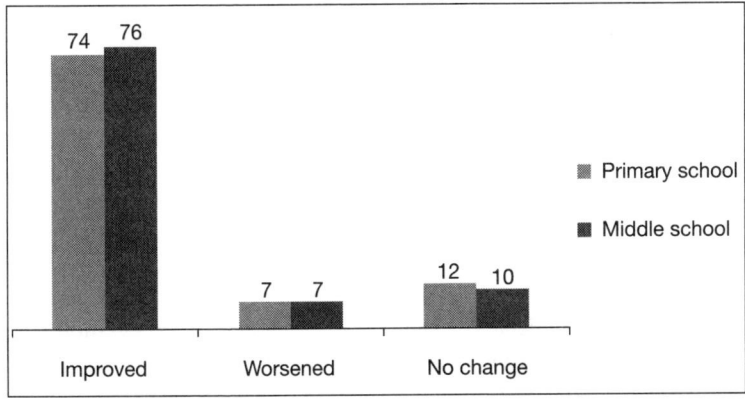

Source: Bihar Assembly Election Study 2010.

Notes: All figures are in percent; rest did not respond to this question.

Figure 7.4

Improved condition of government hospitals in the last five years

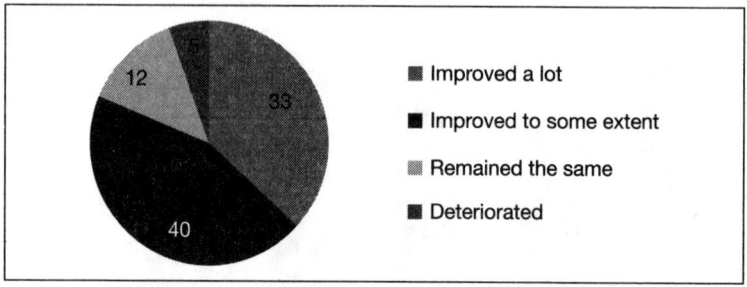

Source: Bihar Assembly Election Study 2010.

Notes: All figures are in percent; figures reported here are for those who mentioned these have improved.

evaluation by the people even about facilities available at government hospitals and primary health centers in villages. In varying degrees, two-thirds of the people believed that there had been improvement in the conditions of government hospitals, while only a very tiny proportion of people (5%) mentioned a negative view. There were another 12% people who believed that things had remained same with regard to government hospitals (see Figure 7.4). People expressed this positive opinion about government hospitals because majority experienced that free medicine and family planning pills were now easily available in government hospitals and primary health centers. They also experienced improved facility regarding various medical tests and better facility for free delivery (see Table 7.4). There was also overwhelming approval for improvement in law and order situation in the otherwise lawless Bihar. More than 90% of the people mentioned that incidences of robbery, theft, and murder or kidnapping had declined during last five years, while only a very small proportion of people held the opposite view. There were few others who did not find any noticeable change in the law and order situation (see Table 7.5). Even with the BJP being in power as an ally of the JD(U), there was a shared feeling that tension between various communities and castes has declined during the last five years. All these indicated enormous approval of development work done by the Nitish Kumar-led JD(U)–BJP government in Bihar during the last five years. The high approval of the work done by the JD(U)–BJP government could be seen

Table 7.4

Perception on improvement in medical facilities in government hospitals

Category of Hospitals	Free Medicine	Facility for Free Delivery	Free Pills for Family Planning	Free Facility for Blood, Urine, and the Like Tests	Facility for Free X-ray
Primary health centers	54	48	41	15	8
Government hospitals	57	63	51	29	23

Source: Bihar Assembly Election Study 2010.

Notes: All figures are in percent; figures reported here are for those who mentioned these have improved.

Table 7.5

Perception on improvement in law and order situation

Categories of Crime	Decreased	Increased	Remained the Same
Incidence of theft	92	3	5
Incidence of robbery	91	5	4
Incidence of kidnapping	93	2	5
Incidence of murder	87	5	8
Tension between religious groups	87	4	9
Tension between different castes	85	5	10

Source: Bihar Assembly Election Study 2010.

Note: All figures are in percent.

even in comparative perspective. Some believe that the ruling coalition government had not done anything dramatic during the last five years, but since the situation was very bad in Bihar, almost everything was at a standstill. In comparative perspective, even the little work done by Nitish government was seen as ushering wonders in the state by the common man on the streets. While it may be true that the rating of work done by the state government may have been slightly higher since people evaluated it in comparison to the prevailing situation in the state during the last decade, at the same time it is important to note that the evaluation was high even compared to how people evaluated the work of their own governments in different states that got re-elected during recent assembly elections (see Figure 7.5).

It was not only due to developmental work that people voted for the ruling JD(U)–BJP government in Bihar, but the ruling alliance also benefitted from high personal popularity of Chief Minister Nitish Kumar. The last 10 years had witnessed the rising personal popularity of Nitish Kumar while the popularity of Lalu Yadav had witnessed a decline during the same period (see Table 7.6). The popularity of Nitish Kumar was not high compared only to Lalu Yadav's popularity; his popularity was high compared to many other chief ministers in different states who had led their party to consecutive electoral successes in their respective states. Nitish Kumar was more or less equally popular compared to Shivraj Singh Chouhan, who led the BJP to successive victory in Madhya Pradesh; Raman Singh, who led the BJP to successive victory in Chhattisgarh; and Narendra Modi, who was about to complete his third term as the chief minister of Gujarat (see Figure 7.6). Although

Figure 7.5

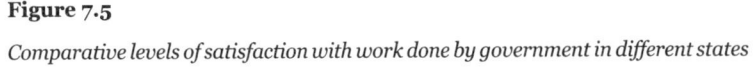

Comparative levels of satisfaction with work done by government in different states

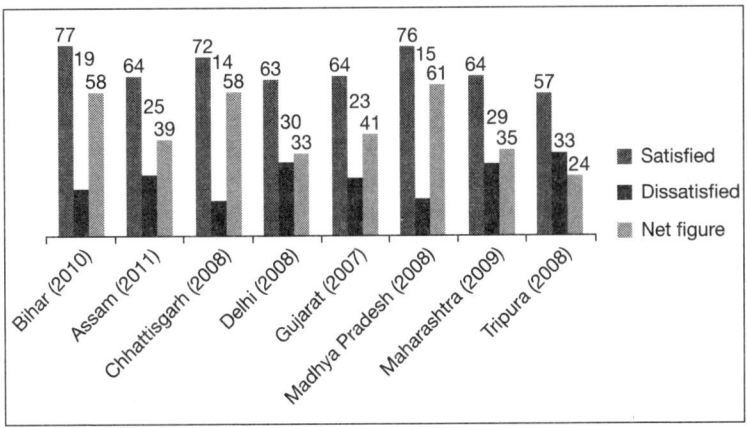

Source: Bihar Assembly Election Study 2010.

Notes: All figures are in percent; net figure is calculated by deducting figures of those who felt dissatisfied from figures of those who felt satisfied. The figure arrived after this calculation is reported as net figure.

Table 7.6

Popularity graph of Nitish Kumar

Leaders	2000	2004	2005 February	2005 October	2009	2010
Lalu Yadav + Rabri Devi	26	29	29	28	23	28
Nitish Kumar	5	22	24	43	60	53

Source: Findings from various post-poll surveys conducted in Bihar after Lok Sabha and assembly elections held in Bihar in respective years.

Sheila Dikshit had won two successive assembly elections (2003 and 2008) after Congress came to power in Delhi after its victory during the 1998 assembly elections, her popularity amongst Delhi's voters was lower compared to Nitish Kumar's popularity in Bihar. There was hardly any doubt that the ruling JD(U)–BJP government got re-elected due to the personal popularity of the chief minister and the developmental work done by the state government. But does that mean that people refrained from voting on caste lines during this election?

Figure 7.6

Rating of Nitish Kumar, higher compared to other chief ministers

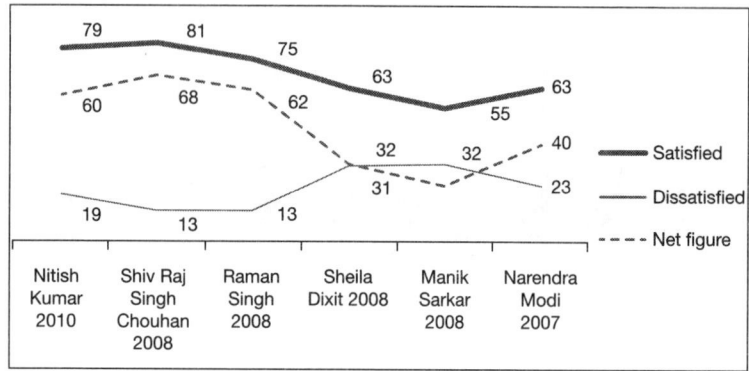

Source: Findings from various post-elections studies conducted in different states after the assembly elections held in that state.

Notes: All figures are in percent; net figure is calculated by deducting figures of those who felt dissatisfied from figures of those who felt satisfied. The figure arrived after this calculation is reported as net figure.

The Voting Patterns: Was Caste-based Mobilization Missing During the 2010 Assembly Elections?

The electoral history of Bihar during the last two decades gives us a glimpse of the decline and the resurgence of the RJD, seen in terms of seats won by the party during various assembly and Lok Sabha elections. The RJD may have won lesser number of seats, but the support base of the party did not decline very much at least until 2005 where it remained ahead of all other parties in terms of votes polled. During the February 2005 assembly elections, the RJD performed badly and won only 75 seats in the assembly, but with 25% of the total votes polled, it was ahead of all other parties in terms of vote share. The October 2005 assembly elections witnessed further decline of the RJD and it lost the assembly elections, but with 23.4% votes it still remained ahead of all other parties in terms of vote share. Until the October 2005 assembly election, which the RJD lost, even if it could not perform well, it still managed to hold on to its traditional support base amongst the Yadavs, the Muslims, and the lower OBCs. But things seem to have changed since the 2009 Lok Sabha elections. Not only did the RJD perform badly, its vote share also declined sharply. It was during the 2009 Lok Sabha elections that the RJD, for the first time, lagged behind the JD(U) even in terms of votes polled, a trend which continued during the 2010 assembly elections. During the 2009 Lok Sabha elections, the RJD polled 19.3% votes, but its vote share declined further to 18.8% during the 2010 assembly elections. Such a sharp decline in the vote share of the RJD was because the party lost its traditional supporters, the Yadavs, the Muslims, and the lower OBC castes. Did such sharp decline in the vote share of the RJD–LJNSP alliance which depended heavily on their caste arithmetic indicate that during the recent elections, the people in Bihar voted only on the issue of development and caste was not an issue?

The support base of the RJD has declined in recent election compared to its vote share in the early and mid-1990s, but the party still remains popular among the Yadavs in Bihar. It is true that even among Yadavs, the popularity of the RJD has declined marginally but still a majority of Yadavs voted for the RJD and its alliance election after election. Even though the vote share of the RJD went down to 19%, still 69% of Yadavs voted for the RJD (see Figure 7.7). A more careful analysis of

Figure 7.7

Voting pattern of Yadavs, Kurmi–Koeris, and upper castes

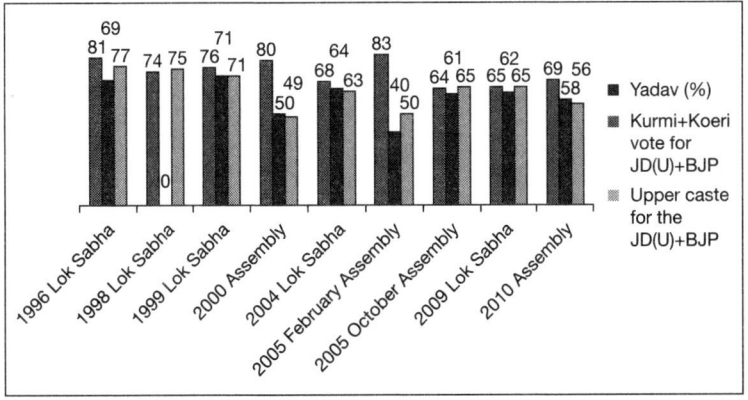

Source: Figures reported here are from various surveys conducted by CSDS, Delhi, in Bihar during various assembly and Lok Sabha elections.

Notes: All figures are in percent; figure for 1996 refers to vote share for the JD since the RJD came into being in 1998; figures reported are vote share for the RJD with its allies; the RJD contested various elections in alliance with different political parties (1996, RJD + CPI + CPM; 1998, RJD + INC + JMM; 1999, RJD + INC; 2000, RJD + CPM + M-COR; 2004, RJD + INC + LJNSP + NCP; 2005 February, RJD + CPI + CPM + NCP; 2005 October, RJD + INC + CPM + NCP; 2009, RJD + LJNSP; 2010, RJD + LJNSP).

how Yadavs voted indicates that the Yadavs remained much more polarized in favor of the RJD in constituencies where the RJD had put up a Yadav candidate. In such constituencies, more than 75% of Yadavs voted in favor of the RJD.

If on the one hand the Yadavs have remained polarized in favor of the RJD, voters belonging to the other two dominant OBC castes, the Kurmis and the Koeris, remained polarized in favor of the JD(U)–BJP alliance. The two parties had contested all the elections in Bihar since 1996 as allies. The alliance had performed well in some elections, while in others it did not. But irrespective of the electoral performance, the Kurmis and the Koeris voted for the JD(U)–BJP alliance in big numbers. While overall 58% of the voters from Kurmi and Koeri castes voted in favor of the JD(U)–BJP alliance, the polarization of voters from these two dominant OBC castes in favor of the JD(U)–BJP alliance was much higher in constituencies where the alliance had put up a candidate from these two castes. In constituencies where the JD(U)–BJP alliance candidate was either a Kurmi or a Koeri, an extremely high 95% voters from the two castes voted for the ruling alliance (see Figure 7.7).

The alliance of the JD(U) with the BJP helped in consolidation of the upper caste votes in their favor, evident clearly from the findings of the post-poll data. Majority of the upper castes voters had voted for the JD(U)–BJP alliance election after election. The upper caste polarization in favor of JD(U)–BJP was more in the early 1990s when the alliance was newly formed, then it witnessed some decline soon after that but the support of the alliance amongst the upper caste went up again in the last five years as evident from the data collected from elections during last five years (see Figure 7.7).

The upper caste and the three dominant OBC castes remained polarized in favor of one party or the other, irrespective of the changing fortunes of political party or alliance, but the Dalits had remained divided between the two alliances, the RJD-led alliance and the JD(U)–BJP alliance. Over several elections, the RJD managed to get just about one-third of Dalit votes. Even the alliance of the RJD with the LJNSP, which is popular amongst the Dalit voters due to the personal popularity of its leader Ram Vilas Paswan, failed in mobilizing the Dalit votes in favor of the RJD. During the 2004 Lok Sabha election, the RJD alliance managed to get more votes from the Dalits compared to the JD(U)–BJP alliance, but even in that election a sizable proportion of Dalits voted for other political parties and the independent candidates. During the two assembly elections held in 2005, the LJNSP contested elections independently without any ally. These elections witnessed splitting of the Dalit votes

Figure 7.8

Voting pattern of Dalits

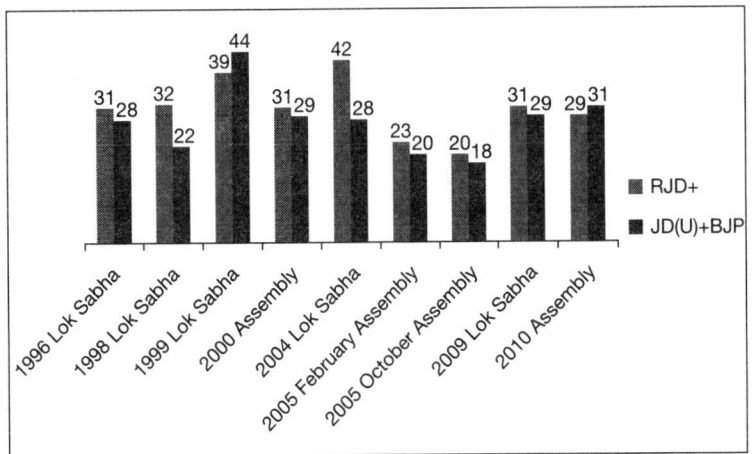

Source: Figures reported here are from various surveys conducted by CSDS, Delhi, in Bihar during various assembly and Lok Sabha elections.

Notes: All figures are in percent; figure for 1996 refers to vote share for the JD since the RJD came into being in 1998; figures reported here are vote share for the RJD with its allies; the RJD contested various elections in alliance with different political parties (1996, RJD+CPI+CPM; 1998, RJD+INC+JMM; 1999, RJD+INC; 2000, RJD+CPM+M-COR; 2004, RJD+INC+LJNSP+NCP; 2005 February, RJD+CPI+CPM+NCP; 2005 October RJD+INC+CPM+NCP; 2009, RJD+LJNSP; 2010, RJD+LJNSP).

amongst various political parties. During the assembly elections held in February 2005, both the RJD and the JD(U)–BJP alliance managed to corner about one-fifth of the Dalit vote, while the LJNSP managed to get 14% of their votes. The assembly elections held within a gap of few months (October 2005) hardly witnessed any change in voting patterns amongst the Dalits except for their greater polarization in favor of the LJNSP. During this election, 28% of the Dalits voted for the LJNSP. The alliance of the LJNSP with the RJD during the 2009 Lok Sabha and the 2010 assembly elections failed in mobilizing the Dalit vote in favor of the RJD alliance. Findings of the survey indicated that the 2010 assembly elections did not witness an overall shift of the Dalits in favor of the JD(U)–BJP and the alliance only got marginally more votes from them compared to the RJD–LJNSP alliance (see Figure 7.8). Did this mean that Nitish Kumar failed to mobilize Dalit votes in favor of his party/alliance even with his Mahadalit policy?

It would be early to conclude that Nitish Kumar failed in mobilizing the Dalits in favor of his party even after Mahadalit policy. According to the Mahadalit policy, the state government classified them into two categories, the lower Dalits with regard to the levels of social, economic, and educational attainment and upper Dalits who are better off in similar terms. Under such classification of the 14 Dalit castes in Bihar, all the 13 Dalits castes were classified as Mahadalit except Dusadh, the caste to which LJNSP leader Ram Vilas Paswan belonged. Under this Mahadalit policy, the state government extended various benefits to the castes belonging to the Mahadalit category. In a nutshell, it meant special treatment to all the 13 Dalit castes except the Dusadhs. While it is true that amongst Dalits, the Dusadhs are the most affluent, keeping only the Dusadhs out of the Mahadalit group meant appeasing all Dalit castes except Dusadh.

The findings of the survey indicated that Nitish Kumar did benefit from the Mahadalit policy. Although the Dalit voters had remained divided and never consolidated behind Ram Vilas Paswan, with the policy of Mahadalit, Nitish Kumar to a great extent managed to consolidate the Dalits votes in favor of the ruling alliance except for the Dusadh, though a still large proportion of Dalits voted for other political parties such as the CPI, CPM, or CPML. Large numbers among them also voted for independent candidates. Amongst Dusadh voters, 21% voted for the ruling JD(U)–BJP alliance, while 55% voted for the RJD–LJNSP alliance. On the contrary, amongst all the other Dalit caste voters, 35% voted for the ruling JD(U)–BJP alliance and only 16% voted for the RJD–LJNSP alliance. Large proportion of 44% Dalits voted for candidates of other smaller parties and independents (see Table 7.7).

While the RJD got support from voters cutting across caste–communities, the MY alliance (popularly known as MY factor) formed the backbone of the electoral strength of the RJD. Findings of the survey indicated that Muslim voters had voted for the RJD and its allies in huge

Table 7.7

Divided Dalit vote: Assembly election, 2010

Caste Category	RJD+	NDA+	Congress	Other Parties and Independents
Dusadh	55	21	8	16
Other Dalits	16	35	5	44

Source: Bihar Assembly Elections 2010.

Note: All figures are in percent.

numbers, election after election. Even during the October 2005 assembly elections, which the RJD lost and the JD(U)–BJP government was formed in Bihar, 58% of Muslims voted for the RJD. But things seem to have changed since the 2005 assembly elections. Although the RJD lost that election, the party still managed to poll sizable proportion of votes, mainly because the Yadavs and Muslim voted for the RJD in big numbers. The 2009 Lok Sabha elections witnessed a shift in the Muslim vote bank of the RJD. During the 2009 Lok Sabha elections, only 30% of the Muslim voted for the RJD. The 2010 assembly election did not witness any shift in the Muslim support for the RJD and in that election, 32% of the Muslim voted for the RJD. Although the RJD lost its Muslim support enormously, the JD(U)–BJP alliance failed to attract the Muslim voters in its favor in similar proportion. Although Congress did not perform well, the party managed to attract the Muslim voters in constituencies dominated by Muslim voters. In 14 assembly seats where the Muslims constituted more than 35% of voters, Congress polled 16.4% votes, a little more than double the vote share of the party in the entire state, and in these constituencies, the vote share of the RJD–LJNSP alliance was 17.6%, nearly 8% less compared to the vote share of the alliance in the entire state (see Figure 7.9). This was in spite of the fact that

Figure 7.9

The Muslims voting pattern for JD–RJD alliance

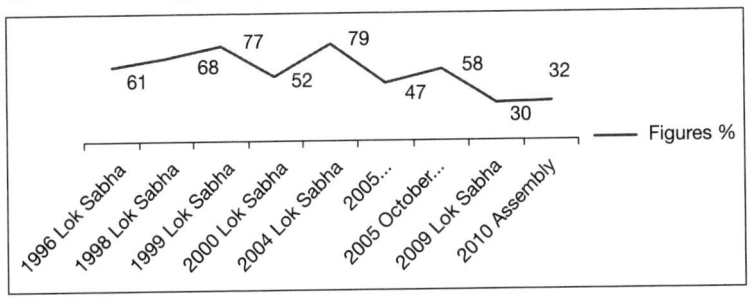

Source: Figures reported here are from various surveys conducted by CSDS, Delhi, in Bihar during various assembly and Lok Sabha elections.

Notes: All figures are in percent; figure for 1996 refers to vote share for the JD since the RJD came into being in 1998; figures reported are vote share for the RJD with its allies amongst Muslims the RJD contested various elections in alliance with different political parties (1996, RJD+CPI+CPM; 1998, RJD+INC+JMM; 1999, RJD+INC; 2000, RJD+CPM+M-COR; 2004, RJD+INC+LJNSP+NCP; 2005 February, RJD+CPI+CPM+NCP; 2005 October, RJD+INC+CPM+NCP; 2009, RJD+LJNSP; 2010, RJD+LJNSP).

the RJD–LJNSP alliance had put up 10 Muslim candidates in these 14 Muslim-dominated assembly constituencies. The Congress also did not lag behind and had given tickets to 12 Muslims in these 14 assembly constituencies. The vote share of the JD(U)–BJP alliance was nearly 8% less compared to the alliance average vote share in those constituencies. Besides this, findings of the survey also indicated that a large proportion of Muslim voters (37%) voted for the Congress candidates in these 14 Muslim-dominated assembly constituencies, while only 17% Muslim voted for the RJD–LJNSP alliance. A large proportion amongst the Muslims (35%) voted for strong independent candidates in these Muslim-dominated constituencies. More Muslims voted for the RJD–LJNSP candidates in constituencies where Muslims were in the range of about 15–30% of total electorate. While the ruling JD(U)–BJP alliance got less votes in assembly constituencies where Muslims were more than 35% of total electorates, the vote share of the ruling alliance was evenly spread in all other constituencies. Does that mean that Nitish Kumar failed to mobilize the Muslim voters in his favor even when his various welfare policies were aimed at the social and economic upliftment of the lower class Muslims, popularly known as "Pasmanda Muslims"?

While it may be difficult to say if the Muslims resorted to strategic voting during the 2010 assembly elections, the findings of the survey indicate a definite splitting of the Muslim vote. It is true that the RJD lost a sizable support among the Muslim voters, but the party still remained the first choice of Muslim voters in constituencies where the RJD candidate was contesting against a BJP or JD(U) candidate. In such constituencies, 41% of the Muslims voted for the RJD, while in constituencies where RJD was in contest against the JD(U) candidate, 37% Muslim voted for the RJD and 29% voted for the JD(U). In such constituencies, 21% Muslim voted for the Congress. While the RJD managed to hold on to its Muslim support to some extent, it could not manage to transfer its Muslim support to its alliance partner, the LJNSP. In constituencies where the LJNSP contested as part of seat-sharing arrangement with the RJD, the Muslim deserted the RJD alliance and voted for the Congress in sizable numbers (see Table 7.8).

Besides the three dominant OBC castes, there are various other OBC castes which constitute nearly one-fifth (20%) of the total voters in Bihar. Due to the numerical strength, they are seen as important vote banks by political parties. While the political parties may eye on the lower OBC as a vote bank, but since the lower OBC constitute of various castes, many of the voters of different lower OBC caste vote differently. While the

Table 7.8

The fractured Muslim vote: Assembly election, 2010

Contest Type	RJD+	NDA+	Congress
RJD vs JD(U)	37	29	21
RJD vs BJP	41	18	16
LJNSP vs JD(U)	19	21	20
LJNSP vs BJP	20	7	37

Source: Bihar Assembly Elections 2010.

Note: All figures are in percent.

smaller sample size does not allow us data to such detailed analysis, the very fact that the votes of the lower OBC had remained divided between the RJD and the JD(U) alliances indicates that various castes within the lower OBC castes had voted differently election after election. The shift in the vote of the lower OBC castes in favor of the JD(U) alliance began during the October 2005 assembly elections and continued even after that. One could clearly see the decisive shift of the lower OBC voters in favor of the ruling JD(U)–BJP alliance during the 2009 Lok Sabha and the 2010 assembly elections. During these two elections, 58 and 55% of lower OBC castes respectively voted for the JD(U)–BJP alliance, giving them a decisive lead, while only a very small proportion of the lower OBC castes voted for the RJD alliance (see Table 7.9).

Conclusion

Few things which emerged from the findings of 2010 elections were that one may have had dispute on the extent of development that had taken place in Bihar during the last five years, but one could hardly dispute that for the common man in Bihar, things had improved and it was not the same Bihar where they lived five years ago. One could also debate on the extent of impact that the development may have had on the voting decision of people during the 2010 assembly election, but one can hardly question if development was one of the dominant issues in the mind of the voters. Also, it is true that the caste-based support base of political parties had loosened a bit, but it may be incorrect to say that the 2010 assembly elections witnessed complete disappearance of caste-based

Table 7.9

The voting patterns amongst lower OBC

Year of Election	RJD+	JD(U) + BJP
1996 Lok Sabha	37	36
1998 Lok Sabha	26	41
1999 Lok Sabha	30	45
2000 assembly	35	25
2004 Lok Sabha	38	36
2005 February assembly	24	26
2005 October assembly	22	48
2009 Lok Sabha	12	58
2010 assembly	13	55

Source: Figures reported in the table are from various surveys conducted by CSDS, Delhi, in Bihar during various assembly and Lok Sabha elections.

Notes: All figures are in percent; figure for 1996 refers to vote share for the JD since the RJD came into being in 1998; figures reported in the table are vote share for the RJD with its allies amongst Muslims; the RJD contested various elections in alliance with different political parties (1996, RJD+CPI+CPM; 1998, RJD+INC+JMM; 1999, RJD+INC; 2000, RJD+CPM+M-COR; 2004, RJD+INC+LJNSP+NCP; 2005 February, RJD+CPI+CPM+NCP; 2005 October, RJD+INC+CPM+NCP; 2009, RJD+LJNSP; 2010, RJD+LJNSP).

voting and that the ruling party refrained from using caste as a tool for voter's mobilization. While the ruling JD(U)–BJP alliance used development as trump card, it may be incorrect to say to that the ruling alliance completely abstained from caste-based mobilization. The Mahadalit and Pasmanda Muslim were clear and successful attempts of the ruling alliance to break the vote bank of the RJD among Muslims and Dalits. This election may not end the argument and counter-argument on development vs caste, but the last five years had certainly changed the popular perception of Bihar at least in the minds of the people who live in Bihar. A large majority of people living in Bihar believe that things have changed during the last five years. Nearly 72% of people living in Bihar saw Bihar on the top half of the developmental ladder, while only 29% people placed Bihar on the same developmental ladder five years ago. Only 13% people believed that Bihar is at the bottom of the developmental ladder, an opinion which was shared by the majority only five years ago. It is true that development had not reached all sectors, it may have been a mere showcasing and facelift by the ruling alliance, but such a strong perception of the people about things having improved should have some consonance with reality. It is unlikely that such shared perception will be completely delinked from the reality.

References

Gupta, C.D. (2010, December 25). Unravelling Bihar's growth miracle. *Economic & Political Weekly*, *45*(52), 50–62.

Kumar, S. (2005). Bihar assembly elections: RJD needs an alliance for victory. *Economic and Political Weekly,* 40(3), 190–193.

Nagraj, R., & Rahman, A. (2010, February 20). Booming Bihar: Fact or fiction. *Economic & Political Weekly*, *45*(8), 10–11.

8

The Question of Development or Identity: Elections During 2014–2015

The 2014 Lok Sabha elections seem to have marked a new beginning in the politics of Bihar. If the last two decades (1989–2009) of politics were marked by massive social and political mobilization of people belonging to the OBCs, the 2014 elections marked the beginning of a massive consolidation of the upper castes in favor of the Narendra Modi-led BJP. This was also supported by mobilization of sections of the OBC and Dalit voters in favor of the BJP and its allies, a result of BJP's alliance with Ram Vilas Paswan-led LJNSP and Upendra Kushwaha's RLSP. One cannot deny that people's strong desire for change in national government due to their massive dissatisfaction with the Congress-led UPA government resulted in large number of people voting for the BJP by default as they saw it as a viable national alternative. At the same time, the BJP's carefully crafted alliance with other parties aimed at building social coalition of voters from different castes helped them in registering a massive victory in Bihar. The opposition parties/alliance RJD–Congress on the one hand and the JD(U) on the other hand not only lost badly but also failed to put up a strong contest against the BJP–LJNSP–RLSP alliance. In the early 1990s, it was Lalu Prasad Yadav who benefitted from the mobilization of the OBCs and remained the undisputed leader of Bihar for nearly one and a half decade (1989–2004). In the later half of the 1990s, the JD(U) led by Nitish Kumar (in alliance with BJP) managed to mobilize the OBCs in Bihar and emerged as a strong leader in Bihar. In the recently held 2014 Lok Sabha elections, the BJP with its allies managed to turn the table upside down and swept the polls in Bihar by forming similar coalitions.

The Results

In a three-cornered electoral contest, the BJP and its allies registered a remarkable victory in Bihar by winning 31 of the total 40 Lok Sabha seats and polled 38.8% votes. The BJP on its own won 22 of the 30 seats it contested, while its ally, the LJNSP, won 6 of the 7 seats. The BJP's other ally RLSP won three of the four Lok Sabha seats. The RJD–Congress alliance together polled 29.8% votes and won only seven seats. The ruling party JD(U) performed badly by winning only two seats, and its vote share was as low as 15.8%.

The BJP and its allies performed well in almost all the regions of Bihar, but still the alliance has been relatively stronger in some regions compared to other, while its opponents have been able to put up some contest in some regions. The BJP and its allies swept the election in Tirhut region, winning all the 12 seats. Here, the alliance polled 44.1% votes, nearly 5% higher compared to its average vote share in the state. The alliance also performed very well in Magadh region, winning 9 of the 10 seats, with 40.7% votes. The RJD–Congress alliance performed well in the East region of Bihar which had a sizable Muslim population. Of the seven Lok Sabha seats in this region, the RJD–Congress alliance managed to win five seats and polled 35.2% votes, nearly 5% more compared to its average vote share in the state. More than the concern about the JD(U) performing badly in the entire state, the bigger worry for the party was its poor performance in the Magadh region, its own stronghold.

How does one look at this vote in Bihar? Some believe that this was a vote for development, while others say that this is an aspirational vote. There was a general belief that the voters stood above considerations of caste and religion and voted for the BJP and its allies in large numbers. Does such a rejection of the ruling party in the state raise questions about the development work done by the JD(U) government in the state or does it imply that there can be critical political circumstances when a reasonably good record of developmental work done by the government does not matter? Does it also imply that the Bihar voter is making a clear distinction between the Lok Sabha polls and an assembly poll? The voters of Bihar have not rejected the good work done by the Nitish Kumar-led JD(U) government, but voted for the BJP and its allies in such a big number only because these were Lok Sabha elections; they could still make a comeback toward the ruling JD(U) in the assembly elections that were held in the year 2015.

When the electoral process began in early January and the BJP had started making headways in Bihar, the voters had indicated somewhat different voting preferences for the Lok Sabha elections and for the assembly elections in a hypothetical scenario that was given to them regarding assembly elections being held at the same time. The voters had indicated somewhat different voting preference for the Lok Sabha and the assembly elections in case both are held together. But as the days passed, the findings of the surveys conducted over a period of time indicated a changing voting preference amongst the voters. More and more voters seemed inclined to vote for the BJP for both the Lok Sabha and the assembly elections. The distinction shown by the voters in their voting preference in early January or late December seemed to have blurred by the end of April. By the end of April one cannot say for sure voters of Bihar would vote the same way they have voted during the Lok Sabha elections, but the results of the Lok Sabha elections clearly indicated, voters voting the way they had indicated in the surveys. It seems that as the campaign progressed, the BJP's popularity increased and voters somehow were ready to prefer voting for the BJP even during the assembly elections. It is difficult to say till the final results are out, but the findings of the CSDS post-poll survey does indicate the ruling party will face a tough political challenge in Bihar. There are initial indications that even if voters of Bihar may approve of the developmental work done by the ruling JD(U) government, they may be willing to vote them out for an even better government (expected).

Does this massive victory of the BJP alliance and poor performance of the JD(U) indicate the beginning of an end to the Nitish Kumar-led JD(U) government in Bihar? Does this defeat of the JD(U) indicate rejection of the notion of work done by the state government during the last few years? The vote share of the JD(U) and the seats it managed to win in the Lok Sabha elections does not indicate complete rejection of the work done by the ruling JD(U) government. The findings of the post-poll survey data indicate that people may not be as happy as they were some years ago with the developmental work done by the ruling JD(U) government; at the same time, one should not conclude that people are critical about the work done by the Nitish Kumar-led government in Bihar, though many of them may not have voted for the ruling party in these elections.

In some states, more so in states ruled by parties other than the BJP, people voted for the BJP in big numbers as they had been fed up by the relatively poor record of developmental work done by the state government. But in Bihar, there had been a mixed response of the people on how they evaluated the work done by the Nitish Kumar government. Although the positive endorsement of the work done by the state government was not as strong as it was a few years ago, especially after the government completed its first term in office (2005–2010), overall there was a positive evaluation of the state government. Although opinions of the people get colored on the basis of their political choices, even then more people believed that the condition of government schools had improved during the last five years. There were also positive views of the people with regard to the situation of supply of electricity, as more believed that it had improved. The views were not that positive on the issue of women safety or employment generation. Large numbers of people were correct in making a distinction that the responsibility of providing facility of school and electricity belonged to the state government, while the issue of women safety or employment was the joint responsibility of both the central and the state governments. Sizable number of voters also confirmed that they individually or someone in their family had benefitted from various schemes such as Indira Awas Yojana, NREGA, National Rural Health Mission, and Old Age Pension. Large numbers of them also believed that it is the state government which was responsible for giving them these benefits. So, overall there was a shared belief that the performance of the state government had been good if not excellent. Hence, if people had only voted for development, the ruling JD(U) should not have performed as badly as they did. A large number of people voted on issues other than development, their desire for change of the government at the center, and their preference for Narendra Modi as the next prime minister of India, but still it would be incorrect to say that the caste-based mobilization was missing in this election and caste hardly played any role in these elections.

Those who saw the results in Bihar either only as rejection of the "good" work done by the state government or only as an aspirational vote could have misread the verdict. The electoral verdict in Bihar was a mix of beginning of some dissatisfaction with the work done by the Nitish Kumar government during the last few years and a strong desire for change at the center. This desire for change could be interpreted as a growing aspiration, but one would be misreading the verdict if this verdict is seen as merely an aspirational vote. By forming an alliance with other political parties, the BJP did try to work out a social coalition of voters belonging to different castes, especially those unattached to the RJD or the JD(U) with the hope that it would be able to bring them to their fold.

It is true that voters from various castes voted for the BJP and its allies, but at the same time the carefully crafted alliance helped the BJP in building a solid vote bank of various castes and communities, which has been instrumental in the BJP's massive victory in Bihar in 2014.

The massive victory of the BJP and its alliance was a result of the BJP's well-crafted alliance with the LJNSP and RLSP in order to expand its support base by forming a social coalition. The ruling JD(U) had broken its alliance from the BJP before the elections, and the BJP could have never imagined to form an alliance with the RJD or the Congress. The BJP found Ram Vilas Paswan and Upendra Kushwaha as its favorite allies. It is not sure if the BJP would be able to mobilize the voters belonging to the dominant OBC castes, the Kurmis, or the Yadavs and almost sure of not being able to mobilize the Muslims. The BJP's alliance with the LJNSP and RLSP was clearly an effort to form a social coalition of the upper castes, Dalits, and sections of OBCs, mainly the Koeris. The BJP was not alone in forming alliances with political parties keeping in mind the social coalition which such political alliance would bring in, as the RJD also entered into an alliance with the Congress keeping in mind the MY alliance which has paid political dividends to Lalu Yadav in the past, especially in the mid-1990s. On the other hand, the JD(U) was hoping that besides its core support amongst the Kurmis, it would manage to get votes from various sections of society (read caste) due to its development work done in Bihar during last few years (see Figure 8.1).

The findings of the post-poll survey data indicate that the political alliance formed by various parties did help in forming strong social coalition. This helped the party/alliance in mobilizing votes in their favor from particular castes. The BJP did benefit from its alliance with the LJNSP and RLSP, as this election witnessed a sharp shift in the voting preference of the Dalits more so amongst the Dusadh (Paswans) in Bihar (see Figure 8.2 and Table 8.1). This election witnessed the sharpest polarization of the upper castes voter in favor of the BJP and its allies (see Table 8.1). Findings of the survey indicate that 78% of the upper castes voted for the BJP alliance. Even in the past when the BJP contested the elections in alliance with the JD(U), they attracted large number of upper caste votes. In the early 1990s, more than 70% upper castes voted for the BJP–JD(U) alliance, but these elections witnessed unprecedented polarization of the upper castes in favor of the BJP alliance (see Figure 8.3).

The alliance also helped the BJP in mobilizing voters belonging to the lower backward castes. Findings of the survey indicate that majority

Figure 8.1

Split of Kurmi–Koeri vote between JD(U) and BJP in 2014

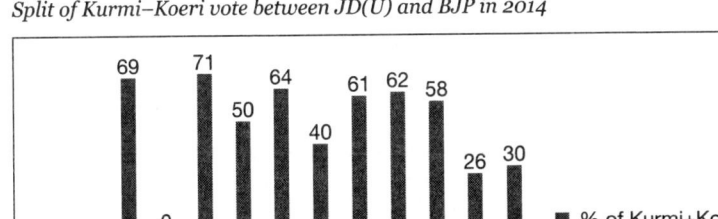

Source: Figures reported here are from various surveys conducted by CSDS, Delhi, in Bihar during various assembly and Lok Sabha elections.

Notes: Figure for BJP+ refers to Kurmi+Koeri vote for the BJP+JD(U) from 1996 until 2010; figure for 2014 indicates BJP+LJNSP+RLSP.

of the lower OBC castes voted for the BJP alliance, much bigger than their voting for any party or alliance in the past with minor exceptions. Amongst the lower OBCs, 53% voted for the BJP alliance, while only 18% voted for the JD(U), the party which championed the cause of the lower OBCs in Bihar. Only 10% of them voted for the RJD–Congress alliance (see Table 8.2).

The BJP's strategy of forming an alliance with the LJNSP did pay dividends. Amongst all Dalit castes, 42% voted for the BJP and its alliance, while only 10% voted for the RJD–Congress alliance, and 20% of them voted for the JD(U) in spite of the ruling party's effort for social and economic development of people belonging to these castes by declaring them as Mahadalit. The BJP was even more successful in mobilizing the voters from the Paswan caste (Dusadh) within the Dalits due to its alliance with Ram Vilas Paswan. Findings of the survey indicated that amongst the Dusadh, 68% voted for the BJP and its allies, while 10% of them voted for the RJD–Congress alliance, with only 6% voting for the JD(U).

The alliance between political parties did not only benefit the BJP in forming social coalition, as the RJD having formed an alliance with the Congress resulted in a strong polarization of the Yadavs and Muslims in

Figure 8.2

Fragmentation in the Dalit vote

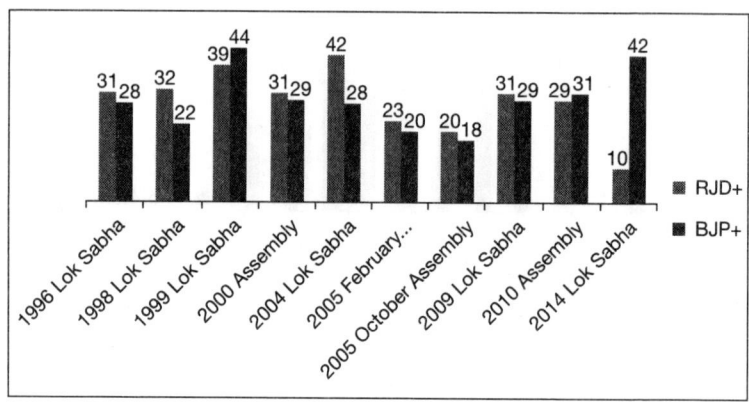

Source: Figures reported here are from various surveys conducted by CSDS, Delhi, in Bihar during various assembly and Lok Sabha elections.

Notes: All figures are in percent; figure for 1996 refers to vote share for the JD since the RJD came into being in 1998; figures reported here are vote share for the RJD with its allies; the RJD contested various elections in alliance with different political parties (1996, RJD+CPI+CPM; 1998, RJD+INC+JMM; 1999, RJD+INC; 2000, RJD+CPM+M-COR; 2004, RJD+INC+LJNSP+NCP; 2005 February, RJD+CPI+CPM+NCP; 2005 October, RJD+INC+CPM+NCP; 2009, RJD+LJNSP; 2010, RJD+LJNSP); figures for BJ+ in 2014 include BJP, LJNSP, and RLSP and for RJD+ include RJD and Congress in 2014.

Table 8.1

BJP's alliance with Paswan (Lok Sabha 2014) helped in getting Dalit vote

Caste Category	RJD+	BJP+	JD(U)
Dusadh/Paswan	10	68	6
Other Dalit castes	10	33	25

Source: CSDS Data Unit.

Notes: All figures are in percent; figures for BJP+ in 2014 include BJP, LJNSP, and RLSP and figures for RJD+ include RJD and Congress.

favor of the RJD–Congress alliance (see Tables 8.3 and 8.4). The survey data indicated that 64% of the Yadavs voted for the RJD–Congress alliance. By forming an alliance with the Congress, the RJD was able to present this alliance as a viable alternative that could challenge the BJP in Bihar. This to a great extent helped in keeping the Yadavs polarized

Figure 8.3

Sharpest polarization of the upper castes for BJP+ in 2014

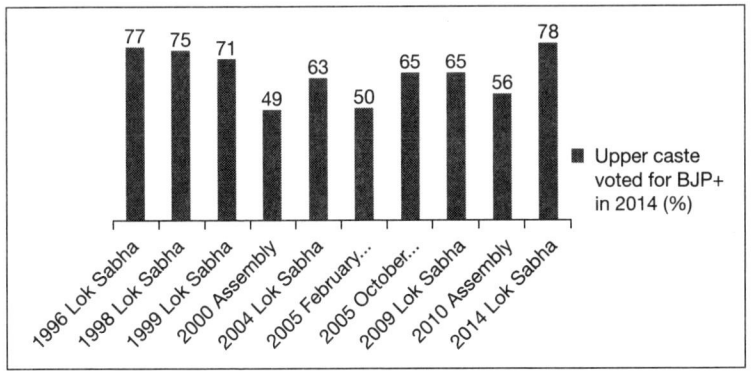

Source: Figures reported here are from various surveys conducted by CSDS, Delhi, in Bihar during various assembly and Lok Sabha elections.

Notes: Figure for BJP+ refers to Dalit vote for the BJP+JD(U) from 1996 until 2010; figure for 2014 indicates BJP+LJNSP+RLSP.

in favor of the RJD and prevented the shifting of the Yadav vote from the RJD to the BJP alliance. The alliance of the RJD with the Congress helped the party in holding on to its Yadav support bases which otherwise may have shifted toward the BJP alliance in sizable proportions, as it happened in the neighboring Uttar Pradesh. The BJP did try to mobilize the Yadav votes in Bihar, but was not very successful as only 18% of Yadavs voted for the BJP and its alliance.

The RJD's alliance with Congress helped Lalu Yadav in regaining its Muslim support bases which the party had started losing slowly and gradually. During the 2009 Lok Sabha and 2010 assembly elections, only 30% of the Muslim voted for the RJD. In most elections held in the past, majority of the Muslim voted for the RJD. Its alliance with the Congress helped in Muslim consolidation behind the RJD–Congress alliance as 64% of the Muslim voted for this alliance. The RJD–Congress alliance failed to attract any other castes in its favor. The situation of the ruling JD(U) was even worse, it failed to attract voters from even a single caste in sizable numbers.

Looking at these trends and patterns of voting, it would be difficult to say that caste-based mobilization was missing in these elections and people voted only on the issue of development. Caste mobilization did play a role in these elections, earlier it was engineered by RJD, now it worked in favor of the BJP.

Table 8.2

The 2014 Lok Sabha elections' decisive shift in the lower OBC vote toward the BJP in 2014

Year of Election	RJD+	JD(U)+BJP
1996 Lok Sabha	37	36
1998 Lok Sabha	26	41
1999 Lok Sabha	30	45
2000 assembly	35	25
2004 Lok Sabha	38	36
2005 February assembly	24	26
2005 October assembly	22	48
2009 Lok Sabha	12	58
2010 assembly	13	55
2014 Lok Sabha	10	53

Source: Figures reported in the table are from various surveys conducted by CSDS, Delhi, in Bihar during various assembly and Lok Sabha elections.

Notes: All figures are in percent; figure for 1996 refers to vote share for the JD since the RJD came into being in 1998; figures reported in the table are vote share for the RJD with its allies amongst Muslims; the RJD contested various elections in alliance with different political parties (1996, RJD+CPI+CPM; 1998, RJD+INC+JMM; 1999, RJD+INC; 2000, RJD+CPM+M-COR; 2004, RJD+INC+LJNSP+NCP; 2005 February, RJD+CPI+CPM+NCP; 2005 October, RJD+INC+CPM+NCP; 2009, RJD+LJNSP; 2010, RJD+LJNSP); figures for B+ in 2014 include BJP, LJNSP, and RLSP.

The 2015 assembly election again changed the scenario, and Nitish Kumar's work along with RJD and Congress helped him to re-establish his political gain.

Nitish Kumar's Development in Bihar, Paid Dividends

The long suspense about Bihar elections came with the JD(U)–RJD–Congress alliance, popularly referred as "Mahagathbandhan" or "GA," pulling a stunning victory. This verdict gave Chief Minister Nitish Kumar a third term in office. The alliance gave a spectacular performance by winning 178 seats with 41.9% of the popular votes. The BJP-led NDA was badly defeated and was restricted to only 58 seats with 34.1% votes. In this bipolar contest, the other parties, namely, Samajwadi Party, Pappu

Table 8.3

Yadavs have remained polarized in favor of RJD+

Year of Election	(%)
1996 Lok Sabha	81
1998 Lok Sabha	74
1999 Lok Sabha	76
2000 assembly	80
2004 Lok Sabha	68
2005 February assembly	83
2005 October assembly	64
2009 Lok Sabha	65
2010 assembly	69
2014 Lok Sabha	64

Source: Figures reported in the table are from various surveys conducted by CSDS, Delhi, in Bihar during various assembly and Lok Sabha elections.

Notes: Figure for 1996 refers to vote share for the JD since the RJD came into being in 1998; figures reported in the table are vote share for the RJD with its allies; the RJD contested various elections in alliance with different political parties (1996, RJD+CPI+CPM; 1998, RJD+INC+JMM; 1999, RJD+INC; 2000, RJD+CPM+M-COR; 2004, RJD+INC+LJNSP+NCP; 2005 February, RJD+CPI+CPM+NCP; 2005 October, RJD+INC+CPM+NCP; 2009, RJD+LJNSP; 2010, RJD+LJNSP); figures for RJ+ in 2014 refer to RJD+Congress.

Yadav's Jan Adhikar Morcha, NCP, and Bahujan Samaj Party were completely marginalized. The independents and the smaller parties together polled 24% votes and managed to win only seven seats. In the previous assembly polls that the JD(U) and BJP fought together, the two parties had got 115 and 91 seats respectively. The RJD and the Congress, which had fought on their own, bagged 22 and 04 seats respectively. These elections grabbed a lot of media attention as it saw aggressive campaigning by the parties with many harsh comments from both sides. Both the alliances left no stone unturned in order to win the elections. The highlight of this election was the coming together of the JD(U), RJD, and Congress. Not only that, they all also agreed to project Nitish Kumar as their chief ministerial candidate. The post-poll survey by Lokniti-CSDS indicated that though both arithmetic and the chemistry worked wonderfully well for the two partners, they seem to have worked a tad more for the RJD than the JD(U) (Kumar & Sardesai, 2015).

Table 8.4

The 2014 Lok Sabha election witnessed Muslims coming back to RJD

Year of Election	%
1996 Lok Sabha	61
1998 Lok Sabha	68
1999 Lok Sabha	77
2000 assembly	52
2004 Lok Sabha	79
2005 February assembly	47
2005 October assembly	58
2009 Lok Sabha	30
2010 assembly	32
2014 Lok Sabha	64

Source: Figures reported in the table are from various surveys conducted by CSDS, Delhi, in Bihar during various assembly and Lok Sabha elections.

Notes: Figure for 1996 refers to vote share for the JD since the RJD came into being in 1998; figures reported in the table are vote share for the RJD with its allies amongst Muslims; the RJD contested various elections in alliance with different political parties (1996, RJD+CPI+CPM; 1998, RJD+INC+JMM; 1999, RJD+INC; 2000, RJD+CPM+M-COR; 2004, RJD+INC+LJNSP+NCP; 2005 February, RJD+CPI+CPM+NCP; 2005 October, RJD+INC+CPM+NCP; 2009, RJD+LJNSP; 2010, RJD+LJNSP).

Lalu Yadav's RJD finished ahead of Nitish Kumar's JD(U) in terms of both seats and votes. This happened despite both parties contesting on an equal number of seats and, more importantly, despite Nitish Kumar being a much more popular leader and the one in whose name votes were sought by the GA. What then explains this surprising outcome?

The GA's spectacular victory can be credited to impressive performance by all the three partners. Of the 101 seats contested, the RJD managed to win 80 seats, while of the similar number of seats contested, the JD(U) managed to win 71 seats. It was interesting to note that despite contesting on an equal number of seats, the RJD finished ahead of the JD(U). The Congress which contested 41 seats managed to win 27 seats (see Table 8.5). This was a huge improvement compared to its tally of four seats in the previous assembly. In fact, these elections were the first piece of good news for the party since its defeat in the 2014 general elections. The earlier chapters have shown how the performance of the party had deteriorated over the years. From nine seats in October 2005, four in

Table 8.5

Party-wise performance in the 2015 assembly election

Alliance	Vote Share (in %)	Seat Share
GA	41.9	178
JD(U)	14.4	71
RJD	21.5	80
Congress	6.0	27
NDA	34.1	58
BJP	24.1	53
LJNSP	3.5	2
RLSP	3.6	2
HAM	2.9	1
Socialist Secular Morcha	5.0	—
Left Front	3.8	3
BSP	3.6	—
Others	11.6	4

Source: CSDS Data Unit.

Note: Others also include independents.

2010, and not a single seat in 2014 Lok Sabha elections, the performance in these elections was a positive thing for the party. When this alliance was formed, there were speculations that it may not work at the ground as the core supporters of the JD(U) and RJD may not vote for the alliance partners, but there was successful transfer of votes by the alliance partners to each other and this led to the victory of the GA.

The NDA managed to win only 58 assembly seats. Not only did its allies perform badly, but its own performance was also disappointing. Of the 160 seats which the BJP contested, it managed to win 53 and 24.1% votes. Although the BJP ended up with maximum votes as a result of contesting the maximum number of seats (160), its vote share declined by 5% compared to 29% in the 2014 Lok Sabha elections. This is a continuation of the trend witnessed in all the assembly elections held after the 2014 Lok Sabha election, where the BJP's vote declined in all the subsequent five assembly elections. It is important to note that in terms of seats, the BJP was reduced to the third position, with the RJD being at first and the JD(U) at second positions. What made the situation worse for BJP was the performance of its allies. The LJNSP managed to win

2 seats of the 40 seats contested, while of the 20 seats which Hindustan Awam Party contested, Jitan Ram Manjhi was the lone winner. Among the NDA alliance partners, the worst performance was by Upendra Kushwaha-led RLSP which managed to win only 2 of the 23 seats contested. Not only the allies failed in transferring votes to each other, it seems that the NDA also failed to consolidate the Dalit vote which it had hoped to achieve by having an alliance with the two Dalit leaders, Ram Vilas Paswan and Jitan Ram Manjhi.

The Important Issue of Caste vs Development

Caste and development story came to acquire center stage in the state assembly elections of 2015. Although development became an important issue in this election, there were two other factors that were important. First, the verdict of Bihar assembly elections was clearly a vote for the development work done by the Nitish Kumar government during his last two terms, and not for what Prime Minister Narendra Modi promised. Second, the results should not be seen as merely the victory of caste alliances and electoral arithmetic crafted by the JD(U)–RJD and Congress as a result of their alliance. Even for the section of voters who voted for the GA on caste identity, it was backed by their firm belief that in the past, Lalu Yadav had been instrumental in giving them the voice, self-respect, and pride. These voters added a different meaning to development from their own dictionary.

Development was also seen as the biggest issue while voting in the 2015 assembly elections; 29% voters stated this as the issue, with 16% quoting price rise. Prior to the elections, both the NDA and GA began their campaign on issues related to development and economy, but soon caste and religion became the focal point (Verma & Sardesai, 2015). In this field, the GA was in a good position as caste was Lalu's domain and development was Nitish's, where the former was the biggest caste leader that the state had seen and he enthralled the audiences with his style and humor. Nitish, on the other hand, engaged his audience by talking about his development agenda and made it a point to focus on his achievements as the chief minister of the state (Bagchi, 2015). The NDA's campaign revolved around Modi who engaged the people in both caste rhetoric and development discourse which often led to Modi

Table 8.6

Caste vs development?

	2010 (%)	2015 (%)
Caste mattered more than development while voting	28	36
Development mattered more	61	54

Source: CSDS Data Unit.

Note: Rest gave no response.

underperforming on both the counts (Bagchi, 2015). Findings from the CSDS post-poll survey show that there was a sharp polarization of the voters regarding caste in the elections compared to the previous assembly election. Table 8.6 clearly shows that in comparison to the last assembly election, the 2015 elections saw an 8% increase among respondents who said that caste issues were more important for them in this election.

Both the alliances gave a lot of importance to development and tried to attract voters by playing the card to their advantage. Narendra Modi had played this card even in the Lok Sabha 2014 elections, but the GA seemed to benefit from it more as the people of Bihar felt that Bihar is no longer backward. When people were asked whether in the last five years there had been development in their state, 86% said that there had been development (27% said that a lot of development took place and 59% said that some development took place). Only 11% said no development had taken place in the last five years. This also impacted the voting choice of the people. Table 8.6 shows that many people in Bihar felt that their state had developed in the last 10 years. The voters were asked to rate their state's development on a scale of 1 to 10, with 1 being most developed and 10 being least developed. Most people chose to place Bihar in 4th–7th band, while 18% rated the state as underdeveloped, whereas this figure was 65% in 2005 (see Table 8.7).

There was a clear consolidation of voters on caste lines behind one alliance or the other. Where the NDA was supported by upper caste voters, the GA was supported by the Yadavs–Muslims–Kurmis. Among the upper castes, 84% voted for the NDA. Never had Bihar seen such a massive polarization of the upper caste voters in favor of the NDA. Sixty-eight percent among the Yadavs and 71% among the Kurmis voted for the GA, while the NDA managed to get only a small section of votes from these castes (see Figure 8.4). The NDA had hoped to mobilize the lower OBC voters in their favor but they seemed to have failed

Table 8.7

Increasing self-pride of Bihar among Biharis on the scale of development

Voters Who Saw Bihar As...	2005 October (%)	2010 (%)	2015 (%)
Highly developed (1–3)	9	16	22
Moderately developed (4–7)	19	55	47
Underdeveloped (8–10)	65	27	18

Source: CSDS Data Unit.

Note: Rest gave no response.

Figure 8.4

Voting pattern of various castes and communities

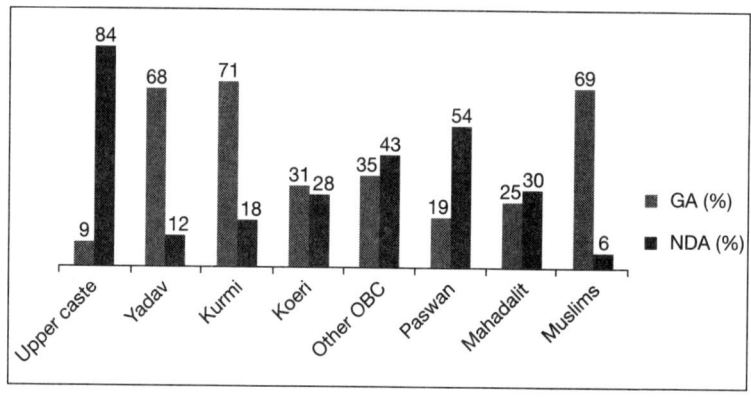

Source: CSDS Data Unit.

in mobilizing them. Among the EBC voters, 43% voted for the NDA, while 35% voted in favor of the GA. The NDA had also hoped to mobilize the Dalit votes in their favor, as it had both Dalit leaders on their side. While the NDA managed to get a sizable number of Paswan votes (54%), the Mahadalit votes got badly split between the GA, the NDA, and other parties mainly the BSP. As expected, the Muslims remained consolidated behind the GA. This polarization of voters on caste lines is reflective of deeper tensions among various castes within the state.

The caste arithmetic also worked well for two alliance partners, though a little more to the RJD than the JD(U). The Kurmis (Nitish's community members) voted in the same number for the RJD as they did for the JD(U) (see Figure 8.5). Kurmi consolidation behind the RJD and the JD(U) was almost equal at 69% and 67%, respectively. On the other

Figure 8.5

Voting pattern of different castes for GA on JD(U)- and RJD-contested seats

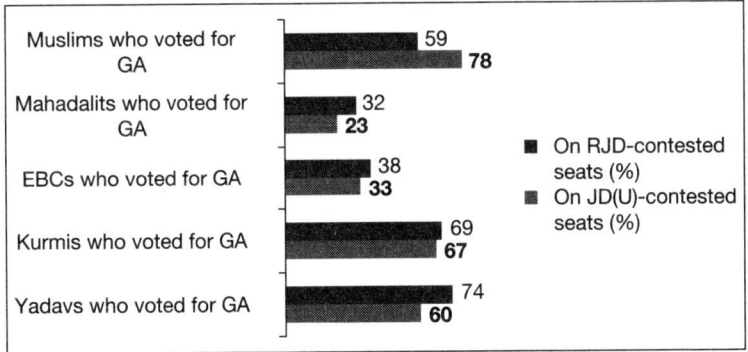

Source: CSDS Data Unit.

hand, on seats where the JD(U) contested, Yadav consolidation behind the JD(U) was relatively less at 60% (Kumar & Sardesai, 2015). Nitish Kumar was more effective in transferring his core base to the RJD than Lalu was in shifting his base to the JD(U).

A clear class divide between the rich and the poor was also evident in Bihar in the 2015 assembly elections (see Table 8.8). In a state where approximately two-thirds of the population are poor and lower-middle class (based on assets owned, house type, and household income), the GA had a massive advantage among poor and lower class sections of voters. The NDA, on the other hand, received significant electoral support from primarily the middle and upper-middle classes. Amongst the upper-middle class voters, 52% voted in favor of the NDA, while amongst the middle class, 36% voted for it. The GA remained extremely popular among the lower-middle class voters, with 46% voting in their favor. The dramatic verdict seems to have successfully communicated that socially inclusive agenda which addresses downtrodden sections has a greater electoral appeal than a developmental model without details and just rhetoric.

The long five-week campaign made a huge impact on the electoral outcome. The NDA was certainly ahead in the electoral race when the elections were announced, but it lost the momentum during the campaign. With every passing week and day, the NDA alliance kept losing its popular support, while the GA kept gaining and the tone of the BJP campaign changing from promising development in the very beginning to personal attack. This did not go well with the voters in Bihar.

Table 8.8

The rich vs the poor in Bihar, 2015

	Voted GA (%)	Voted NDA (%)	Lead of GA over NDA (%)
Poor	41	29	+12
Lower-middle class	46	33	+13
Middle class	39	36	+3
Upper-middle class	36	52	–16

Source: CSDS Data Unit.

The one issue which turned out to be the game changer for the BJP was the statement regarding a need for a fresh look into the issue of reservation by the RSS chief Mohan Bhagwat. This created an uncertainty in the minds the OBC and the Dalits who were beneficiaries of reservation. The lower OBC who seemed somewhat divided at the beginning of the campaign went on to polarize in favor of the GA which championed the cause of reservation for the OBC. The long campaign resulted in a shift among the lower OBC and Dalits away from the BJP, and massive consolidation of the Yadavs and the Kurmis in favor of the GA.

Leadership Factor in Bihar

One of the chief reasons for the victory of the GA was also the leadership factor, mainly Nitish Kumar's popularity. Some political analysts also believed that voters show a tendency to prefer different parties at center and in states. Leadership factor did play an important role in favor of Nitish Kumar in these elections. His record as a chief minister had been clean and the focus on development seemed to have carried the day. Nitish Kumar was much ahead of the other leaders in the chief ministerial race. Forty percent favored Nitish Kumar as their chief minister, while Sushil Modi was favored by 14% and Lalu Yadav by 7%. Over three-fourths of those who voted for the GA mentioned Nitish Kumar as their preferred chief minister. As far as the NDA was concerned, a little over one-third expressed their preference for Sushil Modi and another one-fourth for Jitan Ram Manjhi and Ram Vilas Paswan. The fact that the GA projected a chief ministerial face clearly made a visible difference (Shastri & Attri, 2015).

Figure 8.6

Effectiveness of Nitish Kumar and Narendra Modi on various parameters

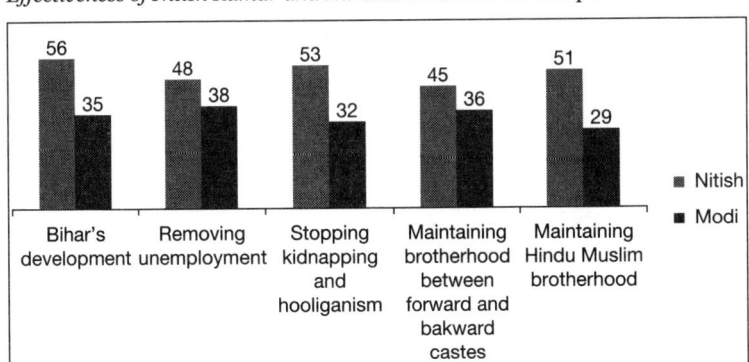

Source: CSDS Data Unit.

Note: All figures are in percent. The rest are those who said "both," "neither," or gave no answer.

Nitish Kumar was also seen as the best chief minister the state has had. More than half the respondents (56%) named him as the best chief minister, while only 9% went to Lalu Yadav. All the other leaders secured only single digit support.

The declaration of Nitish Kumar as the chief ministerial candidate worked for the GA, but on the other hand, the NDA chose not to declare the chief ministerial candidate and contested the election under Narendra Modi's name. This could be one reason for the big defeat of the NDA. Although the BJP did not have any face to match up the charisma of Nitish Kumar, with the support of the allies they could have declared a chief ministerial candidate. Non-declaration of the chief ministerial candidate also led to overexposure of Modi in the elections. It would not be wrong to say that the election became more of Nitish vs Modi. But even Modi's name did not help as Nitish's popularity rating was much higher than that of Modi. On finding out how voters ranked both of them on various indicators, Nitish Kumar did better than Modi on all five dimensions related to development, removing unemployment, stopping kidnapping and hooliganism, maintaining brotherhood between forward and backward caste, and maintaining Hindu–Muslim brotherhood (see Figure 8.6). The people clearly had a lot of confidence on Nitish Kumar and this further helped in the victory of the GA.

Figure 8.7

Opinion on economic conditions of the people

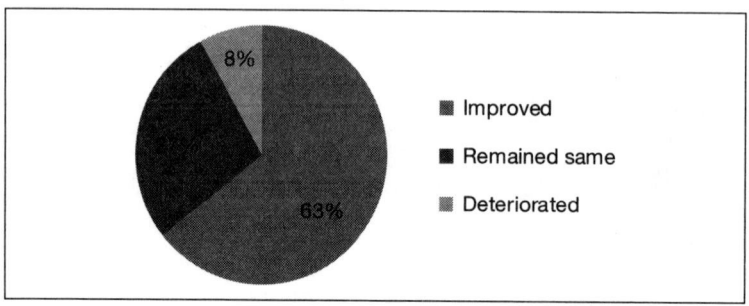

Improved

Remained same

Deteriorated

Source: CSDS Data Unit.

Note: Rest had no opinion. The categories of improved "a lot" and "somewhat" have been merged together to form "Improved." Categories of "somewhat deteriorated" and "deteriorated a lot" have been merged to form "Deteriorated."

Governance

A significant factor other than development that played a role in the elections was the issue of governance. From the aforementioned analysis, it is clear that Nitish's efforts to target important issues in the state had paid dividends as the people of Bihar felt that he was a better choice for the state. An important question, though, that remained was whether the economic condition of people in the last five years had improved or deteriorated. A majority (63%) felt that their economic conditions had improved either somewhat or a lot; 27% felt that there was no difference in their economic condition and that it remained same. Those who felt that their condition had deteriorated, the number dropped down to single digit as 8% felt this (see Figure 8.7). The satisfaction with the JD(U) government in the last five years was also high; as high as 80% were satisfied (either fully of somewhat) with the JD(U). Only 17% said that they were dissatisfied. The satisfaction was also high for the performance of the BJP-led central government in Delhi over the last one and a half year, with 72% being satisfied with the government. But this did not help the NDA in Bihar, because, for the voters in Bihar, the performance of the state government mattered more than the central government's performance. Forty-one percent looked at the work done by the state government while voting and for 26% the work done by the central government

Table 8.9

Performance of state and central governments on voting

While Voting Whose Performance Mattered More to You?	GA (%)	NDA (%)
State government	**58**	21
Central government	27	**57**
Both	33	38
Neither	16	16

Source: CSDS Data Unit.

Note: Rest had no opinion.

was more important. This trend was also visible clearly in their voting pattern. Those who stated that work done by the state government mattered more voted for the GA, and those who said the central government voted for the NDA (see Table 8.9).

Impact of Age and Gender on Voting

Young voters were also important when it came to voting. In the 2014 Lok Sabha elections, the BJP intelligently focused on the young voters by the means of social media, messaging, and also by projecting Narendra Modi as the leader of the youth (Vaishnav & Khosla, 2015). This helped the party in 2014 and there was a hope that the party will again be successful in capturing vote from this particular section. When we take a look at the age-wise classification of vote share of the two alliances, we see that the GA was supported by people of all groups. It received 40% and above vote share from people of all the age groups (see Table 8.10). The GA got more support from the older voters compared to the younger ones. The BJP on the other hand was favored by young voters compared to older ones. First time voters were seen an important voting bloc, as 20 million voters below 30 years were likely to cast their vote in assembly election of 2015 (Waghmare, 2015). If we see the voting pattern of those who were first time voters, an equal proportion of them voted for the NDA and the GA. Thirty-seven percent of first timers voted equally for both the alliances.

In the 2015 elections, there was an increase in women voter turnout from 54.5% in 2010 to 59.9%. Even in the 2010 elections, it was said

Table 8.10

Vote share across age groups

	GA (%)	NDA (%)
Up to 25 years	40	36
26–35 years	44	34
36–45 years	41	36
46–55 years	42	33
56 years and above	42	30

Source: CSDS Data Unit.

Table 8.11

Assessment of Nitish's popularity by gender

	Men (%)	Women (%)
Those who chose Nitish over Modi for Bihar's development	57	54
Those who chose Nitish over Modi for stopping kidnappings	54	52
Those who said they like Nitish Kumar	71	68
Those who were satisfied with Nitish government's work	81	79

Source: CSDS Data Unit.

that women were the key to Nitish's victory. In his first term as chief minister (2005–2010), he had made an endeavor to empower women through policies like 50% reservation in village panchayats across the state. He had made efforts to improve the female literacy rates by focusing on girls' education, offering cash rewards to them for their achievement in school exams, and distributing books, uniform, and bicycles to them. Although the turnout increased in 2015 elections, it is important to see whether this increased turnout led to Nitish's victory. There was no difference among men and women while voting for the GA, as both remained at 42%. Even when voters were asked to rate on his governance and developmental work, men rated him a bit higher than women (see Table 8.11).

One cannot deny fully that the GA did not have an advantage amongst the women, because, when we look at the women across different socioeconomic groups, the alliance did have a greater advantage. The first-time women voters voted in greater proportion for the GA (Mishra & Aasaavari, 2015). In terms of caste as well, gender mattered (see Table 8.12).

Table 8.12

Gender-wise support for the GA among socioeconomic groups

	Men (%)	Women (%)
Age Groups		
First-time voters (18–22 years)	35	39
Rest (above 22 years)	42	42
Economic Class		
Poor	40	43
Others	42	42
Castes/Communities		
Upper castes	8	9
Yadavs	69	66
Kurmis	68	73
Other OBCs	34	36
Paswans	17	20
Mahadalits	26	24
Muslims	68	69

Source: CSDS Data Unit.

What Cost the NDA?

On the one hand, where the arithmetic and the chemistry worked very well for the GA, the centralized nature of BJP's campaign seemed to have cost the NDA. The BJP went into the campaign with their two popular faces, Prime Minister Narendra Modi and the party president Amit Shah. The local leadership was completely sidelined which was obvious from the posters and the hoarding which were put up during the campaign. The Nitish–Lalu duo used this to their advantage and made "Bihari" vs the "Bahari" an issue of the campaign. The BJP also suffered due to their strategy of not declaring their chief ministerial candidate, though it is uncertain to say that things may have been even slightly better had the BJP declared its chief ministerial candidate. If these were not enough, the soaring prices of pulses had angered a section of voters who blamed the central government more than the state government, and decided to vote against the NDA (see Figure 8.8).

Even in the 2014 Lok Sabha elections, the NDA secured 38.8% of the vote, whereas the combined vote base of the GA was over 43%.

Figure 8.8

Central government held responsible more for price rise

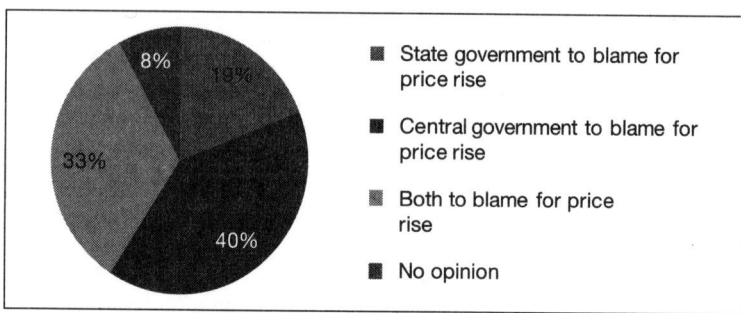

	State government to blame for price rise
State government to blame for price rise	Central government to blame for price rise
	Both to blame for price rise
	No opinion

Source: CSDS Data Unit.

Note: Rest gave no opinion.

Table 8.13

BJP allies got lesser support

NDA Contested	Total Seats	NDA		GA	
		Won	Vote (%)	Won	Vote (%)
BJP contested	157	53	37.4	102	41.7
BJP allies contested	86	5	27.9	76	42.1

Source: CSDS Data Unit.

The BJP's social arithmetic was simple. It wanted to build a coalition of upper caste, lower OBCs, and Dalits to counter the Muslim–Yadav–Kurmi consolidation behind the GA. But the CSDS post-poll data shows that NDA managed to retain its vote base among the lower OBCs and Kurmi–Koeris; its vote share among Dalits (Paswan and other Dalit communities) and Yadavs declined significantly (Verma & Mehta, 2015). The BJP had expected to do well among Dalits with the help of Ram Vilas Paswan and Jitan Ram Manjhi, but it did not help as the BJP performed poorly in comparison to the GA in the seats it contested. The allies, on the other hand, performed even worse (Verma & Mehta, 2015; see Table 8.13). The NDA was not able to perform well in the rural areas as well and from the available 213 seats, it secured only 41 seats, that is, 32.7% in comparison to urban areas where, from 30 seats it got 17 seats (43.1%).

There were many things that worked in favor of the GA, and the most important factor was the carefully grafted alliance of the JD(U), RJD, and Congress. Had Lalu and Nitish contested separately, there would have been a repeat of the 2014 Lok Sabha elections and a division of the "anti-BJP" votes. If Nitish had fought the elections alone, it would have been difficult for him to counter the BJP. An alliance with Lalu helped him as Lalu Yadav had a wider social base. The alliance also helped the RJD as the party had no popular face to take on Narendra Modi, and Congress had neither a popular face nor a wide social base. So the alliance was very strategically crafted and was the main reason for the success. The BJP tried to form a coalition with the LJNSP, HAM, and RLSP but it did not help the NDA. Also, a clear projection of the chief ministerial candidate helped the GA. The non-projection of a chief ministerial candidate from the NDA further helped the GA.

The Recent Turnaround

The summer of 2017 witnessed a turnaround in Bihar politics. Bihar's Chief Minister Nitish Kumar resigned, breaking the alliance with the RJD, but took oath as the chief minister again within 24 hours of his resignation. Soon after breaking alliance with the RJD, Nitish Kumar returned back to his previous ally, the BJP, and formed a new government in coalition with the BJP. While the charges of corruption followed by raids against Tejashwi Yadav and other members of Lalu Yadav turned to be the final point of breaking the alliance between them, it is also true that the relations between them had been less than cordial ever since they formed the government together.

There had been differences between the two coalition partners on whether it was an issue of appointment to top positions or policy legislation on important matters. The coalition partners did have differences when both parties took slightly different stands on important issues, whether it was the *Sharabbandi* (prohibition) or when the RJD leader Shahabuddin was released on bail and issued statements criticizing Nitish Kumar. Even senior RJD leader Raghuvansh Prasad Singh did not miss any opportunity of criticizing Nitish Kumar. He even went on to criticize Nitish Kumar of weakening the alliance by supporting demonetization.

Nitish Kumar, though, after being on the receiving end, went on an offensive. First he refused to reconsider his stand on extending support to the NDA candidate even when the opposition fielded Meera Kumar, the "daughter of Bihar," which did make Lalu unhappy with Nitish Kumar. But there was very little he could do to persuade him and change his decision.

Eventually, when the deputy chief minister and some other leaders of the RJD were in trouble, being charged of involvement in corruption, Nitish Kumar asserted his commitment of zero tolerance for corruption, clearly indicating his least sympathy for his deputy. Nitish Kumar made it very clear that he would prefer to resign to save his image, rather than running a corrupt government, which he finally did.

It is true that Nitish Kumar was hardly left with any options, as remaining in company with Tejashwi Yadav would have sent out the signal of his compromising with the issue of corruption and his image may have got dented, not forming the government in alliance with the BJP would have meant forcing the state for a mid-term assembly elections which would have meant the BJP sweeping the state, registering a thumping victory. He finally opted for breaking the alliance with the RJD and forming a new government in alliance with the BJP in the hope that he would manage to gain in his reputation of fighting against corruption.

What Nitish Kumar failed to realize was that his image as an honest leader might have got some boost nationally, but having formed the government in alliance with the BJP, within hours of breaking the alliance with the RJD, would also damage his image. With this decision, he managed to attract the tag of being an absolute opportunistic leader. Two of his widely acclaimed traits—honesty and integrity—are turning out to be a liability for him. In order to uphold his honest image, he ended up compromising on secularism, equally important for upholding democratic principles. His new political move would hardly help Nitish Kumar in expanding his electoral support base.

It may be possible to mobilize a sizable number of urban voters with a clean image, but is unlikely to be helpful in a primarily rural, caste-based society like in Bihar where identities play an important role. There is hardly any doubt that Nitish Kumar is the "Sushaasan Babu" for a plurality of Biharis, but this image may not be enough to win elections. Even when the Mahagathbandan contested the election under the leadership of Nitish Kumar, his own party's performance was worse than the RJD whose leaders have a far less clean image. The "clean image" was insufficient for mustering votes for the JD(U), but helped ally RJD in gaining beyond core voters. Nitish Kumar may have been able to save the chief minister's chair and may even have ensured its continuation beyond the 2020 election, but the premium he paid for this insurance of the chief minister's chair was very big.

References

Bagchi, S. (2015). A tale of two campaigns. The Hindu Centre for Politics and Public Policy. Retrieved February 5, 2016, from http://www.thehinducentre.com/the-arena/current issues/article7826538.ece

Kumar, S., & Sardesai, S. (2015). Bihar post-poll survey: Why did Lalu's party fare better than Nitish's despite the latter's immense popularity? *The Indian Express*. Retrieved March 2, 2016, from http://indianexpress.com/article/india/india-news-india/bihar-post-poll-survey-nitish-kumars-core-vote-transfers-better-than-lalus-does/

Mishra, J., & Aasaavari, A. (2015). Bihar post poll survey: Women did make impact but only to an extent. *The Indian Express*. Retrieved June 24, 2015, from http://indianexpress.com/article/india/india-news-india/bihar-post-poll-survey-women-did-make-impact-but-only-to-an-extent/

Shastri, S., & Attri, V. (2015). Bihar rates its favourite CM Nitish Kumar as more capable than PM Narendra Modi. *The Indian Express*. Retrieved March 2, 2016, from http://indianexpress.com/article/india/india-news-india/post-poll-survey-bihar-rates-it-favourite-cm-nitish-kumar-as-more-capable-than-pm-narendra-modi/

Vaishnav, M., & Khosla, S. (2015). A complete guide to Bihar elections. *Quartz India*. Retrieved June 27, 2016, from http://qz.com/516722/a-complete-guide-to-the-bihar-elections/

Verma, R., & Mehta, N. (2015). Dalits dump NDA, rural Bihar stays out of its reach. *The Indian Express*. Retrieved January 2, 2016, from http://indianexpress.com/article/india/india-news-india/bihar-post-poll-survey-dalits-dump-nda-rural-bihar-stays-out-of-its-reach/

Verma, R., & Sardesai S. (2015). Bihar post-poll survey: Both caste and development, viewed through identity lens. *The Indian Express*. Retrieved April 5, 2016, from http://indianexpress.com/article/india/india-news-india/bihar-post-poll-survey-both-caste-and-development-viewed-through-identity-lens/

Waghmare, A. (2015). Four factors that will likely decide Bihar polls. *The Wire*. Retrieved April 3, 2016, from http://thewire.in/13634/four-factors-that-will-likely-decide-bihar-polls/

Index

About the Series Editors and Author

Series Editors

Suhas Palshikar taught politics at Savitribai Phule Pune University and has been associated with Lokniti, Programme on Comparative Democracy of the CSDS. He is also the Chief Editor of the journal *Studies in Indian Politics*. He has co-edited two volumes on electoral politics: *Party Competition in Indian States: Electoral Politics in Post-Congress Polity* (2014) and *Electoral Politics in India: The Resurgence of the Bharatiya Janata Party* (2017). His most recent publication is *Indian Democracy* (2017).

Rajeshwari Deshpande is a Professor of Politics at the Savitribai Phule Pune University. She is a member of the editorial managing team of the journal *Studies in Indian Politics* and coordinates a forum on "Teaching and Learning Political Science in India" for the same journal. She has published over 20 research articles in journals/edited volumes in English as well as in Marathi. She has edited the book *Politics of Welfare: Comparisons Across Indian States* with Louise Tillin and K.K. Kailash (2015).

Author

Sanjay Kumar is Professor and Director of Centre for the Study of Developing Societies (CSDS) since 2014. His core area of research is electoral politics, but he has also been engaged in research on Indian youth, state of democracy, and slums of Delhi. He has directed several national-level studies, most important being the series of National Election Study (NES) conducted by Lokniti–CSDS since 1996.

Earlier, he had authored *Changing Electoral Politics in Delhi: From Caste to Class*; co-authored (with Peter Ronald de Souza and Sandeep Shastri) *Indian Youth in a Transforming World: Attitudes and Perceptions*; edited *Indian Youth and Electoral Politics: An Emerging Engagement;* and co-edited (with Suhas Palshikar and Sanjay Lodha) *Electoral Politics in India: Resurgence of the Bharatiya Janata Party* and (with Christophe Jaffrelot) *Rise of the Plebeians? The Changing Face of Indian Legislative Assemblies.* He has contributed chapters in several edited volumes and research journals and writes regularly for national newspapers. He is also a known face on Indian television as an expert on elections.